CIMA

OPERATIONAL

PAPER F1

FINANCIAL OPERATIONS

PRACTICE & REVISION KIT

Our Kit has a **brand new look** for CIMA's new 2010 syllabus.

In this edition we:

- Discuss the **best strategies** for revising and taking your F1 exam
- Show you how to be well prepared for the **2010 exams**
- Give you **lots of great guidance** on tackling questions
- Show you how you can **build your own exams**
- Provide you with **two** mock exams

BPP's **i-Pass** product also supports this paper.

FOR EXAMS IN 2010

BPP LEARNING MEDIA

First edition January 2010

ISBN 9780 7517 7521 1

British Library Cataloguing-in-Publication Data
A catalogue record for this book
is available from the British Library

Published by

BPP Learning Media Ltd
BPP House, Aldine Place
London W12 8AA

www.bpp.com/learningmedia

Printed in the United Kingdom

Your learning materials, published by BPP Learning Media Ltd, are printed on paper sourced from sustainable, managed forests.

All our rights reserved. No part of this publication may be reproduced, stored in a retrieval system or transmitted, in any form or by any means, electronic, mechanical, photocopying, recording or otherwise, without the prior written permission of BPP Learning Media Ltd.

We are grateful to the Chartered Institute of Management Accountants for permission to reproduce past examination questions. The answers to past examination questions have been prepared by BPP Learning Media Ltd.

©
BPP Learning Media Ltd
2010

A note about copyright

Dear Customer

What does the little © mean and why does it matter?

Your market-leading BPP books, course materials and e-learning materials do not write and update themselves. People write them: on their own behalf or as employees of an organisation that invests in this activity. Copyright law protects their livelihoods. It does so by creating rights over the use of the content.

Breach of copyright is a form of theft – as well as being a criminal offence in some jurisdictions, it is potentially a serious breach of professional ethics.

With current technology, things might seem a bit hazy but, basically, without the express permission of BPP Learning Media:

- Photocopying our materials is a breach of copyright

- Scanning, ripcasting or conversion of our digital materials into different file formats, uploading them to facebook or emailing them to your friends is a breach of copyright

You can, of course, sell your books, in the form in which you have bought them – once you have finished with them. (Is this fair to your fellow students? We update for a reason.) But the e-products are sold on a single user licence basis: we do not supply 'unlock' codes to people who have bought them second-hand.

And what about outside the UK? BPP Learning Media strives to make our materials available at prices students can afford by local printing arrangements, pricing policies and partnerships which are clearly listed on our website. A tiny minority ignore this and indulge in criminal activity by illegally photocopying our material or supporting organisations that do. If they act illegally and unethically in one area, can you really trust them?

Contents

	Page
Finding questions and using the Practice and Revision Kit	
Question index	iv
Topic index	vi
Using your BPP Learning Media Practice and Revision Kit	vii
Passing F1	
Revising F1	viii
Passing the F1 exam	ix
The exam paper	xi
What the examiner means	xii
Planning your question practice	
BPP's question plan	xiv
Build your own exams	xvi
Questions and answers	
Questions	1
Answers	93
Exam practice	
Mock exam 1	
• Questions	189
• Plan of attack	201
• Answers	203
Mock exam 2	
• Questions	215
• Plan of attack	227
• Answers	229
Mathematical tables	241
Review form & free prize draw	

Stop press

Because of publishing deadlines, BPP Learning Media has been unable to include CIMA's pilot paper for the 2010 syllabus in this Kit. BPP Learning Media will be posting its solutions to pilot papers online before the May 2010 exams. Please see http://www.bpp.com/learningmedia/news-and-events/cima2010.asp for details.

Question index

Questions set under the old syllabus's P7 *Financial Accounting and Tax Principles* (FATP) exam are included because their style and content are similar to those that appear in the Paper F1 exam.

		Marks	Time allocation Mins	Page number Question	Page number Answer
Part A: Regulation and Ethics of Financial Reporting					
1	Objective test questions: The regulatory framework	39	70	3	95
2	Objective test questions: External audit	30	54	5	96
3	Objective test questions: Ethics	22	40	8	96
4	Section B questions: Regulation	25	45	10	97
5	Section B questions: External audit	20	36	11	99
6	Section B questions: Ethics	15	27	12	101
Part B: Single Company Financial Statements					
7	Objective test questions: Presentation	24	43	13	102
8	Section B questions: Presentation	10	18	15	103
9	Objective test questions: Statements of cash flows	24	43	16	104
10	Section B questions: Statements of cash flows	5	9	19	105
11	HZ (FATP 5/09/amended)	25	45	20	105
12	Tex (FATP pilot paper/amended)	25	45	21	108
13	AG (FATP 5/05/amended)	25	45	23	111
14	CJ (FATP 5/06/amended)	25	45	25	113
15	DN (FATP 11/06/amended)	25	45	26	115
16	Lemming Inc	25	45	28	118
17	Objective test questions: Non-current assets, inventories and construction contracts I	27	49	29	119
18	Objective test questions: Non-current assets, inventories and construction contracts II	35	63	32	120
19	Section B questions: Non-current assets, inventories and construction contracts	30	54	35	121
20	Geneva	15	27	37	124
21	Objective test questions: Capital transactions and financial instruments	26	47	37	125
22	Objective test questions: Accounting standards I	36	65	40	126
23	Objective test questions: Accounting standards II	48	86	44	126
24	Section B questions: Accounting standards I	40	72	48	128
25	Section B Questions: Accounting standards II	40	72	51	131
26	AZ (FATP Pilot paper/amended)	25	45	53	136
27	AF (FATP 5/05/amended)	25	45	54	139
28	Murdoch Co	25	45	55	141
29	BG (FATP 11/05/amended)	25	45	56	143
30	DM (FATP 11/06/amended)	25	45	57	146
31	DZ (FATP 5/07/amended)	25	45	58	149
32	EY (FATP 11/07/amended)	25	45	60	152
33	FZ (FATP 5/08/amended)	25	45	62	155
34	GZ (FATP 11/08/amended)	25	45	64	158

	Marks	Time allocation Mins	Page number Question	Page number Answer
Part C: Group Financial Statements				
35 Objective test questions: Group financial statements	21	38	66	162
36 Goose and Gander	25	45	69	164
37 Parsley	25	45	70	166
38 Molecule	25	45	71	168
39 Tom, Dick and Harry	25	45	72	169
Part D: Principles of Business Taxation				
40 Objective test questions: General principles of taxation	49	88	74	171
41 Objective test questions: International tax	33	59	76	172
42 Objective test questions: Indirect taxes	29	52	79	173
43 Objective test questions: Company taxation	37	67	81	174
44 Objective test questions: Deferred tax	41	74	85	177
45 Section B questions: Taxation I	25	45	88	180
46 Section B questions: Taxation II	25	45	89	181
47 Section B questions: Taxation III	25	45	89	183

Mock exam 1
Questions 48 to 51

Mock exam 2
Questions 52 to 55

Planning your question practice

Our guidance from page xiv shows you how to organise your question practice, either by attempting questions from each syllabus area or by **building your own exams** – tackling questions as a series of practice exams.

Topic index

Listed below are the key Paper F1 syllabus topics and the numbers of the questions in this Kit covering those topics.

If you need to concentrate your practice and revision on certain topics or if you want to attempt all available questions that refer to a particular subject you will find this index useful.

Syllabus topic	Question numbers
Consolidated financial statements	35, 36, 37, 38, 39
Company taxation	27, 43, 45(c), 47(b), 47(e)
Construction contracts	17, 14(b), 18, 19(f), 20, 25(c), 32
Deferred tax	27, 29, 44, 45(c), 47(a), 47(b), 47(c), 47(d)
Discontinued operations	24 (g), 24(h), 28, 33
Employee tax	40
Ethics	3, 6
Events after the reporting period	22, 23
External audit	2, 5
Financial instruments	21, 24(d), 27
General tax principles	40, 45(a), 46(b)
IAS 1	7, 8
IAS 8	7
IAS 12	44, 47(d),
Indirect taxation	42, 45(b), 45(e), 46(a)
Intangible assets	19(a), 19(d), 25(e), 31, 33
International tax	41, 46(d)
Inventories	17, 18, 19(b)
Impairment of assets	17, 18, 19(d), 19(e), 28, 37, 39, 40
Leasing	22, 23, 24(a), 25(b), 25(d), 25(f), 27, 29(b), 30, 33
Non-current assets	17, 18, 24(h)
Operating segments	22
Property, plant and equipment	19(c), 19(d), 19(e), 23, 26, 28, 29, 30, 31, 32, 33
Provisions	22, 23, 24(b), 24(c), 24(g), 25(a), 26, 28, 29, 33
Regulatory framework	1, 4
Related parties	23, 24(d), 25(g)
Research and development	5(a), 13, 19(a), 25(e), 31
Revenue recognition	23, 24(f)
Share capital transactions	21, 30, 32, 33
Statement of cash flows	9, 10, 11(b), 12(a), 13, 14(a), 15(a), 16(b)
Statement of changes in equity	26, 27, 30, 31, 32, 33
Statement of comprehensive income	8(b), 16(a), 26, 27, 28, 29(a), 30, 31, 32, 33
Statement of financial position	12(b), 15(b), 26, 27, 28, 29(a), 30, 31, 32, 33
Withholding tax	40, 45(d), 46(c)

Using your BPP Learning Media Practice and Revision Kit

Tackling revision and the exam

You can significantly improve your chances of passing by tackling revision and the exam in the right ways. Our advice is based on feedback from CIMA. We focus on Paper F1; we discuss revising the syllabus, what to do (and what not to do) in the exam, how to approach different types of question and ways of obtaining easy marks.

Selecting questions

We provide signposts to help you plan your revision.

- A full **question index**
- A **topic index**, listing all the questions that cover key topics, so that you can locate the questions that provide practice on these topics, and see the different ways in which they might be examined
- **BPP's question plan**, highlighting the most important questions
- **Build your own exams**, showing you how you can practise questions in a series of exams

Making the most of question practice

We realise that you need more than questions and model answers to get the most from your question practice.

- Our **Top tips** provide essential advice on tackling questions and presenting answers
- We show you how you can pick up **Easy marks** on questions, as picking up all readily available marks can make the difference between passing and failing
- We include **marking guides** to show you what the examiner rewards
- We summarise **Examiner's comments** to show you how students coped with the questions
- We refer to the **BPP 2009 Study Text** for detailed coverage of the topics covered in each question

Attempting mock exams

There are two mock exams that provide practice at coping with the pressures of the exam day. We strongly recommend that you attempt them under exam conditions as they reflect the question styles and syllabus coverage of the exam. To help you get the most out of doing these exams, we provide guidance on how you should have approached the whole exam.

Our other products

BPP Learning Media also offers these products for practising and revising for the F1 exam:

Passcards	Summarising what you should know in visual, easy to remember, form
Success CDs	Covering the vital elements of the F1 syllabus in less than 90 minutes and also containing exam hints to help you fine tune your strategy
i-Pass	Providing computer-based testing in a variety of formats, ideal for self-assessment
i-Learn	Allowing you to learn actively with a clear visual format summarising what you must know

You can purchase these products by visiting www.bpp.com/mybpp

Revising F1

This is a very wide-ranging syllabus, but with not a great deal of depth in some areas. For instance, the tax section of the paper does not use any specific tax regime, so the questions are just 'general'.

The format of the paper allows the examiner to cover a large part of the syllabus, so you cannot afford to neglect any area.

Areas to concentrate on are:

- Statements of cash flows
- Leases and construction contracts
- Taxation and deferred tax
- The IASB *Framework*
- Single company financial statements. You must know the correct IAS 1 formats.
- Consolidated financial statements

Question practice

You should use the Passcards and any brief notes you have to revise these topics, but you mustn't spend all your revision time passively reading. Question practice is vital; doing as many questions as you can in full will help develop your ability to analyse scenarios and produce relevant discussion and recommendations. The question plan on page xiv tells you what questions cover so that you can choose questions covering a variety of topics.

Passing the F1 exam

Displaying the right qualities

The examiners will expect you to display the following qualities.

Qualities required	
Produce neat workings and readable answers	If you produce no workings, the marker can give you no credit for using the right method. If the marker cannot read what you have written they can give you no marks at all.
Carry out standard calculations	You must be able to deal with simple tax and financial instrument calculations.
Demonstrate understanding of the basics	Deferred tax and construction contracts can be complex, but you will only get fairly simple questions, so make sure you understand the principles.

Avoiding weaknesses

The examiners have identified weaknesses that occur in many students' answers at every sitting. You will enhance your chances significantly if you ensure you avoid these mistakes:

- Failing to provide what the question verbs require (discussion, evaluation, recommendations) or to write about the topics specified in the question requirements
- Inability to carry out calculations
- Not showing workings in 3-4 mark questions
- Repeating the same material in different parts of answers
- Regurgitation of definitions and lists with no application to the question
- Brain dumping all that is known about a topic (no credit is given for this)
- Failing to answer sufficient questions because of poor time management
- Not answering all parts of questions
- Not using the information provided in the question accurately
- Attempting to question spot

Using the reading time

Use the reading time to analyse the adjustments needed in the Section C questions and go over the requirements of the Section B questions deciding which parts to answer first.

Tackling questions

Numerical questions

Expect to see numbers throughout the paper. Approach them methodically and show all workings clearly.

Discussion questions

Remember that **depth of discussion** is also important. Discussions will often consist of paragraphs containing 2-3 sentences. Each paragraph should:

- **Make a point**
- **Explain the point** (you must demonstrate **why** the point is important)
- **Illustrate the point** (with material or analysis from the scenario, perhaps an example from real-life)

Gaining the easy marks

The first few marks are always the easiest to gain in any question. This applies particularly to Section B. Spend the same amount of time on each Section B question. This will give you a good chance of scoring marks on each question. Your Section C questions carry a lot of marks. Make sure you begin by getting down the format and filling in any numbers which don't require calculation.

The exam paper

Format of the paper

		Number of marks
Section A:	Around 7-9 multiple choice and other objective test questions, 2-4 marks each	20
Section B:	6 compulsory questions, 5 marks each	30
Section C:	2 compulsory questions, totalling 50 marks	50
		100

Time allowed: 3 hours plus 20 minutes reading time.

Section A will always contain some multiple choice questions but will not consist solely of multiple choice questions. For 3 or 4-mark questions, marks are given for correct workings.

Section B questions will be mainly written discussion, although some calculations may be included. This section will require breadth of syllabus knowledge and also good time management skills.

The **Section C** questions will cover statements of comprehensive income, statements of financial position, statements of cash flows for a single company and simple consolidated statement of comprehensive income and statement of financial position.

What the examiner means

The table below has been prepared by CIMA to help you interpret exam questions.

Learning objective	Verbs used	Definition
1 Knowledge		
What you are expected to know	• List	• Make a list of
	• State	• Express, fully or clearly, the details of/facts of
	• Define	• Give the exact meaning of
2 Comprehension		
What you are expected to understand	• Describe	• Communicate the key features of
	• Distinguish	• Highlight the differences between
	• Explain	• Make clear or intelligible/state the meaning or purpose of
	• Identify	• Recognise, establish or select after consideration
	• Illustrate	• Use an example to describe or explain something
3 Application		
How you are expected to apply your knowledge	• Apply	• Put to practical use
	• Calculate/compute	• Ascertain or reckon mathematically
	• Demonstrate	• Prove the certainty or exhibit by practical means
	• Prepare	• Make or get ready for use
	• Reconcile	• Make or prove consistent/compatible
	• Solve	• Find an answer to
	• Tabulate	• Arrange in a table
4 Analysis		
How you are expected to analyse the detail of what you have learned	• Analyse	• Examine in detail the structure of
	• Categorise	• Place into a defined class or division
	• Compare and contrast	• Show the similarities and/or differences between
	• Construct	• Build up or complete
	• Discuss	• Examine in detail by argument
	• Interpret	• Translate into intelligible or familiar terms
	• Prioritise	• Place in order of priority or sequence for action
	• Produce	• Create or bring into existence
5 Evaluation		
How you are expected to use your learning to evaluate, make decisions or recommendations	• Advise	• Counsel, inform or notify
	• Evaluate	• Appraise or assess the value of
	• Recommend	• Propose a course of action

Useful websites

The websites below provide additional sources of information of relevance to your studies for Paper F1 – Financial Operations.

- BPP www.bpp.com

   For details of other BPP material for your CIMA studies

- CIMA www.cimaglobal.com

   The official CIMA website

- *Financial Times* www.ft.com
- *The Economist* www.economist.com
- *Wall Street Journal* www.wsj.com

Using your BPP products

This Kit gives you the question practice and guidance you need in the exam. Our other products can also help you pass:

- **Learning to Learn Accountancy** gives further valuable advice on revision
- **Passcards** provide you with clear topic summaries and exam tips
- **Success CDs** help you revise on the move
- **i-Pass CDs** offer tests of knowledge against the clock
- **Learn Online** is an e-learning resource delivered via the Internet, offering comprehensive tutor support and featuring areas such as study, practice, email service, revision and useful resources

You can purchase these products by visiting www.bpp.com/mybpp.

Planning your question practice

We have already stressed that question practice should be right at the centre of your revision. Whilst you will spend some time looking at your notes and the Paper F1 Passcards, you should spend the majority of your revision time practising questions.

We recommend two ways in which you can practise questions.

- Use **BPP Learning Media's question plan** to work systematically through the syllabus and attempt key and other questions on a section-by-section basis
- **Build your own exams** – attempt the questions as a series of practice exams

These ways are suggestions and simply following them is no guarantee of success. You or your college may prefer an alternative but equally valid approach.

BPP's question plan

The plan below requires you to devote a **minimum of 40 hours** to revision of Paper F1. Any time you can spend over and above this should only increase your chances of success.

STEP 1 **Review your notes** and the chapter summaries in the Paper F1 **Passcards** for each section of the syllabus.

STEP 2 **Answer the key questions** for that section. These questions have boxes round the question number in the table below and you should answer them in full. Even if you are short of time you must attempt these questions if you want to pass the exam. You should complete your answers without referring to our solutions.

STEP 3 **Attempt the other questions** in that section. For some questions we have suggested that you prepare **answer plans or do the calculations** rather than full solutions. Planning an answer means that you should spend about 40% of the time allowance for the questions brainstorming the question and drawing up a list of points to be included in the answer.

STEP 4 **Attempt Mock exams 1 and 2** under strict exam conditions.

Syllabus section	2009 Passcards chapters	Questions in this Kit	Comments	Done ☑
The regulatory framework	1	1, 4	The MCQs are fairly simple here. The Section B questions invite you to spend a lot of time, so *don't do it* – practise answering these question with notes and bullet points.	☐
External audit and ethics	2, 3	2, 3 5, 6	Make sure you know the different types of audit report qualification and be very strict and to the point on the Section B questions.	☐
Financial accounts – presentation	4, 5	7-8	This area is very important – IAS 1 and IAS 8. Do all of the MCQs. Make sure you can write out the formats.	☐
Statements of cash flows	9	9, 10	These are good revision for the various components of the statement, so do them before attempting the longer questions.	☐
Statements of cash flows	9	11-16	These are Section C questions on statements of cash flows. This is not a difficult topic. Do all of these questions and make sure you can produce *net cash flow from operating activities* using both methods.	☐
Non-current assets, inventories and construction contracts	6, 7, 11	17–20	These are fairly complex topics. If you have trouble with the MCQs, go back to the Study Text and revise the area.	☐
Capital transactions and financial instruments	12	21	These MCQs cover most of the important issues in this area. Make sure you understand how to deal with redemption of capital and purchase of own shares.	☐
Accounting standards	8, 10	22-25	These questions cover IAS 10, IAS 24, IAS 37 and IAS 17. These are all important because they are relatively *easy* to learn and apply, so if they come up they will be easy marks. Make sure you can calculate finance lease interest payments using both methods.	☐
Financial statements	4, 5	26-34	Section C will have an accounts preparation question, so practice on these. Make sure you can do all of them.	☐
Group financial statements	13, 14, 15, 16	35-39	This is a new topic at this level so it needs a lot of practice. Do all of these questions.	☐
General principles of taxation	17, 18	40-42	Answer all of these MCQs. There will be more than one question on each topic, so you will get lots of practice.	☐
		45, 46	These are Section B-type questions. Make sure you do not spend more than 9 minutes on each.	☐
Company taxation	19	43, 44	Answer all of these MCQs. Make sure you really understand the adjustments necessary to get from accounting profit to taxable profit and can do it easily.	☐
		47	These are Section B questions on company tax. Deferred tax is the most difficult aspect. Just make sure you understand the basics.	☐

Build your own exams

Having revised your notes and the BPP Passcards, you can attempt the questions in the Kit as a series of practice exams. You can organise the questions in the following way:

	Marks
7-10 objective test questions	20
6 Section B questions	30
2 Section C questions	50
	100

This Kit contains 16 banks of objective test questions – numbers 1, 2, 3, 7, 9, 17, 18, 21, 22, 23, 35, 40, 41, 42, 43, 44.

For Section A of your exam, select from each of these to a total of 20 marks. If you do a 3 or 4-mark question, reduce the number of questions accordingly.

For Section B, do 6 sub-questions from the following questions – 4, 5, 6, 8, 10, 19, 24, 25, 45, 46, 47. Make sure you do at least one question from Part A, one from Part B, one from Part C and one from Part D – see the Question and Answer Checklist.

For Section C, do one of the following: 11, 12, 13, 14, 15, 16, 26, 27, 28, 29, 30, 31, 32, 33, 34 and one of 36, 37, 38, 39.

Also make sure you do the two mock exams.

STOP PRESS!

Consolidated accounts: fair value adjustments and additional depreciation charges

Remember that goodwill is calculated as the difference between the consideration transferred and the fair value of net assets acquired by the group.

If there is a difference between the fair value and the book value of the net assets, then a **fair value adjustment** is required.

There are two possible ways of achieving this.

(a) The **subsidiary company** might **incorporate any necessary revaluations** in its own books of account. In this case, we can proceed directly to the consolidation, taking asset values and reserves figures straight from the subsidiary company's statement of financial position.

(b) The **revaluations** may be made as a **consolidation adjustment without being incorporated** in the subsidiary company's books. In this case, we must make the necessary adjustments to the subsidiary's statement of financial position as a working. Only then can we proceed to the consolidation.

If the revaluations relate to depreciating assets, there may be **additional depreciation** to be charged as a result.

In your exam, you may need to calculate the additional depreciation charge. Remember that to calculate the additional depreciation charge, you need to divide the fair value adjustment (ie the revalued amount less the original book value) by the remaining useful life.

QUESTIONS

Part A: Regulation and Ethics of Financial Reporting

Questions 1 to 6 cover Regulation and Ethics of Financial Reporting, the subject of Part A of the BPP Study Text for Paper F1.

1 Objective test questions: The regulatory framework — 70 mins

1. Guidance on the application and interpretation of International Financial Reporting Standards is provided by:

    A The IASB
    B The IASC Foundation
    C The IFRIC
    D The Standards Advisory Council (2 marks)

2. Which of the following is *not* an advantage of global harmonisation of accounting standards?

    A Priority given to different user groups in different countries
    B Easier transfer of accounting staff across national borders
    C Ability to comply with the requirements of overseas stock exchanges
    D Better access to foreign investor funds (2 marks)

3. The IASB has recently revised and improved a number of standards. One of the major purposes of these revisions has been:

    A To make the standards more relevant to developing countries
    B To eliminate alternative treatments of items in accounts
    C To give preparers of accounts more choice
    D To comply with the demands of pressure groups (2 marks)

4. The International Accounting Standards Board's *Framework for the Preparation and Presentation of Financial Statements* defines five elements of financial statements. Three of the elements are asset, liability and income.

    List the other TWO elements. (2 marks)

5. Which two of the following, per the *Framework*, are *underlying assumptions* relating to financial statements?

    1 The accounts have been prepared on an accruals basis
    2 Users are assumed to have sufficient knowledge to be able to understand the financial statements
    3 The accounting policies used have been disclosed
    4 The business is expected to continue in operation for the foreseeable future
    5 The information is free from material error or bias

    A 1 and 3
    B 2 and 3
    C 1 and 4
    D 3 and 5 (2 marks)

6. Which two of the following are not elements of financial statements per the *Framework*?

    1 Profits
    2 Assets
    3 Income
    4 Equity
    5 Losses
    6 Expenses

	A	2 and 4
	B	1 and 5
	C	3 and 4
	D	5 and 6

(2 marks)

7 According to the *Framework*, the income statement measures:

A Financial position
B Performance
C Profitability
D Financial adaptability

(2 marks)

8 Which two of the following are underlying assumptions in the International Accounting Standards Board's *Framework for the Preparation and Presentation of Financial Statements*?

1 Accruals
2 Relevance
3 Comparability
4 Going concern
5 Reliability

A 1 and 5
B 2 and 5
C 3 and 4
D 1 and 4

(2 marks)

9 The International Accounting Standards Board's *Framework for the Preparation and Presentation of Financial Statements* defines elements of financial statements. In no more than 30 words define an asset.

(2 marks)

10 The term GAAP is used to mean

A Generally accepted accounting procedures
B General accounting and audit practice
C Generally agreed accounting practice
D Generally accepted accounting practice

(2 marks)

11 Which one of the following is responsible for governance and fundraising in relation to the development of International Accounting Standards?

A International Accounting Standards Board
B International Financial Reporting Interpretations Committee
C International Accounting Standards Committee Foundation Trustees
D Standards Advisory Council

(2 marks)

12 The setting of International Accounting Standards is carried out by co-operation between a number of committees and boards, which include:

1 International Accounting Standards Committee Foundation (IASC Foundation)
2 Standards Advisory Council (SAC)
3 International Financial Reporting Interpretations Committee (IFRIC)

Which of the above reports to, or advises, the International Accounting Standards Board (IASB)?

	Reports to:	Advises:
A	1 and 3	2
B	1 and 2	3
C	3	2
D	2	1

(2 marks)

13 The IASB's *Framework for the Preparation and Presentation of Financial Statements* provides definitions of the elements of financial statements. One of the elements defined by the Framework is 'expenses'.

In no more than **35** words, give the IASB Framework's definition of expenses. (2 marks)

14 According to the International Accounting Standards Board's (IASB) *Framework for the Preparation and Presentation of Financial Statements* (Framework), what is the objective of financial statements?

   Write your answer in nor more than **35** words. **(2 marks)**

15 Financial statements prepared using International Standards and the International Accounting Standards Board's (IASB *Framework for the Preparation and Presentation of Financial Statements* (Framework) are presumed to apply two of the following four underlying assumptions

   1 Relevance
   2 Going concern
   3 Prudence
   4 Accruals

   Which two of the above are underlying assumptions according to the IASB's *Framework*?

   A 1 and 2 only
   B 2 and 3 only
   C 3 and 4 only
   D 2 and 4 only **(2 marks)**

16 Which of the following are functions of the International Accounting Standards Committee Foundation?

   1 Issuing International Accounting Standards
   2 Approving the annual budget of the International Accounting Standards Committee (IASC) and its committees
   3 Enforcing International Accounting Standards
   4 Reviewing the strategy of the IASC
   5 Publishing an annual report on the activities of the IASC and IASB

   A 1, 2 and 5
   B 2 and 4
   C 1, 3 and 5
   D 2, 4 and 5 **(2 marks)**

17 The International Accounting Standards Board's (IASB) *Framework for the Preparation and Presentation of Financial Statements* (Framework), sets out four qualitative characteristics of financial information.

   Two of the characteristics are relevance and comparability. List the other TWO characteristics. **(2 marks)**

18 State the TWO underlying assumptions outlined in the International Accounting Standard Board's (IASB) *Framework for the Preparation and Presentation of Financial Statements*. **(2 marks)**

19 The process leading to the publication of an International Financial Reporting Standard (IFRS) has a number of stages.

   List the THREE stages that normally precede the final issue of an IFRS. **(3 marks)**

   (Total = 39 marks)

2 Objective test questions: External audit   54 mins

1 The International Standard on Auditing 701 *Modifications to the Independent Auditor's Report,* classifies modified audit reports into 'matters that do not affect the auditor's opinion' and 'matters that do affect the auditor's opinion'. This latter category is further sub-divided into three categories

   List these three categories **(3 marks)**

2   An external auditor gives a qualified audit report that is a 'disclaimer of opinion'.

    This means that the auditor

    A   Has been unable to agree with an accounting treatment used by the directors in relation to a material item.

    B   Has been prevented from obtaining sufficient appropriate audit evidence.

    C   Has found extensive errors in the financial statements and concludes that they do not show a true and fair view.

    D   Has discovered a few immaterial differences that do not affect the auditor's opinion. **(2 marks)**

3   There is a major uncertainty facing Z, a limited liability company. Actions are pending against the company for allegedly supplying faulty goods, causing widespread damage.

    The directors have fully described the circumstances of the case in a note to the financial statements.

    What form of audit report is appropriate in this case?

    A   Qualified opinion – limitation on auditors' work
    B   Disclaimer of opinion
    C   Unqualified report with an additional explanatory paragraph
    D   Qualified opinion – disagreement **(2 marks)**

4   Which of the following matters are normally covered by the auditors' report?

    1   Whether the company has kept proper accounting records

    2   Whether the accounts are in agreement with the accounting records

    3   Whether the accounts have been prepared in accordance with the relevant legislation and accounting standards

    4   Whether other information presented with the financial statements is consistent with them

    A   1 and 2 only
    B   1, 2 and 3 only
    C   3 and 4 only
    D   All four matters are normally covered **(2 marks)**

5   A company's auditors find insufficient evidence to substantiate the company's cash sales, which are material in amount.

    What form of qualification of the audit report would normally be appropriate in this situation?

    A   Qualified opinion – disagreement
    B   Qualified opinion – limitation on auditors' work
    C   Disclaimer of opinion
    D   Qualified opinion – adverse opinion **(2 marks)**

6   A company's accounting records were largely destroyed by fire shortly after the year end. As a result, the financial statements contain a number of figures based on estimates.

    What form of qualification of the audit report would be appropriate in this situation?

    A   Qualified opinion – disagreement
    B   Qualified opinion – limitations on auditors' work
    C   Disclaimer of opinion
    D   Qualified opinion – adverse opinion **(2 marks)**

7 An auditor forms the opinion that a company's trade receivables are overstated by a material amount because of the company's failure to provide for a balance due from a company that has ceased trading.

   What form of qualification of the audit report would normally be appropriate in this case?

   A   Qualified opinion – disagreement
   B   Qualified opinion – limitation on auditors' work
   C   Disclaimer of opinion
   D   Qualified opinion – adverse opinion (2 marks)

8 When carrying out an audit an external auditor must satisfy himself of a number of matters. Which of the following are not one of those matters?

   A   The accounts have been prepared by a qualified accountant
   B   Proper accounting records have been kept
   C   The accounts have been prepared in accordance with local legislation and relevant accounting standards
   D   The accounts are in agreement with accounting records (2 marks)

9 If an external auditor does not agree with the directors' treatment of a material item in the accounts, the first action they should take is to:

   A   Give a qualified opinion of the financial statements
   B   Give an unqualified opinion of the financial statements
   C   Force the directors to change the treatment of the item in the accounts
   D   Persuade the directors to change the treatment of the item in the accounts (2 marks)

10 The external auditor has a duty to report on the truth and fairness of the financial statements and to report any reservations. The auditor is normally given a number of powers by statute to enable the statutory duties to be carried out.

   List three powers that are usually granted to the auditor by statute. (3 marks)

11 Which one of the powers listed below is unlikely to be granted to the auditor by legislation?

   A   The right access at all times to the books, records, documents and accounts of the entity
   B   The right to be notified of, attend and speak at meetings of equity holders
   C   The right to correct financial statements if the auditor believes the statements do not show a true and fair view
   D   The right to require officers of the entity to provide whatever information and explanations thought necessary for the performance of the duties of the auditor (2 marks)

12 Which one of the following statements would be correct when an independent auditor's report gives an adverse opinion?

   A   The effect of the disagreement with management is so pervasive that the financial statements are misleading and, in the opinion of the auditor, do not give a true and fair view.
   B   A disagreement with management over material items needs to be highlighted using an 'except for' statement.
   C   An opinion cannot be given because insufficient information or access to records has been given to the auditor.
   D   A disagreement with management over material items means that an unqualified report must be issued. (2 marks)

13 The external auditors have completed the audit of GQ for the year ended 30 June 2008 and have several outstanding differences of opinion that they have been unable to resolve with the management of GQ. The senior partner of the external auditors has reviewed these outstanding differences and concluded that individually and in aggregate the differences are not material.

Which ONE of the following audit opinions will the external auditors use for GQ's financial statements for the year ended 30 June 2008?

    A   An unqualified opinion
    B   An adverse opinion
    C   An emphasis of matter
    D   A qualified opinion (2 marks)

14 In no more than 25 words, state the objective of an external audit. (2 marks)

(Total = 30 marks)

3 Objective test questions: Ethics — 40 mins

1 A professional accountant in business may be involved in a wide variety of work. Which of these functions will he **not** be carrying out?

    A   Preparing financial statements
    B   Auditing financial statements
    C   Preparing budgets and forecasts
    D   Preparing the management letter provided to the auditors (2 marks)

2 A professional accountant is required under the CIMA Code to comply with five fundamental principles. These include:

    A   Integrity, Objectivity, Reliability
    B   Professional competence and due care, Confidentiality, Integrity
    C   Morality, Objectivity, Professional behaviour
    D   Efficiency, Confidentiality, Professional competence and due care (2 marks)

3 Which of these is least likely to constitute a threat to compliance with the fundamental principles for an accountant in public practice?

    A   The opportunity for personal gain
    B   Intimidation from the directors
    C   Conflict of interest
    D   Confidentiality of information (2 marks)

4 A number of different circumstances may create self-interest threats for the accountant in public practice. Which of these is not a self-interest threat?

    A   Undue dependence on fees from a client
    B   Rotation of audit partners
    C   Close business relationship with a client
    D   Concern about the possibility of losing a client (2 marks)

5 Self-review threats for the accountant in public practice can include:

    A   Accepting gifts from a client
    B   Being threatened with dismissal
    C   Having prepared the original financial statements that are now the subject of the audit engagement
    D   A member of the audit team having a family relationship with a director of the audit client (2 marks)

6 What is meant by an advocacy threat when encountered by the accountant in public practice?

   A A situation where a professional accountant promotes a position or opinion to the point that subsequent objectivity may be compromised

   B A situation where an accountant in public practice is threatened with legal action

   C A situation where a close relationship causes a professional accountant to become too sympathetic to the interests of others

   D A situation where a previous judgement needs to be re-evaluated by the professional accountant responsible for that judgement **(2 marks)**

7 Which of these situations will give rise to a conflict of interest for the professional accountant in public practice?

   A Being under pressure to reduce the amount of work performed in order to reduce fees

   B Reporting on the operation of financial systems after being involved in their design

   C A professional accountant having a financial interest in an entity which is a major competitor of a client

   D A member of the audit team having long association with the client **(2 marks)**

8 Which of the following is an advantage of a principles-based ethical code?

   A It can easily be legally enforced.

   B It provides rules to be followed in all circumstances

   C It encourages compliance by requiring a professional person to actively consider the issues.

   D It can be narrowly interpreted, making it easy for the professional to see whether or not the Code has been violated. **(2 marks)**

9 What is meant by the fundamental principle of 'professional behaviour'?

   A Compliance with relevant laws and regulations and avoidance of any action that discredits the profession

   B Being straightforward and honest in all professional and business relationships

   C Not allowing professional judgement to be affected by bias, undue influence or business considerations

   D Maintaining a high level of technical expertise through continuing professional development
   (2 marks)

10 Which of the following is **not** a circumstance where disclosure of confidential information is permitted under the CIMA Code?

    A Disclosure of information when authorised by the client
    B Disclosure of information to advance the interests of a new client
    C Disclosure of information to protect the professional interests of an accountant in a legal action
    D Disclosure of information when required by law **(2 marks)**

11 Which of these is **not** a source of ethical codes for accountants?

    A IFAC
    B CIMA
    C APB
    D HMRC **(2 marks)**

Total = 22 marks

4 Section B questions: Regulation — 45 mins

(a) The International Accounting Standards Board (IASB) *Framework for the Preparation and Presentation of Financial Statements (Framework)* defines the elements of financial statements.

Required

Explain each of the elements, illustrating each with an example. **(5 marks)**

`P7 5/08`

(b) The IASB's *Framework* identifies four principal qualitative characteristics of financial information.

Required

Identify and explain each of the four principal qualitative characteristics of financial information listed in the IASB's *Framework*. **(5 marks)**

`P7 11/05`

(c) C is a small developing country which passed legislation to create a recognised professional accounting body two years ago. At the same time as the accounting body was created, new regulations governing financial reporting requirements of entities were passed. However, there are currently no accounting standards in C.

C's government has asked the new professional accounting body to prepare a report setting out the country's options for developing and implementing a set of high quality local accounting standards. The government request also referred to the work of the IASB and its International Financial Reporting Standards.

Required

As an advisor to the professional accounting body, outline three options open to C for the development of a set of high quality local accounting standards. Identify one advantage and one disadvantage of each option. **(5 marks)**

`P7 5/06`

(d) *The Framework for the Preparation and presentation of Financial Statements* (Framework) was first published in 1989 and was adopted by The International Accounting Standards Board (IASB)

Explain the purposes of the *Framework*. **(5 marks)**

`P7 5/07`

(e) EK publishes various types of book and occasionally produces films which it sells to major film distributors.

  (i) On 31 March 20X7, EK acquired book publishing and film rights to the next book to be written by an internationally acclaimed author, for $1 million. The author has not yet started writing the book but expects to complete it in 20X9.

  (ii) Between 1 June and 31 July 20X7, EK spent $500,000 exhibiting its range of products at a major international trade fair. This was the first time EK had attended this type of event. No new orders were taken as a direct result of the event, although EK directors claim to have made valuable contacts that should generate additional sales or additional funding for films in the future. No estimate can be made of additional revenue at present.

  (iii) During the year, EK employed an external consultant to redesign EK's corporate logo and to create advertising material to improve EK's corporate image. The total cost of the consultancy was $800,000.

EK's directors want to treat all of the above items of expenditure as assets.

Required

Explain how EK should treat these items of expenditure in its financial statements for the year ended 31 October 20X7 with reference to the International Accounting Standard Board's (IASB) *Framework for the Preparation and Presentation of Financial Statements (Framework)* and relevant International Financial Reporting Standards. **(5 marks)**

P7 5/08

(Total = 25 marks)

5 Section B questions: External audit — 36 mins

(a) Selected balances in HF's financial records at 30 April 20X9 were as follows:

	$000
Revenue	15,000
Profit	1,500
Property, plant and equipment – net book value	23,000
Inventory	1,500

After completing the required audit work the external auditors of HF had the following observations:

(1) Inventory with a book value of $500 is obsolete and should be written off.

(2) Development expenditure net book value of $600,000, relating to the development of a new product line, has been capitalised and amortised in previous years but the project has now been abandoned, (after 30 April X9).

(3) Decommissioning costs relating to HF's production facilities, estimated to be $5,000,000 in 17 years time is being provided for, over 20 years, at $250,000 a year.

Assume there are no other material matters outstanding.

As external auditor you have just completed a meeting with HF management. At the meeting HF management decided the following:

- Item (1) is not material, so it is not necessary to write off the obsolete inventory.
- Item (2) the development expenditure should be written off against current year profits.
- Item (3) the decommissioning cost will continue to be provided for over 20 years.

Required

(i) Explain whether or not the management's decisions taken in the meeting are correct for items (1) and (2). **(2 marks)**

(ii) Explain whether you agree with the management's treatment of the decommissioning costs in item (3) and explain the type of audit report that should be issued, giving your reasons. **(3 marks)**

(Total = 5 marks)

P7 5/09

(b) Explain the circumstances in which an audit report will express each of the following:

(i) A qualified opinion
(ii) A disclaimer of opinion
(iii) An adverse opinion **(5 marks)**

(c) An auditor, in carrying out his statutory duty, may sometimes find himself to be in conflict with the directors of the company. What statutory rights does he have to assist him in discharging his responsibility to the shareholders? **(5 marks)**

(d) DC is carrying out three different construction contracts. The balances and results for the year to 30 September 2006 were as follows:

Contract	1	2	3
Contract end date	30 Sept 2013	31 Dec 2010	30 Sept 2010
	$m	$m	$m
Profit/(loss) recognised for year	2	2.3	(0.6)
Expected total profit/(loss) on contract	12	5.0	(3.0)

DC's management have included $3.7m profit in the profit for the year ended 30 September 2006.

No allowance has been made in the income statement for the future loss expected to arise on contract 3, as management consider the loss should be offset against the expected profits on the other two contracts.

EA & Co are DC's external auditors. EA & Co consider that the profit in relation to long term contracts for the year ended 30 September 2006 should be $1.3m, according to IAS 11 *Construction Contracts*. Assume that EA & Co have been unable to persuade DC's management to change their treatment of the long term contract profit/loss.

Required

(i) Explain the objective of an external audit.

(ii) Identify, with reasons, the type of audit report that would be appropriate for EA & Co to use for DC's financial statements for the year ended 30 September 2006. Briefly explain what information should be included in the audit report in relation to the contracts.

Your answer should refer to appropriate International Standards on Auditing (ISA). **(5 marks)**

P7 11/06

(Total = 20 marks)

6 Section B questions: Ethics — 27 mins

(a) The CIMA Code of Ethics sets out fundamental principles and a conceptual framework for applying them. How does this approach work and how does it differ from a rules-based system? **(5 marks)**

(b) Explain what is meant by conflict of interest and how the professional accountant in public practice should deal with this threat. **(5 marks)**

(c) Explain what is meant by the concept of independence and why it is important for the accountant in public practice. **(5 marks)**

(Total = 15 marks)

Part B: Single Company Financial Accounts

Questions 7 to 34 cover Single Company Financial Accounts, the subject of Part B of the BPP Study Text for Paper F1.

7 Objective test questions: Presentation — 43 mins

1. Which, if any, of the following statements about limited liability companies are correct, according to IAS 1 (revised)?

   1. Companies must produce their financial statements within one year after their reporting period.
   2. The accounting policies adopted by a company must be disclosed by note.
   3. The accounting records of a limited liability company must be open to inspection by a member of the company at all times.

   A   2 only
   B   2 and 3 only
   C   1 and 3 only
   D   None of the statements is correct   **(2 marks)**

2. Which of the following items can appear in a company's statement of changes in equity, according to IAS 1 (revised) *Presentation of financial statements*?

   1. Total comprehensive income for the period
   2. Dividends paid
   3. Surplus on revaluation of properties
   4. Proceeds of issuance of share capital

   A   All four items
   B   1, 2 and 3 only
   C   1, 3 and 4 only
   D   2 and 4 only   **(2 marks)**

3. Which of the following items are required by IAS 1 (revised) *Presentation of financial statements* to be disclosed in the financial statements of a limited liability company?

   1. Authorised share capital
   2. Finance costs
   3. Staff costs
   4. Depreciation

   A   1 and 4 only
   B   1, 2 and 3 only
   C   2, 3 and 4 only
   D   All four items   **(2 marks)**

4. Which of the following constitute a change of accounting policy according to IAS 8 *Accounting policies, changes in accounting estimates and errors?*

   1. A change in the basis of valuing inventory
   2. A change in depreciation method
   3. Depreciation that was previously treated as part of cost of sales is now shown under administrative expenses
   4. Adopting an accounting policy for a new type of transaction not previously dealt with

		A	1 and 2	
		B	2 and 3	
		C	1 and 3	
		D	2 and 4	(2 marks)

5 Which of the following items would qualify for treatment as a change in accounting estimate, according to IAS 8 (revised) *Accounting policies, changes in accounting estimates and errors*?

    1   Provision for obsolescence of inventory
    2   Correction necessitated by a material error
    3   A change as a result of the adoption of a new International Accounting Standard
    4   A change in the useful life of a non-current asset

	A	All four items	
	B	2 and 3 only	
	C	1 and 3 only	
	D	1 and 4 only	(2 marks)

6 A change in accounting policy is accounted for by:

	A	Changing the current year figures but not previous year's figures	
	B	Retrospective application	
	C	No alteration of any figures but disclosure in the notes	
	D	No alteration of any figures nor disclosure in the notes	(2 marks)

7 Which one of the following would be regarded as a change of accounting policy under IAS 8 *Accounting policies, changes in accounting estimates and errors*?

	A	An entity changes its method of depreciation of machinery from straight line to reducing balance.
	B	An entity has changed its method of valuing inventory from FIFO to weighted average.
	C	An entity changes its method of calculating the provision for warranty claims on its products sold.
	D	An entity disclosed a contingent liability for a legal claim in the previous year's accounts. In the current year, a provision has been made for the same legal claim. **(2 marks)**

8 Shah changes the depreciation method for its motor vehicles from the straight line method to the reducing balance method. How would this be treated in the financial statements?

	A	Changing the current year figures but not previous year's figures	
	B	Retrospective application	
	C	No alteration of any figures but disclosure in the notes	
	D	No alteration of any figures nor disclosure in the notes	(2 marks)

9 IAS 8 – *Accounting Policies, Changes in Accounting Estimates and Errors* specifies the definition and treatment of a number of different items. Which of the following is NOT specified by IAS 8?

	A	The effect of a change in an accounting estimate	
	B	Prior period adjustments	
	C	Provisions	
	D	Errors	(2 marks)

10 IAS 1 (revised) *Presentation of financial statements* requires some items to be disclosed on the face of the financial statements and others to be disclosed in the notes.

    1   Depreciation
    2   Revenue
    3   Closing inventory
    4   Finance cost
    5   Dividends

Which two of the above have to be shown on the face of the statement of comprehensive income, rather than in the notes:

A   1 and 4
B   3 and 5
C   2 and 3
D   2 and 4   **(2 marks)**

11   IAS 1 (revised) *Presentation of Financial Statements* encourages an analysis of expenses to be presented on the face of the statement of comprehensive income. The analysis of expenses must use a classification based on either the nature of expense, or its function, within the entity such as:

1   Raw materials and consumables used;
2   Distribution costs;
3   Employee benefit costs;
4   Cost of sales;
5   Depreciation and amortisation expense.

Which of the above would be disclosed on the face of the statement of comprehensive income if a manufacturing entity uses analysis based on function?

A   1, 3 and 4
B   2 and 4
C   1 and 5
D   2, 3 and 5   **(2 marks)**

12   Which one of the following would be regarded as a chance of accounting estimate according to IAS 8 *Accounting policies, changes in accounting estimates and errors*?

A   An entity started valuing inventory using the weighted average cost basis. Inventory was previously valued on the FIFO basis.
B   An entity started revaluing its properties, as allowed by IAS 16 *Property, plant and equipment*. Previously, all property, plant and equipment had been carried at cost less accumulated depreciation.
C   A material error in the inventory valuation methods caused the closing inventory at 31 March 2008 to be overstated by $900,000.
D   An entity created a provision for claims under its warranty of products sold during the year. 5% of sales revenue had previously been set as the required provision amount. After an analysis of three years sales and warranty claims the calculation of the provision amount has been changed to a more realistic 2% of sales.

(2 marks)

(Total = 24 marks)

8 Section B questions: Presentation   18 mins

(a)   Suggest reasons why companies should be expected to publish accounts using standard formats saying why and to whom the specific information shown in the formats would be useful.   **(5 marks)**

(b)   The following is an extract from the trial balance of CE at 31 March 20X6:

	$'000	$'000
Administration expenses	260	
Cost of sales	480	
Interest paid	190	
Interest bearing borrowings		2,200
Inventory at 31 March 20X6	220	
Property, plant and equipment at cost	1,500	
Property, plant and equipment, depreciation to 31 March 20X5		540
Distribution costs	200	
Revenue		2,000

Notes:

(i) Included in the closing inventory at the year end was inventory at a cost of $35,000, which was sold during April 20X6 for $19,000.

(ii) Depreciation is provided for on property, plant and equipment at 20% per year using the reducing balance method. Depreciation is regarded as cost of sales.

(iii) A member of the public was seriously injured while using one of CE's products on 4 October 20X5. Professional legal advice is that CE will probably have to pay $500,000 compensation.

Required

Prepare CE's statement of comprehensive income for the year ended 31 March 20X6 down to the line 'profit before tax'. **(5 marks)**

P7 5/06

(Total = 10 marks)

9 Objective test questions: Statements of cash flows — 43 mins

1. The following is an extract from a statement of cash flows prepared by a trainee accountant.

	$'000
Cash flows from operating activities	
Profit before taxation	3,840
Adjustments for	
Depreciation	(1,060)
Loss on sale of building	210
	2,990
Increase in inventories	(490)
Decrease in trade payables	290
Net cash from operating activities	2,790

Which of the following criticisms of this extract are correct?

1 Depreciation should have been added, not deducted.
2 Loss on sale of building should have been deducted, not added.
3 Increase in inventories should have been added, not deducted.
4 Decrease in trade payables should have been deducted, not added.

A   1 and 4
B   2 and 3
C   1 and 3
D   2 and 4 **(2 marks)**

2. In the year ended 31 December 20X4 a company sold some plant which had cost $100,000 for $20,000. At the time of sale the carrying value of the plant was $18,000.

Which of the following correctly states the treatment of the transaction in the company's statement of cash flows?

	Proceeds of sale	*Profit on sale*
A	Cash inflow under financing activities	Deducted from profit in calculating cash flow from operating activities.
B	Cash inflow under investing activities	Added to profit in calculating cash flow from operating activities.
C	Cash inflow under financing activities	Added to profit in calculating cash flow from operating activities.
D	Cash inflow under investing activities	Deducted from profit in calculating cash flow from operating activities.

(2 marks)

3   Which of the following items should not appear in a company's statement of cash flows?

    1   Proposed dividends
    2   Dividends received
    3   Bonus issue of shares
    4   Surplus on revaluation of a non-current asset
    5   Proceeds of sale of an investment not connected with the company's trading activities

    A   1, 2, 3 and 5
    B   3 and 4 only
    C   1, 3 and 4
    D   2 and 5   (2 marks)

4   Which, if any, of the following statements about statements of cash flows are correct according to IAS 7 *Statement of Cash Flows*?

    1   The direct and indirect methods produce different figures for operating cash flow.
    2   In calculating operating cash flow using the indirect method, an increase in inventory is added to operating profit.
    3   Figures shown in the statement of cash flows should include sales taxes.
    4   The final figure in the statement of cash flows is the increase or decrease in cash at bank.

    A   1 and 4
    B   2 and 3
    C   2 only
    D   None of the statements is correct.   (2 marks)

5   The statement of financial position of R, a limited liability company, at 31 December 20X3 and 20X4 included these figures.

	31 December 20X3 $m	31 December 20X4 $m
Property, plant and equipment: cost	40	50
Accumulated depreciation	(10)	(14)
	30	36

    The statement of comprehensive income for the year ended 31 December 20X4 showed the following figures.

    Depreciation charge for year $6m
    Loss on sales of property, plant and equipment $1m

    The company purchased new property, plant and equipment costing $16m during the year.

    What figure should appear in the company's statement of cash flows for 20X4 for receipts from the sale of property, plant and equipment?

    A $3m
    B $5m
    C $4m
    D   The figure cannot be calculated from the information provided.   (2 marks)

6   A statement of cash flows shows the increase or decrease in cash and cash equivalents in the period.

    Which of the following items are included in this movement?

    1   Cash at bank

    2   Overdraft at bank

    3   Current asset investments readily convertible into known amounts of cash and which can be sold without disrupting the company's business.

    4   Equity investments.

A All four items
B 1, 2 and 3 only
C 1 and 2 only
D 1 and 3 only (2 marks)

7   Which of the following should appear in a statement of cash flows according to IAS 7 *Statement of Cash Flows*?

1   Dividends paid on preference shares
2   Interest capitalised as part of the cost of a non-current asset
3   Cash flows resulting from share issues

A   All three items
B   1 and 2 only
C   1 and 3 only
D   2 and 3 only (2 marks)

8   The IAS 7 format for a statement of cash flows using the indirect method opens with adjustments to net profit before taxation to arrive at cash flow from operating activities.

Which of the following lists consists only of items that would be deducted in that calculation?

A   Loss on sale of non-current assets, increase in inventories, decrease in trade payables
B   Depreciation, increase in trade receivables, decrease in trade payables
C   Increase in trade receivables, profit on sale of non-current assets, decrease in trade payables
D   Profit on sale of non-current assets, increase in trade payables, decrease in trade receivables

(2 marks)

9   A company's accounting records contain the following figures.

	$'000
Sales for year	3,600
Purchases for year	2,400
Receivables: 31 December 20X2	600
31 December 20X3	700
Payables: 31 December 20X2	300
31 December 20X3	450
Salaries and other expenses paid during 20X3, excluding interest	760

What figure should appear in the company's statement of cash flows for 20X3 for cash generated from operations, based on these figures?

A $490,000
B $390,000
C $1,250,000
D   None of these figures (2 marks)

10 At 30 September 20X5, BY had the following balances, with comparatives:

As at 30 September	20X5 $'000	20X4 $'000
Non-current tangible assets		
Property, plant and equipment	260	180
Equity and reserves		
Property, plant and equipment revaluation surplus	30	10

The statement of comprehensive income for the year ended 30 September 20X5 included:

Gain on disposal of an item of equipment $10,000
Depreciation charge for the year $40,000

Notes to the accounts:

Equipment disposed of had cost $90,000. The proceeds received on disposal were $15,000.

Calculate the property, plant and equipment purchases that BY would show in its statement of cash flows for the year ended 30 September 20X5, as required by IAS 7 *Statement of Cash Flows*. **(4 marks)**

11 At 1 October 20X4, BK had the following balance:

Accrued interest payable $12,000 credit

During the year ended 30 September 20X5, BK charged interest payable of $41,000 to its statement of comprehensive income. The closing balance on accrued interest payable account at 30 September 20X5 was $15,000 credit.

How much interest paid should BK show on its statement of cash flows for the year ended 30 September 20X5?

A $38,000
B $41,000
C $44,000
D $53,000

(2 marks)

P7 11/05

(Total = 24 marks)

10 Section B question: Statements of cash flows   9 mins

The following financial information relates to FC for the year ended 31 March 20X8.

FC
STATEMENT OF COMPREHENSIVE INCOME FOR THE YEAR ENDED 31 MARCH 20X8

	$'000
Revenue	445
Cost of sales	(220)
Gross profit	225
Other income	105
	330
Administrative expenses	(177)
Finance costs	(20)
Profit before tax	133
Income tax expense	(43)
Profit for the year	90

The following administrative expenses were incurred in the year.

	$'000
Wages	70
Other general expenses	15
Depreciation	92
	177
Other income:	
Rentals received	45
Gain on disposal of non-current assets	60
	105

Statement of financial position extracts at:

	31 March 20X8	31 March 20X7
	$'000	$'000
Inventories	40	25
Trade receivables	50	45
Trade payables	(30)	(20)

Required

Prepare FC's statement of cash flows for the year ended 31 March 20X8, down to the line 'Cash generated from operations', using the direct method.

(5 marks)

P7 5/08

11 HZ (FATP 5/09/amended) — 45 mins

The accountant of HZ started preparing the financial statements for the year ended 31 March 20X9, but was suddenly taken ill. The **draft** financial statements for HZ for the year ended 31 March 20X9 are given below:

HZ STATEMENTS OF FINANCIAL POSITION AT 31 MARCH 20X9 (DRAFT)   31 MARCH 20X8 (FINAL)

	$000	$000	$000	$000
Assets				
Non-current assets				
Property, plant and equipment	5,854		6,250	
Goodwill	217		350	
Other intangible assets	198	6,269	170	6,770
Current assets				
Inventories	890		750	
Trade receivables	924		545	
Cash and cash equivalents	717		300	
		2,531		1,595
Total assets		8,800		8,365
Equity and liabilities				
Equity share capital	2,873		2,470	
Share premium account	732		530	
Revaluation surplus	562		400	
Retained earnings	1,623		1,840	
Total equity		5,790		5,240
Non-current liabilities				
10% loan notes	–		1,250	
5% loan notes	700		700	
Deferred tax	312		250	
Total non-current liabilities		1,012		2,200
Current liabilities				
Trade payables	744		565	
Income tax	117		247	
Suspense account	1,000		–	
Provision	120		–	
Accrued interest	17		113	
Total current liabilities		1,998		925
Total equity and liabilities		8,800		8,365

STATEMENT OF COMPREHENSIVE INCOME FOR THE YEAR ENDED 31 MARCH 20X9 (DRAFT)

	$000
Revenue	9,750
Cost of sales	(5,200)
Gross profit	4,550
Distribution costs	(1,195)
Administrative expenses	(2,990)
Profit from operations	365
Finance costs	(60)
Profit before tax	305
Income tax expense	(182)
Profit for the year	123

Additional information:

(i) Non-current tangible assets include properties which were revalued upwards during the year.

(ii) Non-current tangible assets disposed of in the year had a net book value of $98,000; cash received on their disposal was $128,000. Any gain or loss on disposal has been included under cost of sales.

(iii) During the year goodwill became impaired. The impairment was charged to cost of sales.

(iv) Depreciation charged for the year was $940,000, included in cost of sales.

(v) On 1 April 20X8, HZ issued 806,000 $0.50 equity shares at a premium of 50%.

(vi) On 1 April 20X8, HZ issued 1,000,000 5% cumulative $1 preferred shares at par, redeemable at 10% premium on 1 April 20Y8. Issue costs of $70,000 have been paid and included in administrative expenses. The constant annual rate of interest is 6·72%. The cash received for the issue of the preferred shares has been debited to cash and credited to suspense.

(vii) The other intangible assets relate to research and development expenditure.

Development expenditure of $170,000 was incurred and paid in the year ended 31 March 20X7; the remaining expenditure was incurred in the year ended 31 March 20X9. At 31 March 20X8, the expenditure met the IAS 38 criteria for deferral. When development expenditure was assessed at 31 March 20X9, it was clear that the expenditure incurred in 20X6/X7 no longer met the IAS 38 criteria, but the expenditure incurred in 20X8/X9 did still meet the requirements. No action has yet been taken to write off any development expenditure.

(viii) On 1 May 20X8, HZ purchased and cancelled all its 10% loan notes at par plus accrued interest (included in finance costs).

(ix) Ordinary dividends paid during the year were $290,000 and preferred share dividends paid were $50,000.

(x) HZ has been advised that it is probably going to lose a court case and has provided $120,000 for the estimated cost of this case. This is included in administrative expenses.

Required

(a) Explain the accounting adjustments required by HZ to clear the balance on the suspense account at 31 March 20X9 and calculate a revised profit before tax for the year ended 31 March 20X9. (Note a detailed statement of comprehensive income is NOT required) **(5 marks)**

(b) Prepare statement of cash flows, using the indirect method, for HZ for the year ended 31 March 20X9, in accordance with IAS 7 *Statement of cash flows*. **(20 marks)**

Notes to the financial statements are not required, but all workings must be clearly shown. Do NOT prepare a statement of accounting policies.

(Total = 25 marks)

12 Tex (FATP Pilot paper/amended)   45 mins

The following information has been extracted from the draft financial statements of Tex, a manufacturing company.

TEX
STATEMENT OF COMPREHENSIVE INCOME FOR THE YEAR ENDED 30 SEPTEMBER 20X1

	$'000
Revenue	15,000
Cost of sales	(9,000)
Gross profit	6,000
Other operating expenses	(2,300)
	3,700
Finance cost	(124)
Profit before taxation	3,576
Income tax expense	(1,040)
Profit for the year	2,536

TEX
STATEMENT OF FINANCIAL POSITION AS AT 30 SEPTEMBER 20X1

	20X1		20X0	
	$'000	$'000	$'000	$'000
Assets				
Property, plant and equipment		18,160		14,500
Current assets				
Inventories	1,600		1,100	
Trade receivables	1,500		800	
Bank	150		1,200	
		3,250		3,100
Total assets		21,410		17,600
Equity and liabilities				
Equity:				
Share capital		10,834		7,815
Retained earnings		6,536		5,000
		17,370		12,815
Non-current liabilities				
Interest-bearing borrowing	1,700		2,900	
Deferred tax	600		400	
		2,300		3,300
Current liabilities				
Trade payables	700		800	
Taxation	1,040		685	
		1,740		1,485
Total equity and liabilities		21,410		17,600

Property, plant and equipment

	Property $'000	Plant $'000	Total $'000
Cost			
30 September 20X0	8,400	10,800	19,200
Additions	2,800	5,200	8,000
Disposals	–	(2,600)	(2,600)
30 September 20X1	11,200	13,400	24,600
Depreciation			
30 September 20X0	1,300	3,400	4,700
Disposals	–	(900)	(900)
Charge for year	240	2,400	2,640
30 September 20X1	1,540	4,900	6,440
Net book value			
30 September 20X1	9,660	8,500	18,160
30 September 20X0	7,100	7,400	14,500

The plant that was disposed of during the year was sold for $730,000.

All additions to property, plant and equipment were purchased for cash.

Dividends paid during the year were $1,000,000.

Required

(a) Prepare Tex's statement of cash flows for the year ended 30 September 20X1. **(13 marks)**

(b) During the year to 30 September 20X2 Tex had the following results:

TEX
STATEMENT OF COMPREHENSIVE INCOME FOR THE YEAR ENDED 30 SEPTEMBER 20X2

	$'000
Revenue	18,000
Cost of sales	(8,900)
Gross profit	9,100
Other operating expenses	(5,000)
	4,100
Finance cost	(120)
Profit before taxation	3,980
Income tax expense	(1,300)
Profit for the year	2,680

Extract from cash book for year to 30 September 20X2:

	$'000
Purchases	9,000
Other operating expenses (all paid by the year end)	2,000
Loan interest paid	120
Cash received from customers	16,700
Cash paid to suppliers	8,300
Tax paid	1,040
Dividend paid	1,000

There are no additions or disposals of property, plant or equipment. Depreciation is charged to other operating expenses in the statement of comprehensive income.

There is no movement on share capital or non-current liabilities.

Required

Prepare the statement of financial position for Tex at 30 September 20X2.

(12 marks)

(Total = 25 marks)

13 AG (FATP 5/05/amended) — 45 mins

The financial statements of AG are given below:

STATEMENT OF FINANCIAL POSITION AS AT

	31 March 20X5			31 March 20X4
	$'000	$'000	$'000	$'000
Non-current assets				
Property, plant and equipment	3,600		3,900	
Goodwill	800		900	
Development expenditure	370	4,770	400	5,200
Current assets				
Inventories	685		575	
Trade receivables	515		420	
Cash and cash equivalents	1,082	2,282	232	1,227
Total assets		7,052		6,427
Equity				
Share capital	2,600		1,900	
Share premium account	750		400	
Revaluation surplus	425		300	
Retained earnings	1,360		1,415	
Total equity		5,135		4,015

STATEMENT OF FINANCIAL POSITION AS AT

	31 March 20X5			31 March 20X4
	$'000	$'000	$'000	$'000
Non-current liabilities				
8% redeemable preference shares	500		–	
10% loan notes	0		1,000	
5% loan notes	500		500	
Deferred tax	250		200	
Total non-current liabilities		1,250		1,700
Current liabilities				
Trade payables	480		350	
Income tax	80		190	
Accrued expenses	107		172	
Total current liabilities		667		712
Total equity and liabilities		7,052		6,427

STATEMENT OF COMPREHENSIVE INCOME FOR THE YEAR ENDED 31 MARCH 20X5

	$'000
Revenue	7,500
Cost of sales	(4,000)
Gross profit	3,500
Distribution costs	(900)
Administrative expenses	(2,400)
Finance costs	(65)
Profit before tax	135
Income tax expense	(90)
Profit for the year	45

Additional information

(a) On 1 April 20X4, AG issued 1,400,000 $0.50 ordinary shares at a premium of 50%.

(b) On 1 May 20X4, AG purchased and cancelled all its 10% loan notes at par.

(c) On 1 October 20X4, AG issued 500,000 $1.00 8% preference shares at par. The preference shares are redeemable at par in 20X9.

(c) Non-current tangible assets include properties which were revalued upwards by $125,000 during the year.

(d) Non-current tangible assets disposed of in the year had a net book value of $75,000; cash received on disposal was $98,000. Any gain or loss on disposal has been included under cost of sales.

(e) Cost of sales includes $80,000 for development expenditure amortised during the year.

(f) Administrative expenses includes $100,000 for goodwill written-off during the year.

(g) Depreciation charged for the year was $720,000.

(h) The accrued expenses balance includes interest payable on the loan notes of $87,000 at 31 March 20X4 and $12,000 at 31 March 20X5. Dividends on the redeemable 8% preference shares were paid on 31 March 20X5.

(i) The income tax expense for the year to 31 March 20X5 is made up as follows:

	$'000
Corporate income tax	40
Deferred tax	50
	90

(j) Dividends paid on ordinary shares during the year were $100,000.

Required

Prepare a statement of cash flows, using the indirect method, for AG for the year ended 31 March 20X5, in accordance with IAS 7 *Statement of cash flows*. **(25 marks)**

14 CJ (FATP 5/06/amended) — 45 mins

The financial statements of CJ for the year to 31 March 20X6 were as follows:

STATEMENTS OF FINANCIAL POSITION AS AT	31 March 20X6 $'000	31 March 20X6 $'000	31 March 20X5 $'000	31 March 20X5 $'000
Assets				
Non-current assets				
Property	19,160		18,000	
Plant and equipment	8,500		10,000	
Available for sale investments	2,100		2,100	
		29,760		30,100
Current assets				
Inventory	2,714		2,500	
Trade receivables	2,106		1,800	
Cash at bank	11,753		0	
Cash in hand	409		320	
		16,982		4,620
Total assets		46,742		34,720
Equity and liabilities				
Equity				
Ordinary shares $0.50 each	12,000		7,000	
Share premium	10,000		5,000	
Revaluation surplus	4,200		2,700	
Retained earnings	2,809		1,510	
		29,009		16,210
Non-current liabilities				
Interest bearing borrowings	13,000		13,000	
Provision for deferred tax	999	13,999	800	13,800
Current liabilities				
Bank overdraft	0		1,200	
Trade and other payables	1,820		1,700	
Corporate income tax payable	1,914		1,810	
		3,734		4,710
Total equity and liabilities		46,742		34,720

STATEMENT OF COMPREHENSIVE INCOME FOR THE YEAR TO 31 MARCH 20X6

	$'000
Revenue	31,000
Cost of sales	(19,000)
Gross profit	12,000
Administrative expenses	(3,900)
Distribution costs	(2,600)
	5,500
Finance cost	(1,302)
Profit before tax	4,198
Income tax expense	(2,099)
Profit for the year	2,099
Other comprehensive income:	
Gain on property revaluation	1,500
Total comprehensive income for the year	3,599

Additional information

(a) On 1 April 20X5, CJ issued 10,000,000 $0.50 ordinary shares at a premium of 100%.

(b) Properties were revalued by $1,500,000 during the year.

(c) Plant disposed of in the year had a net book value of $95,000; cash received on disposal was $118,000.

(d) Depreciation charged for the year was properties $2,070,000 and plant and equipment $1,985,000.

(e) The trade and other payables balance includes interest payable of $650,000 at 31 March 20X5 and $350,000 at 31 March 20X6.

(f) Dividends paid during the year, $800,000 comprised last year's final dividend plus the current year's interim dividend.

Dividends payable are not accrued.

(g) Income tax expense comprises:

	$
Corporate income tax	1,900,000
Deferred tax	199,000
	2,099,000

Required

(a) Prepare CJ's statement of cash flows for the year ended 31 March 20X6, in accordance with IAS 7 *Statement of cash flows*. **(15 marks)**

(b) CJ commenced a long-term contract in early 20X6. The details are as follows:

	$'000
Total contract price	5,000
Costs to date	700
Expected further costs to complete	2,500
Progress billings	500
Percentage completed	20%

CJ did not include any of these amounts in its financial statements. No payment has yet been received and it has not yet made any payments to its suppliers or subcontractors.

Required

Redraft CJ's statement of financial position at 31 March 20X6 to include the results of the long-term contract. Ignore any tax implications. (This does not affect your answer to (a).) **(10 marks)**

(Total = 25 marks)

15 DN (FATP 11/06/amended) — 45 mins

DN's draft financial statements for the year ended 31 October 20X6 are as follows:

DN
STATEMENT OF COMPREHENSIVE INCOME FOR THE YEAR TO 31 OCTOBER 20X6

	$'000	$'000
Revenue		2,600
Cost of sales		
Parts and sub-assemblies	(500)	
Labour	(400)	
Overheads	(400)	
		(1,300)
Gross profit		1,300
Administrative expenses	(300)	
Distribution costs	(100)	
		(400)
Profit from operations		900
Finance cost		(110)
Profit before tax		790
Income tax expense		(140)
Profit for the year		650
Other comprehensive income		
Gain on revaluation of property		300
Total comprehensive income for the year		950

DN
STATEMENT OF FINANCIAL POSITION AS AT

	31 October 20X6 $'000	31 October 20X6 $'000	31 October 20X5 $'000	31 October 20X5 $'000
Assets				
Non-current assets				
Property, plant and equipment		4,942		4,205
Current assets				
Inventories	190		140	
Trade receivables	340		230	
Cash and cash equivalents	2,318		45	
		2,848		415
Total assets		7,790		4,620
Equity and liabilities				
Equity				
Equity shares of $0.50 each	1,300		1,000	
Share premium	300		0	
Revaluation surplus	400		0	
Retained earnings	2,060		1,410	
Total equity		4,060		2,410
Non-current liabilities				
Bank loans (various rates)		3,500		2,000
		7,560		4,410
Current liabilities		230		210
Total equity and liabilities		7,790		4,620

Additional information

(a) Property, plant and equipment comprises:

	20X6 $'000	20X5 $'000
Property	3,100	2,800
Plant and equipment	1,842	1,405

(b) Plant and equipment sold during the year for $15,000 had a carrying amount of $10,000. The profit on disposal of $5,000 has been included in overheads.

(c) Properties were revalued on 31 October 20X6.

(d) DN made an equity share issue on 31 October 20X6.

(e) DN's funding includes a new $1,500,000 bank loan which was drawn down on 30 June 20X6 and is due for repayment on 29 June 20X9

(f) Tax paid for the year was $120,000.

(g) Current liabilities:

	20X6 $'000	20X5 $'000
Trade payables	105	85
Interest payable	55	75
Tax payable	70	50
Total current liabilities	230	210

(h) No dividends were declared or paid during the year.

(i) Overheads include the annual depreciation charge of $100,000 for property and $230,000 for plant and equipment.

Required

(a) Prepare DN's statement of cash flows for the year ended 31 October 20X6, using the indirect method, in accordance with IAS 7 *Statement of cash flows*. **(15 marks)**

(b) Over the next twelve months DN expects to make sales of $3,300,000, which will require purchases of $1,700,000. Inventory levels will remain constant.

It expects to collect $3,100,000 from customers and pay $1,600,000 to suppliers. Interest costs will be the same as 20X6 and the tax charge is estimated at $60,000. DN will clear both tax and interest payable by the year end.

No purchases or disposals of non-current assets are planned. Depreciation will be $330,000 and DN intends to hold other expenses to $500,000, which will be paid in cash.

Required

Draft DN's projected statement of financial position at 31 October 20X7.   **(10 marks)**

(Total = 25 marks)

16 Lemming Inc   45 mins

The statements of financial position at 31 August 20X8 and 20X9 for Lemming Inc are given below.

LEMMING INC
STATEMENTS OF FINANCIAL POSITION AS AT

		31 August 20X8 $'000	31 August 20X8 $'000	31 August 20X9 $'000	31 August 20X9 $'000
Property, plant and equipment	(a)		6,400		8,500
Current assets					
Inventory		1,200		1,400	
Receivables		1,500		1,400	
Cash at bank		200		300	
			2,900		3,100
			9,300		11,600
Equity					
Share capital	(b)		2,000		2,200
Share premium account	(b)		2,340		2,540
Revaluation surplus			–		1,000
Retained earnings			2,400		2,960
			6,740		8,700
Non current liabilities					
10% Loan notes 20Y5	(c)		1,000		1,500
			7,740		10,200
Current liabilities					
Trade payables		800		700	
Taxation		400		500	
Bank overdraft		360		200	
			1,560		1,400
			9,300		11,600

Notes

(a) Movements in property, plant and equipment

	Land $'000	Buildings $'000	Plant and equipment $'000	Total $'000
Cost or valuation				
At 1 September 20X8	2,000	3,000	3,400	8,400
Additions	–	–	2,500	2,500
Disposals	–	–	(1,000)	(1,000)
Revaluation	1,000	–		1,000
At 31 August 20X9	3,000	3,000	4,900	10,900
Accumulated depreciation				
At 1 September 20X8	–	400	1,600	2,000
Charge for year	–	60	1,140	1,200
Disposals	–	–	(800)	(800)
At 31 August 20X9	–	460	1,940	2,400

	Net book value				
	At 31 August 20X9	3,000	2,540	2,960	8,500
	At 1 September 20X8	2,000	2,600	1,800	6,400

(b) Issue of shares – 400,000 $0.50 ordinary shares were issued for a $0.50 premium on 1 September 20X8. All shares were fully paid up by the year end.

(c) Issue of loan notes – A further $500,000 of 10% loan notes was issued at par on 1 September 20X8. Interest on all loan notes is paid on 28 February and 31 August each year.

(d) Plant sold during the year realised $250,000.

(e) The tax charge for the year was $500,000.

(f) Sales revenue for the year to 31 August 20X9 was $14,050,000 and purchases were $10,690,000.

(g) Operating expenses of $700,000 were paid during the year.

Required

(a) Prepare the statement of comprehensive income for Lemming Inc for the year ended 31 August 20X9.

(b) Prepare the statement of cash flows of Lemming Inc for the year ended 31 August 20X9, complying as far as possible with IAS 7 *Statement of cash flows,* using the indirect method.

(25 marks)

17 Objective test questions: Non-current assets, inventories and construction contracts I
49 mins

1   The components of the cost of a major item of equipment are given below.

	$
Purchase price	780,000
Import duties	117,000
Sales tax (refundable)	78,000
Site preparation	30,000
Installation	28,000
Initial operating losses before the asset reaches planned performance	50,000
Estimated cost of dismantling and removal of the asset, recognised as a provision under IAS 37 *Provisions, contingent liabilities and contingent assets*	100,000
	1,183,000

What amount may be recognised as the cost of the asset, according to IAS 16 *Property, plant and equipment?*

A $956,000
B $1,105,000
C $1,055,000
D $1,183,000

(2 marks)

2   Which of the following statements about IAS 36 *Impairment of assets* are correct?

1   Non-current assets must be checked annually for evidence of impairment.

2   An impairment loss must be recognised immediately in the income statement, except that all or part of a loss on a revalued asset should be charged against any related revaluation surplus.

3   If individual assets cannot be tested for impairment, it may be necessary to test a group of assets as a unit.

A   1 and 2 only
B   1 and 3 only
C   2 and 3 only
D   1, 2 and 3

(2 marks)

3   Which of the following statements is correct?

   1   Negative goodwill should be shown in the statement of financial position as a deduction from positive goodwill.
   2   IAS 38 allows goodwill to be written off immediately against reserves as an alternative to capitalisation.
   3   As a business grows, internally generated goodwill may be revalued upwards to reflect that growth.
   4   Internally developed brands must not be capitalised.

   A   1 and 4
   B   2 and 3
   C   3 only
   D   4 only   (2 marks)

4   Which of the following accounting policies would contravene International Accounting Standards if adopted by a company?

   1   Goodwill on acquisitions is written off immediately against reserves.
   2   Land on which the company's buildings stand is not depreciated.
   3   Internally generated brands are capitalised at fair value as advised by independent consultants.
   4   In calculating depreciation, the estimated useful life of an asset is taken as half the actual estimated useful life as a measure of prudence.

   A   1, 3 and 4
   B   2 and 4 only
   C   1 and 3 only
   D   All four are unacceptable   (2 marks)

5   Which of the following items should be included in arriving at the cost of the inventory of finished goods held by a manufacturing company, according to IAS 2 *Inventories*?

   1   Carriage inwards on raw materials delivered to factory
   2   Carriage outwards on goods delivered to customers
   3   Factory supervisors' salaries
   4   Factory heating and lighting
   5   Cost of abnormally high idle time in the factory
   6   Import duties on raw materials

   A   1, 3, 4 and 6
   B   1, 2, 4, 5 and 6
   C   3, 4 and 6
   D   2, 3 and 5   (2 marks)

6   Which of the following statements about IAS 2 *Inventories* are correct?

   1   Production overheads should be included in cost on the basis of a company's actual level of activity in the period.
   2   In arriving at the net realisable value of inventories, trade discounts and settlement discounts must be deducted.
   3   In arriving at the cost of inventories, FIFO, LIFO and weighted average cost formulas are acceptable.
   4   It is permitted to value finished goods inventories at materials plus labour cost only, without adding production overheads.

   A   1 only
   B   2 only
   C   3 only
   D   None of them   (2 marks)

Questions

7 The position of a construction contract at 30 June 20X6 is as follows.

	$
Contract price	900,000
At 30 June 20X6	
Costs to date	720,000
Estimated costs to completion	480,000
Progress payments invoiced and received	400,000
Percentage complete	60%

What figures should appear for this contract in the accounts at 30 June 20X6, according to IAS 11 *Construction contracts*?

	Statement of comprehensive income		Statement of financial position	
A	Sales revenue	$540,000	Receivables	$140,000
	Costs	$840,000		
B	Sales revenue	$540,000		
	Costs	$720,000		
C	Sales revenue	$540,000	Amount due from customer	$20,000
	Costs	$840,000		
D	Sales revenue	$540,000	Receivables	$140,000
	Costs	$720,000		

(2 marks)

---

8 The following measures relate to a non-current asset:

(i) Net book value $20,000
(ii) Net realisable value $18,000
(iii) Value in use $22,000
(iv) Replacement cost $50,000

The recoverable amount of the asset is

A $18,000
B $20,000
C $22,000
D $50,000

(2 marks)

---

9 BL started a contract on 1 November 20X4. The contract was scheduled to run for two years and has a sales value of $40 million.

At 31 October 20X5, the following details were obtained from BL's records:

	$m
Costs incurred to date	16
Estimated costs to completion	18
Percentage complete at 31 October 20X5	45%

Applying IAS 11 *Construction contracts*, how much revenue and profit should BL recognise in its statement of comprehensive income for the year ended 31 October 20X5? **(2 marks)**

---

10 CI purchased equipment on 1 April 20X2 for $100,000. The equipment was depreciated using the reducing balance method at 25% per year. CI's year end is 31 March.

Depreciation was charged up to and including 31 March 20X6. At that date, the recoverable amount was $28,000.

Calculate the impairment loss on the equipment according to IAS 36 Impairment of Assets. **(3 marks)**

The following data are given for sub-questions 11 and 12 below

CN started a three year contract to build a new university campus on 1 April 20X5. The contract had a fixed price of $90 million.

CN incurred costs to 31 March 20X6 of $77 million and estimated that a further $33 million would need to be spent to complete the contract.

CN uses the percentage of cost incurred to date to total cost method to calculate stage of completion of the contract.

11 Calculate revenue earned on the contract to 31 March 20X6, according to IAS 11 Construction Contracts.
(2 marks)

12 State how much gross profit/loss CN should recognise in its statement of comprehensive income for the year ended 31 March 20X6, according to IAS 11 Construction Contracts. (2 marks)

13 IAS 16 *Property, Plant and Equipment* requires an asset to be measured at cost on its original recognition in the financial statements.

EW used its own staff, assisted by contractors when required, to construct a new warehouse for its own use.

Which ONE of the following costs would NOT be included in attributable costs of the non-current asset?

A   Clearance of the site prior to work commencing.

B   Professional surveyors' fees for managing the construction work.

C   EW's own staff wages for time spent working on the construction.

D   An allocation of EW's administration costs, based on EW staff time spent on the construction as a percentage of the total staff time.
(2 marks)

(Total = 27 marks)

18 Objective test questions: Non-current assets, inventories and construction contracts II
63 mins

1 A company purchased a machine for $50,000 on 1 January 20X1. It was judged to have a 5-year life with a residual value of $5,000. On 31 December 20X2 $15,000 was spent on an upgrade to the machine. This extended its remaining useful life to 5 years, with the same residual value. During 20X3, the market for the product declined and the machine was sold on 1 January 20X4 for $7,000.

What was the loss on disposal?

A $31,000
B $35,000
C $31,600
D $35,600
(2 marks)

2 A cash generating unit comprises the following:

	$m
Building	20
Plant and equipment	10
Goodwill	5
Current assets	10
	45

Following a downturn in the market, an impairment review has been undertaken and the recoverable amount of the cash generating unit is estimated to be $25m.

What is the carrying value of the building after adjusting for the impairment loss?

A $11m
B $10m
C $12.5m
D $20m
(2 marks)

3 In less than 30 words, define 'impairment'. (2 marks)

4 Which of the following is *not* true regarding IAS 2 *Inventories*?

   A   Fixed production overheads must be allocated to items of inventory on the basis of the normal level of production.

   B   Plant lying idle will lead to a higher fixed overhead allocation to each unit.

   C ✓ An abnormally high level of production will lead to a lower allocation of fixed production overhead to each unit

   D   Unallocated overheads must be recognised as an expense in the period in which they are incurred.

   (2 marks)

5 In less than 20 words define *fair value*. (2 marks)

The following data is to be used to answer sub-questions 6 and 7 below

X acquired the business and assets from the owners of an unincorporated business: the purchase price was satisfied by the issue of 10,000 equity shares with a nominal market value of $10 each and $20,000 cash. The market value of X shares at the date of acquisition was $20 each.

The assets acquired were:

- Net tangible non-current assets with a book value of $20,000 and current value of $25,000.
- Patents for a specialised process valued by a specialist valuer at $15,000.
- Brand name, valued by a specialist brand valuer on the basis of a multiple of earnings at $50,000.
- Publishing rights of the first text from an author that the management of X expects to become a best seller. The publishing rights were a gift from the author to the previous owners at no cost. The management of X has estimated the future value of the potential best seller at $100,000. However, there is no reliable evidence available to support the estimate of the management.

6 In no more than **30 words**, explain the accounting treatment to be used for the publishing rights of the first text. (2 marks)

7 Calculate the value of goodwill to be included in the accounts of X for this purchase. (4 marks)

8 An item of plant and equipment was purchased on 1 April 20X1 and for $100,000. At the date of acquisition its expected useful life was 10 years. Depreciation was provided on a straight line basis, with no residual value.

On April 1 20X3, the asset was revalued to $95,000. On 1 April 20X4, the useful life of the asset was reviewed and the remaining useful life was reduced to 5 years, a total useful life of 8 years.

Calculate the amounts that would be included in the statement of financial position for the asset cost/valuation and provision for accumulated depreciation at 31 March 20X5. (4 marks)

9 IAS 16 *Property, Plant and Equipment* provides definitions of terms relevant to non-current assets. Complete the following sentence, **in no more than 10 words**.

   'Depreciable amount is Cost less residual value (2 marks)

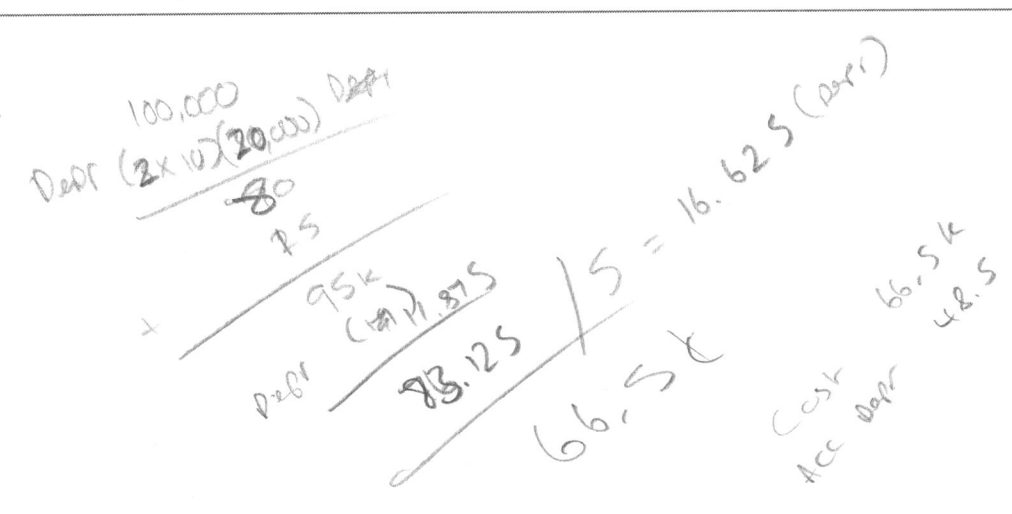

10 Which ONE of the following items would CM recognise as subsequent expenditure on a non-current asset and capitalise it as required by IAS 16 *Property, Plant and Equipment*?

  A CM purchased a furnace five years ago, when the furnace lining was separately identified in the accounting records. The furnace now requires relining at a cost of $200,000. When the furnace is relined it will be able to be used in CM's business for a further five years.

  B CM's office building has been badly damaged by a fire. CM intends to restore the building to its original condition at a cost of $250,000.

  C CM's delivery vehicle broke down. When it was inspected by the repairers it was discovered that it needed a new engine. The engine and associated labour costs are estimated to be $5,000.

  D CM closes its factory for two weeks every year. During this time, all plant and equipment has its routine annual maintenance check and any necessary repairs are carried out. The cost of the current year's maintenance check and repairs was $75,000.
(2 marks)

11 DS purchased a machine on 1 October 20X2 at a cost of $21,000 with an expected useful economic life of six years, with no expected residual value. DS depreciates its machines using the straight line basis.

The machine has been used and depreciated for three years to 30 September 20X5. New technology was invented in December 20X5, which enabled a cheaper, more efficient machine to be produced; this technology makes DS's type of machine obsolete. The obsolete machine will generate no further economic benefit or have any residual value once the new machines become available. However, because of production delays, the new machines will not be available on the market until 1 October 20X7.

Calculate how much depreciation DS should charge to profit or loss for the year ended 30 September 20X6, as required by IAS 16 *Property, Plant and Equipment*.
(3 marks)

12 IAS 38 *Intangible Assets* sets out six criteria that must be met before an internally generated intangible asset can be recognised.

List FOUR of IAS 38's criteria for recognition.
(4 marks)

13 Details from DV's long-term contract, which commenced on 1 May 20X6, at 30 April 20X7:

	$'000
Invoiced to client for work done	2,000
Costs incurred to date:	
Attributable to work completed	1,500
Inventory purchased, but not yet used	250
Progress payment received from client	900
Expected further costs to complete project	400
Total contract value	3,000

DV uses the percentage of costs incurred to total costs to calculate attributable profit.

Calculate the amount that DV should recognise in its statement of comprehensive income for the year ended 30 April 20X7 for revenue, cost of sales and attributable profits on this contract according to IAS 11 *Construction Contracts*.

(4 marks)

(Total = 35 marks)

19 Section B questions: Non-current assets, inventories and construction contracts   54 mins

(a) (i) Discuss the criteria which IAS 38 *Intangible assets* states should be used when considering whether research and development expenditure should be written off in an accounting period or carried forward.

(ii) Discuss to what extent these criteria are consistent with the fundamental accounting assumptions within IAS 1. **(5 marks)**

(b) 'The cost of inventories should comprise all costs of purchase, costs of conversion and other costs incurred in bringing the inventories to their present location and condition' (IAS 2).

This statement results in problems of a practical nature in arriving at the amount at which inventories and short term work in progress are stated in the accounts.

Required

Comment on the above statement identifying and discussing both the accounting policy and the problems 'of a practical nature' that may arise when computing the amount at which inventories and short term work in progress are stated in financial accounts. **(5 marks)**

(c) A new type of delivery vehicle, when purchased on 1 April 20X0 for $20,000, was expected to have a useful life of four years. It now appears that the original estimate of the useful life was too short, and the vehicle is now expected to have a useful life of six years, from the date of purchase. All delivery vehicles are depreciated using the straight-line method and are assumed to have zero residual value.

Required

As the trainee management accountant, draft a memo to the transport manager explaining whether it is possible to change the useful life of the new delivery vehicle. Using appropriate International Accounting Standards, explain how the accounting transactions relating to the delivery vehicle should be recorded in the statement of comprehensive income for the year ended 31 March 20X3 and the statement of financial position at that date **(5 marks)**

P7 Pilot paper

(d) BI owns a building which it uses as its offices, warehouse and garage. The land is carried as a separate non-current tangible asset in the statement of financial position.

BI has a policy of regularly revaluing its non-current tangible assets. The original cost of the building in October 20X2 was $1,000,000; it was assumed to have a remaining useful life of 20 years at that date, with no residual value. The building was revalued on 30 September 20X4 by a professional valuer at $1,800,000.

BI also owns a brand name which it acquired 1 October 20X0 for $500,000. The brand name is being amortised over 10 years.

The economic climate had deteriorated during 20X5, causing BI to carry out an impairment review of its assets at 30 September 20X5. BI's building was valued at a market value of $1,500,000 on 30 September 20X5 by an independent valuer. A brand specialist valued BI's brand name at market value of $200,000 on the same date.

BI's management accountant calculated that the brand name's value in use at 30 September 20X5 was $150,000.

Required

Explain how BI should report the events described above and quantify any amounts required to be included in its financial statements for the year ended 30 September 20X5. **(5 marks)**

P7 11/05

(e) DV purchased two buildings on 1 September 1996. Building A cost $200,000 and had a useful economic life of 20 years. Building B cost $120,000 and had a useful life of 15 years. DV's accounting policies are to revalue buildings every five years and depreciate them over their useful economic lives on the straight line basis. DV does not make an annual transfer from revaluation surplus to retained profits for excess depreciation.

DV received the following valuations from its professionally qualified external valuer:

31 August 2001	Building A	$180,000
	Building B	$75,000
31 August 2006	Building A	$100,000
	Building B	$30,000

Required

Calculate the gains or impairments arising on the revaluation of Buildings A and B at 31 August 2006 and identify where they should be recognised in the financial statements of DV. **(5 marks)**

`P7 11/06`

(f) HS, a contractor, signed a two year fixed price contract on 31 March 20X8 for $300,000 to build a bridge. Total costs were originally estimated at $240,000.

At 31 March 20X9, HS extracted the following figures from its financial records:

	$000
Contract value	300
Costs incurred to date	170
Estimated costs to complete	100
Progress payments received	130
Value of work completed	165

HS calculates the stage of completion of contracts using the value of work completed as a proportion of total contract value.

Required

Calculate the following amounts for the contract that should be shown in HS's financial statements:

Statement of comprehensive income:

- Revenue recognised for the year ended 31 March 20X9;
- Profit recognised for the year ended 31 March 20X9.

Statement of financial position:

- Gross amount due to/from the customer at 31 March 20X9, stating whether it is an asset or liability.

(5 marks)

`P7 5/09`

(Total = 30 marks)

20 Geneva 27 mins

Geneva Co is a company involved in the building industry and often has a number of major construction contracts which fall into two or more accounting periods.

During the year ended 31 December 20X8, Geneva Co enters into three construction contracts as follows:

	Contract Lausanne $'000	Contract Bern $'000	Contract Zurich $'000
Fixed contract price	2,000	2,000	2,000
Payments on account	1,080	950	800
Costs incurred to date	1,000	1,100	640
Estimated costs to complete the contract	600	1,100	1,160
Estimate percentage of work completed	60%	50%	35%

Required

Show how each contract would be reflected in the statement of financial position and statement of comprehensive income of Geneva Co for the year ended 31 December 20X8. **(5 marks each)**

(Total = 15 marks)

21 Objective test questions: Capital transactions and financial instruments 47 mins

1   A company made an issue of 100,000 ordinary shares of 50c at $1.10 each. The cash received was correctly recorded in the cash book but the whole amount was entered into ordinary share capital account.

Which of the following journal entries will correct the error made in recording the issue?

		Debit $	Credit $
A	Share capital account	10,000	
	Share premium account		10,000
B	Cash	60,000	
	Share premium account		60,000
C	Share capital account	60,000	
	Share premium account		60,000
D	Share premium account	60,000	
	Share capital account		60,000

(2 marks)

2   A company issued 1,000,000 $1 shares at $1.50 each payable as follows.

On application (including premium)	70c
On allotment	30c
First and final call	50c

All monies were received except for the call due from a holder of 10,000 shares. These shares were subsequently forfeited and reissued at $1.60 per share.

What *total* will be credited to share premium account as a result of this issue?

A $501,000
B $506,000
C $511,000
D   None of the above

(2 marks)

3   At 1 January 20X4, a company's share capital consisted of 1,000,000 ordinary shares of 50c each, and there was a balance of $800,000 on its share premium account.

   During 20X4, the following events took place.

   1 March   The company made a bonus issue of 1 share for every 2 held, using the share premium account.
   1 July   The company issued 600,000 shares at $2 per share.
   1 October   The company made a rights issue of 1 share for every 3 held at $1.80 per share.

   What are the balances on the company's share capital and share premium accounts at 31 December 20X4?

	Share capital $	Share premium $
A	1,400,000	2,860,000
B	2,800,000	1,460,000
C	1,800,000	2,320,000
D	1,400,000	2,360,000

   (2 marks)

4   A company has forfeited shares for non-payment of calls, but has not yet reissued them.

   How, if at all, will the forfeited shares be shown in the company's statement of financial position?

   A   As a deduction from called up share capital
   B   As an asset under investments
   C   As a current asset under receivables
   D   No item appears in the statement of financial position for the shares

   (2 marks)

5   Which of the following are normally permitted uses for a company's share premium account?

   1   Issuing fully paid bonus shares
   2   Being repaid to members as part of an authorised reduction of share capital
   3   Writing off preliminary expenses of company formation
   4   Writing off subsequent share issue expenses

   A   1, 2 and 4 only
   B   1, 3 and 4 only
   C   2, 3 and 4 only
   D   All four are permitted

   (2 marks)

6   Which of the following statements regarding share issues is incorrect?

   A   **Application** is where potential shareholders apply for shares in the company and send cash to cover their application

   B   **Allotment** is when the company allocates shares to the successful applicants and returns cash to unsuccessful applicants

   C   A **call** is where the purchase value is payable in instalments. The company will 'call' for instalments.

   D   If a shareholder fails to pay a call his allotment is cancelled and his money returned to him. His shares may then be reissued.

   (2 marks)

7   IAS 32 *Financial Instruments – Disclosure and Presentation* classifies issues shares as either equity instruments or financial liabilities. An entity has the following categories of funding in its statement of financial position:

   1   A preference share that is redeemable for cash at a 10% premium on 30 May 2015.
   2   An ordinary share which is not redeemable and has no restrictions on receiving dividends.
   3   A loan note that is redeemable at par in 2020.
   4   A cumulative preference share that is entitled to receive a dividend of 7% a year.

   Applying IAS 32, how would **each** of the above be categorised on the statement of financial position?

	As an equity instrument	As a financial liability
A	1 and 2	3 and 4
B	2 and 3	1 and 4
C	2	1, 3 and 4
D	1, 2 and 3	4

(2 marks)

8   BN is a listed entity and has the following balances included in its opening statement of financial position:

	$000
Equity	
Equity shares, $1 shares, fully paid	750
Share premium	250
Retained earnings	500
	1,500

BN reacquired 100,000 of its shares and classified them as 'treasury shares'. BN still held the treasury shares at the year end.

How should BN classify the treasury shares on its closing statement of financial position in accordance with IAS 32 *Financial instruments – presentation*?

A   As a non-current asset investment.
B   As a deduction from equity.
C   As a current asset investment.
D   As a non-current liability.   (2 marks)

9   R issued 500,000 new $1 equity shares on 1 April 20X2. The issue price of the share was $1.50 per share. Applicants paid $0.20 per share with their applications and a further $0.80 per share on allotment. All money was received on time.

A final call of $0.50 per share was made on 31 January 20X3. One holder of 5,000 shares failed to pay the call by the due date and the shares were forfeited. The forfeited shares were reissued for $1 per share on 31 March 20X3.

Which of the following is the correct set of accounting entries to record the reissue of the forfeited shares?

	Investment in own shares account	Bank account	Investment in own shares account	Share premium account
A	$5,000 credit	$5,000 debit	$2,500 debit	$2,500 credit
B	$5,000 credit	$5,000 debit	0	0
C	$5,000 credit	$5,000 debit	$2,500 credit	$2,500 debit
D	$5,000 debit	$5,000 credit	$2,500 credit	$2,500 debit

(2 marks)

The following data applies to questions 10 and 11.

On 1 January 20X8 PX issued 10m 7% $1 preference shares, redeemable after 4 years at a 5% premium. Issue charges amount to $500,000 and the effective interest rate is 10%.

10   What is the total finance charge on the issue?   (3 marks)

11   At what amount will the preference shares be shown in the statement of financial position at 31 December 20X9?   (3 marks)

12   Which ONE of the following gives the true meaning of "treasury shares"?

A   Shares owned by a country's Treasury
B   An entity's own shares purchased by the entity and still held at the period end
C   An entity's own shares purchased by the entity and resold before the period end at a gain
D   An entity's own shares purchased by the entity and cancelled

(2 marks)

(Total = 26 marks)

22 Objective test questions: Accounting standards I (65 mins)

1. A company leases some plant on 1 January 20X4. The cash price of the plant is $9,000, and the company leases it for four years, paying four annual instalments of $3,000 beginning on 31 December 20X4.

   The company uses the sum of the digits method to allocate interest.

   What is the interest charge for the year ended 31 December 20X5?

   A $900
   B $600
   C $1,000
   D $750
   (2 marks)

2. A company leases some plant on 1 January 20X4. The cash price is $9,000, and the company is to pay four annual instalments of $3,000, beginning on 1 January 20X4.

   The company uses the sum of the digits method to allocate interest.

   What is the interest charge for the year ended 31 December 20X5?

   A $750
   B $500
   C $900
   D $1,000
   (2 marks)

3. Which of the following statements about IAS 10 *Events after the reporting period* are correct?

   1 Notes to the financial statements must give details of all material adjusting events reflected in those financial statements.

   2 Notes to the financial statements must give details of non-adjusting events affecting users' ability to understand the company's financial position.

   3 Financial statements should not be prepared on a going concern basis if after the end of the reporting period the directors have decided to liquidate the company.

   A All three statements are correct.
   B 1 and 2 only
   C 1 and 3 only
   D 2 and 3 only
   (2 marks)

4. A company's statement of comprehensive income showed a profit before tax of $1,800,000

   After the year end and before the financial statements were authorised for issue, the following events took place.

   1 The value of an investment held at the year end fell by $85,000.

   2 A customer who owed $116,000 at the year end went bankrupt owing a total of $138,000.

   3 Inventory valued at cost $161,000 in the statement of financial position was sold for $141,000.

   4 Assets with a carrying value at the year end of $240,000 were unexpectedly expropriated by government.

   What is the company's profit after making the necessary adjustments for these events?

   A $1,399,000
   B $1,579,000
   C $1,664,000
   D None of these figures
   (2 marks)

5   Which of the following events after the reporting period would normally be classified as *adjusting*, according to IAS 10 *Events after the reporting period*?

   1   Destruction of a major non-current asset
   2   Issue of shares and debentures
   3   Discovery of error or fraud
   4   Evidence of impairment in value of a property as at the year end
   5   Purchases and sales of non-current assets

   A   1, 2 and 5 only
   B   3 and 4 only
   C   3, 4 and 5 only
   D   1, 3 and 4 only   (2 marks)

6   Which of the following events after the reporting period would normally be classified as *non-adjusting*, according to IAS 10 *Events after the reporting period*?

   1   Opening new trading operations
   2   Sale of goods held at the year end for less than cost
   3   A customer is discovered to be insolvent
   4   Announcement of plan to discontinue an operation
   5   Expropriation of major assets by government

   A   2 and 3 only
   B   1, 2 and 3 only
   C   2, 3, 4 and 5 only
   D   1, 4 and 5 only   (2 marks)

7   In compiling its financial statements, the directors of a company have to decide on the correct treatment of the following items.

   1   An employee has commenced an action against the company for wrongful dismissal. The company's solicitors estimate that the ex-employee has a 40 per cent chance of success in the action.

   2   The company has guaranteed the overdraft of another company, not at present in any financial difficulties. The possibility of a liability arising is thought to be remote.

   3   Shortly after the year end, a major installation owned by the company was destroyed in a flood. The company's going concern status is not affected.

   What are the correct treatments for these items, assuming all are of material amount?

   A   All three should be disclosed by note.
   B   A provision should be made for item 1 and items 2 and 3 disclosed by note.
   C   Items 1 and 3 should be disclosed by note, with no disclosure for item 2.
   D   Item 1 should be disclosed by note. No disclosure is required for items 2 and 3.   (2 marks)

8   Which of the following statements about IAS 37 *Provisions, contingents liabilities and contingent assets* are correct?

   1   Provisions should be made for constructive obligations (those arising from a company's pattern of past practice) as well as for obligations enforceable by law.

   2   Discounting may be used when estimating the amount of a provision if the effect is material.

   3   A restructuring provision must include the estimated costs of retraining or relocating continuing staff.

   4   A restructuring provision may only be made when a company has a detailed plan for the reconstruction and a firm intention to carry it out.

   A   All four statements are correct
   B   1, 2 and 4 only
   C   1, 3 and 4 only
   D   2, 3 and 4 only   (2 marks)

9   Which of the following criteria must be present in order for a company to recognise a provision?

1   There is a present obligation as a result of past events.
2   It is probable that a transfer of economic benefits will be required to settle the obligation.
3   A reliable estimate of the obligation can be made.

A   All three criteria must be present.
B   1 and 2 only
C   1 and 3 only
D   2 and 3 only **(2 marks)**

10 Which **one** of the following would be treated as a non-adjusting event after the reporting period, as required by IAS 10 *Events after the Reporting Period*, in the financial statements of AN for the period ended 31 January 20X5? The financial statements were approved for publication on 15 May 20X5.

A   Notice was received on 31 March 20X5 that a major customer of AN had ceased trading and was unlikely to make any further payments.

B   Inventory items at 31 January 20X5, original cost $30,000, were sold in April 20X5 for $20,000.

C   During 2004, a customer commenced legal action against AN. At 31 January 20X5, legal advisers were of the opinion that AN would lose the case, so AN created a provision of $200,000 for the damages claimed by the customer. On 27 April 20X5, the court awarded damages of $250,000 to the customer.

D   There was a fire on 2 May 20X5 in AN's main warehouse which destroyed 50% of AN's total inventory. **(2 marks)**

11 DT's final dividend for the year ended 31 October 20X5 of $150,000 was declared on 1 February 20X6 and paid in cash on 1 April 20X6. The financial statements were approved on 31 March 20X6.

The following statements refer to the treatment of the dividend in the accounts of DT:

1   The payment clears an accrued liability set up as at 31 October 20X5.

2   The dividend is shown as a deduction in the statement of comprehensive income for the year ended 31 October 20X6.

3   The dividend is shown as an accrued liability as at 31 October 20X6.

4   The $150,000 dividend was shown in the notes to the financial statements at 31 October 20X5.

5   The dividend is shown as a deduction in the statement of changes in equity for the year ended 31 October 20X6.

Which of the above statements reflect the correct treatment of the dividend?

A   1 and 2
B   1 and 4
C   3 and 5
D   4 and 5 **(2 marks)**

12 List the THREE criteria specified in IAS 37 *Provisions, Contingent Liabilities and Contingent Assets* that must be satisfied before a provision is recognised in the financial statements. **(3 marks)**

13 DH has the following two legal claims outstanding:

- A legal action against DH claiming compensation of $700,000, filed in February 20X7. DH has been advised that it is probable that the liability will materialise.
- A legal action taken by DH against another entity, claiming damages of $300,000, started in March 20X4. DH has been advised that it is probable that it will win the case.

How should DH report these legal actions in its financial statements for the year ended 30 April 20X7?

	Legal action against DH	Legal action taken by DH
A	Disclose by a note to the accounts	No disclosure
B	Make a provision	No disclosure
C	Make a provision	Disclose as a note
D	Make a provision	Accrue the income

(2 marks)

14 Define an operating segment as per IFRS 8 *Operating segments*. **(3 marks)**

15 Which ONE of the following is a criteria for determining a reportable segment under IFRS 8 *Operating segments*?

- A Its revenue is 15% or more of the total revenue of all segments
- B Its revenue is 10% or more of the total revenue of all operating segments
- C Its assets are 10% or more of the combined assets of all operating segments
- D Its assets are 15% or more of the combined assets of all operating segments

(2 marks)

16 Which ONE of the following material items would be classified as a non-adjusting event in HL's financial statements for the year ended 31 December 20X8 according to IAS 10 *Events after the reporting period*?

HL's financial statements were approved for publication on 8 April 20X9.

- A On 1 March 20X9, HL's auditors discovered that, due to an error during the count, the closing inventory had been undervalued by $250,000.
- B Lightning struck one of HL's production facilities on 31 January 20X9 and caused a serious fire. The fire destroyed half of the factory and its machinery. Output was severely reduced for six months.
- C One of HL's customers commenced court action against HL on 1 December 20X8. At 31 December 20X8, HL did not know whether the case would go against it or not. On 1 March 20X9, the court found against HL and awarded damages of $150,000 to the customer.
- D On 15 March 20X9, HL was advised by the liquidator of one of its customers that it was very unlikely to receive any payments for the balance of $300,000 that was outstanding at 31 December 20X8.

(2 marks)

17 Which of the following are required by IFRS 8 *Operating segments* to be disclosed in an entity's financial statements, if they are included in the measure of segment profit or loss to be reported to the chief operating decision maker?

(i)   Revenues from transactions with other operating segments within the entity
(ii) Cost of sales
(iii) Amortisation
(iv) Income tax expense
(v)   Administrative expenses and distribution costs

- A (i), (ii) and (v)
- B (ii), (iii) and (iv)
- C (ii), (iii) and (v)
- D (i), (iii) and (iv)

(2 marks)

(Total = 36 marks)

23 Objective test questions: Accounting standards II — 86 mins

1 IAS 37 *Provisions, contingent liabilities and contingent assets* governs the recognition of contingent items. Which of the following statements about contingencies, if any, are correct according to IAS 37?

1. A contingent liability should be disclosed by note if it is probable that an obligation will arise and its amount can be estimated reliably.
2. A contingent asset should be disclosed by note if it is probable that it will arise.
3. An entity should not recognise a contingent asset.

- A None of the statements is correct.
- B 1 and 2
- C 2 and 3
- D All of the statements are correct. **(2 marks)**

2 IAS 24 *Related party disclosures* governs disclosures required for transactions between a company and parties deemed to be related to it.

Which of the following parties will normally be held to be related parties of a company?

1. Its subsidiary companies
2. Its directors
3. Close family of the company's directors
4. Providers of finance to the company
5. A customer or supplier with whom the company has a significant volume of business

- A All of the parties listed
- B 1, 2, 3 and 4 only
- C 1, 2 and 3 only
- D 3, 4 and 5 only **(2 marks)**

3 Which of the following statements defines a finance lease?

- A A short term hire agreement
- B A long term hire agreement where the legal title in the asset passes on the final payment
- C A long term hire agreement where substantially all the risks and rewards of ownership are transferred
- D A long term hire agreement where the hirer is responsible for maintenance of the asset **(2 marks)**

4 An asset is hired under a finance lease with a deposit of $30,000 on 1 January 20X1 plus 8 six monthly payments in arrears of $20,000 each. The fair value of the asset is $154,000. The finance charge is to be allocated using the sum of the digits method.

What is the finance charge for the year ending 31 December 20X3?

- A $7,000
- B $8,000
- C $10,000
- D $11,000 **(2 marks)**

5 The directors of Robin (year end 31 December 20X6) were informed on 27 February 20X7 that a serious fire at one of the company's factories had stopped production there for at least six months to come. On 3 March 20X7 the directors of Robin were informed that a major customer had gone into liquidation owing a substantial amount to Robin as at the year end. The liquidator was pessimistic about the prospect of recovering anything for unsecured creditors. The financial statements for the year ended 31 December 20X6 were approved on 20 March 20X7.

In accordance with IAS 10 *Events after the reporting period*, how should the two events be treated in the financial statements?

	Fire	Liquidation
A	Accrued in accounts	Disclosed in notes
B	Disclosed in notes	Disclosed in notes
C	Accrued in accounts	Accrued in accounts
D	Disclosed in notes	Accrued in accounts

(2 marks)

6 In which of the following circumstances would a provision be recognised under IAS 37 *Provisions, contingent liabilities and contingent assets* in the financial statements for the year ending 31 March 20X6?

   1   A board decision was made on 15 March to close down a division with potential costs of $100,000. At 31 March the decision had not been communicated to managers, employees or customers.

   2   There are anticipated costs from returns of a defective product in the next few months of $60,000. In the past all returns of defective products have always been refunded to customers.

   3   It is anticipated that a major refurbishment of the company Head Office will take place from June onwards costing $85,000.

   A   1 and 2 only
   B   2 and 3 only
   C   2 only
   D   3 only   (2 marks)

7 According to IAS 24 *Related party disclosures*, which of the following would be presumed to be a related party of Fredo unless it can be demonstrated otherwise?

   A   The bank which has given a loan to Fredo
   B   The husband of the managing director of Fredo
   C   Fredo's major supplier
   D   The assistant accountant of Fredo   (2 marks)

8 List the three criteria set out in IAS 37 *Provisions, Contingent Liabilities and Contingent Assets* for the recognition of a provision.   (3 marks)

9 AP has the following two legal claims outstanding:

   - A legal action claiming compensation of $500,000 filed against AP in March 20X4.
   - A legal action taken by AP against a third party, claiming damages of $200,000 was started in January 20X3 and is nearing completion.

   In both cases, it is more likely than not that the amount claimed will have to be paid.

   How should AP report these legal actions in its financial statements for the year ended 31 March 20X5?

	Legal action against AP	Legal action by AP
A	Disclose by a note	No disclosure
B	Make a provision	No disclosure
C	Make a provision	Disclose as a note
D	Make a provision	Accrue the income

                                                                                                                 (2 marks)

10 Which one of the following would be regarded as a related party of BS?

   A   BX, a customer of BS.
   B   The president of the BS Board, who is also the chief executive officer of another entity, BU, that supplies goods to BS.
   C   BQ, a supplier of BS.
   D   BY, BS's main banker.   (2 marks)

11 An item of machinery leased under a five year finance lease on 1 October 20X3 had a fair value of $51,900 at date of purchase.

   The lease payments were $12,000 per year, payable in arrears.

   If the sum of digits method is used to apportion interest to accounting periods, calculate the finance cost for the year ended 30 September 20X5.   (3 marks)

12 Which one of the following would require a provision to be created by BW at its year end of 31 October 20X5?

A The government introduced new laws on data protection which come into force on 1 January 20X6. BW's directors have agreed that this will require a large number of staff to be retrained. At 31 October 20X5, the directors were waiting on a report they had commissioned that would identify the actual training requirements.

B At the year end, BW is negotiating with its insurance provider about the amount of an insurance claim that it had filed. On 20 November 20X5, the insurance provider agreed to pay $200,000.

C BW makes refunds to customers for any goods returned within 30 days of sale, and has done so for many years.

D A customer is suing BW for damages alleged to have been caused by BW's product. BW is contesting the claim and, at 31 October 20X5, the directors have been advised by BW's legal advisers it is very unlikely to lose the case.

(2 marks)

13 IAS 18 *Revenue recognition* defines when revenue may be recognised on the sale of goods.

List four of the five conditions that IAS 18 requires to be met for income to be recognised. (4 marks)

The following data are given for sub-questions 14 and 15 below

CS acquired a machine, using a finance lease, on 1 January 20X4. The machine had an expected useful life of 12,000 operating hours, after which it would have no residual value.

The finance lease was for a five-year term with rentals of $20,000 per year payable in arrears. The cost price of the machine was $80,000 and the implied interest rate is 7.93% per year. CS used the machine for 2,600 hours in 20X4 and 2,350 hours in 20X5.

14 Using the actuarial method, calculate the non-current liability and current liability figures required by IAS 17 *Leases* to be shown in CS's statement of financial position at 31 December 20X5. (3 marks)

15 Calculate the non-current asset – property, plant and equipment net book value that would be shown in CS's balance sheet at 31 December 20X5. Calculate the depreciation charge using the machine hours method. (2 marks)

16 On 31 March 20X7, DT received an order from a new customer, XX, for products with a sales value of $900,000. XX enclosed a deposit with the order of $90,000.

On 31 March 20X7, DT had not completed credit referencing of XX and had not despatched any goods. DT is considering the following possible entries for this transaction in its financial statements for the year ended 31 March 20X7.

1 Include $900,000 in income statement revenue for the year
2 Include $90,000 in income statement revenue for the year
3 Do not include anything in income statement revenue for the year
4 Create a trade receivable for $810,000
5 Create a trade payable for $90,000

According to IAS 18 *Revenue Recognition*, how should DT record this transaction in its financial statements for the year ended 31 March 20X7?

A 1 and 4
B 2 and 5
C 3 and 4
D 3 and 5

(2 marks)

The following data are given for sub questions 17 and 18 below

Company X closed one of its divisions 12 months ago. It has yet to dispose of one remaining machine. The carrying value of the machine at the date when business ceased was $750,000. It was being depreciated at 25% on a reducing balance basis. Company X has been advised that the fair value of the machine is $740,000 and expects to incur costs of $10,000 in making the sale. It has located a probable buyer but the sale will not be completed before the year end.

17 At what amount should the machine be shown in the year end financial statements of Company X?

- A $750,000
- B $562,500
- C $740,000
- D $730,000

(2 marks)

18 Where should the carrying value of the machine be shown in Company X's statement of financial position?

- A Under non-current assets
- B Under current assets
- C Included within inventory
- D Included within receivables

(2 marks)

19 GD's financial reporting period is 1 September 2007 to 31 August 2008.

Which ONE of the following would be classified as a non-adjusting event according to IAS 10 *Events after the reporting period*?

Assume all amounts are material and that GD's financial statements have not yet been approved for publication.

- A On 30 October 2008, GD received a communication stating that one of its customers had ceased trading and gone into liquidation. The balance outstanding at 31 August 2008 was unlikely to be paid.
- B At 31 August 2008, GD had not provided for an outstanding legal action against the local government administration for losses suffered as a result of incorrect enforcement of local business regulations. On 5 November 2008, the court awarded GD $50,000 damages.
- C On 1 October 2008, GD made a rights issue of 1 new share for every 3 shares held at a price of $175. The market price on that date was $200.
- D At 31 August 2008, GD had an outstanding insurance claim of $150,000. On 10 October 2008, the insurance company informed GD that it would pay $140,000 as settlement. **(2 marks)**

20 Which ONE of the following would **NOT** normally be treated as a related party of HJ in accordance with IAS 24 *Related party disclosures*?

- A XX, HJ's largest customer, accounts for 75% of HJ's turnover
- B HJ2, a subsidiary of HJ, that does not trade with HJ
- C HJA, an associate of HJ
- D A shareholder of HJ, holding 25% of HJ's equity shares

(2 marks)

21 HP entered into an operating lease for a machine on 1 May 20X7 with the following terms:

- Five years non-cancellable lease
- 12 months rent free period from commencement
- Rent of $12,000 per annum payable at $1,000 a month from month 13 onwards
- Machine useful life 15 years

Calculate the amount that should be charged to profit or loss in HP's financial statements in respect of the lease, for each of the years ended 30 April 20X8 and 30 April 20X9.

(3 marks)

(Total = 48 marks)

24 Section B questions: Accounting standards I — 72 mins

(a) The following definitions have been taken from the International Accounting Standards Committee's *Framework for the Preparation and Presentation of Financial Statements*.

- 'An asset is a resource controlled by the entity as a result of past events and from which future economic benefits are expected to flow to the entity.'
- 'A liability is a present obligation of the entity arising from past events, the settlement of which is expected to result in an outflow from the entity of resources embodying economic benefits.'

IAS 17 *Leases* requires lessees to capitalise finance leases in their financial statements.

Required

Explain how IAS 17's treatment of finance leases applies the definitions of assets and liabilities.

(5 marks)

(b) NDL drilled a new oil well, which started production on 1 March 20X3. The licence granting permission to drill the new oil well included a clause that requires NDL to 'return the land to the state it was in before drilling commenced'.

NDL estimates that the oil well will have a 20-year production life. At the end of that time, the oil well will be de-commissioned and work carried out to reinstate the land. The cost of this de-commissioning work is estimated to be $20 million.

Required

As the trainee management accountant, draft a memo to the production manager explaining how NDL must treat the de-commissioning costs in its financial statements for the year to 31 March 20X3. Your memo should refer to appropriate International Accounting Standards. **(5 marks)**

P7 Pilot paper

(c) BJ is an entity that provides a range of facilities for holidaymakers and travellers.

At 1 October 20X4 these included:

- a short haul airline operating within Europe; and
- a travel agency specialising in arranging holidays to more exotic destinations, such as Hawaii and Fiji.

BJ's airline operation has made significant losses for the last two years. On 31 January 20X5, the directors of BJ decided that, due to a significant increase in competition on short haul flights within Europe, BJ would close all of its airline operations and dispose of its fleet of aircraft. All flights for holiday makers and travellers who had already booked seats would be provided by third party airlines. All operations ceased on 31 May 20X5.

On 31 July 20X5, BJ sold its fleet of aircraft and associated non-current assets for $500 million, the carrying value at that date was $750 million.

At the balance sheet date, BJ were still in negotiation with some employees regarding severance payments. BJ has estimated that in the financial period October 20X5 to September 20X6, they will agree a settlement of $20 million compensation.

The closure of the airline operation caused BJ to carry out a major restructuring of the entire entity. The restructuring has been agreed by the directors and active steps have been taken to implement it. The cost of restructuring to be incurred in year 20X5/20X6 is estimated at $10 million.

Required

Explain how BJ should report the events described above and quantify any amounts required to be included in its financial statements for the year ended 30 September 20X5. (Detailed disclosure notes are not required.)

(5 marks)

P7 11/05

(d) CB is an entity specialising in importing a wide range of non-food items and selling them to retailers. George is CB's president and founder and owns 40% of CB's equity shares:

- CB's largest customer, XC, accounts for 35% of CB's revenue. XC has just completed negotiations with CB for a special 5% discount on all sales.
- During the accounting period, George purchased a property from CB for $500,000. CB had previously declared the property surplus to its requirements and had valued it at $750,000.
- George's son, Arnold, is a director in a financial institution, FC. During the accounting period, FC advanced $2 million to CB as an unsecured loan at a favourable rate of interest.

Required

Explain, with reasons, the extent to which each of the above transactions should be classified and disclosed in accordance with IAS 24 *Related Party Disclosures* in CB's financial statements for the period. **(5 marks)**

P7 5/06

(e) CR issued 200,000 $10 redeemable 5% preference shares at par on 1 April 20X5. The shares were redeemable on 31 March 20Y0 at a premium of 15%. Issue costs amounted to $192,800.

Required

(a) Calculate the total finance cost over the life of the preference shares. **(2 marks)**

(b) Calculate the annual charge to the income statement for finance expense, as required by IAS 39 Financial Instruments: Recognition and Measurement, for each of the five years 20X6 to 20Y0. Assume the constant annual rate of interest as 10%. **(3 marks)**

(Total = 5 marks)

P7 5/06

(f) You are in charge of the preparation of the financial statements for DF. You are nearing completion of the preparation of the accounts for the year ended 30 September 20X6 and two items have come to your attention.

(i) Shortly after a senior employee left in April 20X6, a number of accounting discrepancies were discovered. With further investigation, it became clear that fraudulent activity had been going on. DF has calculated that, because of the fraud, the profit for the year ended 30 September 20X5 had been overstated by $45,000.

(ii) On 1 September 20X6, DF received an order from a new customer enclosing full payment for the goods ordered; the order value was $90,000. DF scheduled the manufacture of the goods to commence on 28 November 20X6. The cost of manufacture was expected to be $70,000. DF's management want to recognise the $20,000 profit in the statement of comprehensive income for the year ended 30 September 20X6. It has been suggested that the $90,000 should be recognised as revenue and a provision of $70,000 created for the cost of manufacture.

DF's statement of comprehensive income for the year ended 30 September 20X5 showed a profit of $600,000. The draft statement of comprehensive income for the year ended 30 September 20X6 showed a profit of $700,000. The 30 September 20X5 accounts were approved by the directors on 1 March 20X6.

Required

Explain how the events described above should be reported in the financial statements of DF for the years ended 30 September 20X5 and 20X6. **(5 marks)**

P7 11/06

(g) On 1 June 20X6 the directors of DP commissioned a report to determine possible actions they could take to reduce DP's losses. The report, which was presented to the directors on 1 December 20X6, proposed that DP cease all of its manufacturing activities and concentrate on its retail activities. The directors formally approved the plan to close DP's factory. The factory was gradually shut down, commencing on 5 December 20X6, with production finally ceasing on 15 March 20X7. All employees had ceased working or had been transferred to other facilities in the company, by 29 March 20X7. The plant and equipment was removed and sold for $25,000 (net book value $95,000) on 30 March 20X7.

The factory and building are being advertised for sale but had not been sold by 31 March 20X7. The carrying value of the land and building at 31 March 20X7, based on original cost, was $750,000. The estimated net realisable value of the land and building at 31 March 20X7 was $1,125,000.

Closure costs incurred (and paid) up to 31 March 20X7 were $620,000.

The cash flows, revenues and expenses relating to the factory were clearly distinguishable from DP's other operations. The output of the factory was sold directly to third parties and to DP's retail outlets. The manufacturing facility was shown as a separate segment in DP's segmental information.

Required

With reference to relevant International Accounting Standards, explain how DP should treat the factory closure in its financial statements for the year ended 31 March 20X7. **(5 marks)**

P7 5/07

(h) On 1 September 20X7, the Directors of EK decided to sell EK's retailing division and concentrate activities entirely on its manufacturing division.

The retailing division was available for immediate sale, but EK had not succeeded in disposing of the operation by 31 October 20X7. EK identified a potential buyer for the retailing division, but negotiations were at an early stage. The Directors of EK are certain that the sale will be completed by 31 August 20X8.

The retailing division's carrying value at 31 August 20X7 was:

	$'000
Non-current tangible assets – property, plant and equipment	300
Non-current tangible assets – goodwill	100
Net current assets	43
Total carrying value	443

The retailing division has been valued at $423,000, comprising:

	$'000
Non-current tangible assets – property, plant and equipment	320
Non-current tangible assets – goodwill	60
Net current assets	43
Total carrying value	423

EK's directors have estimated that EK will incur consultancy and legal fees for the disposal of $25,000.

Required

(i) Explain whether EK can treat the sale of its retailing division as a 'discontinued operation', as defined by IFRS 5 *Non-current Assets held for Sale and Discontinued Operations*, in its financial statements for the year ended 31 October 20X7. **(3 marks)**

(ii) Explain how EK should treat the retailing division in its financial statements for the year ended 31 October 20X7, assuming the sale of its retailing division meets the classification requirements for a disposal group (IFRS 5). **(2 marks)**

(Total = 5 marks)

P7 11/07

(Total = 40 marks)

25 Section B questions: Accounting standards II — 72 mins

(a) IAS 37 defines the meaning of a provision and sets out when a provision should be recognised.

Required

Using the IAS 37 definition of a provision, explain how a provision meets the International Accounting Standards Board's *Framework for the Preparation and Presentation of Financial Statements*' definition of a liability. **(5 marks)**

P7 Pilot paper

(b) A lessee leases a non-current asset on a non-cancellable lease contract of five years, the details of which are:

- The asset has a useful life of five years.
- The rental is $21,000 per annum payable at the end of each year.
- The lessee also has to pay all insurance and maintenance costs.
- The fair value of the asset was $88,300.

The lessee uses the sum of digits method to calculate finance charges on the lease.

Required

Prepare statement of comprehensive income and statement of financial position extracts for years one and two of the lease. **(5 marks)**

P7 Pilot paper

(c) AE has a three year contract which commenced on 1 April 20X4. At 31 March 20X5, AE had the following balances in its ledger relating to the contract:

	$'000	$'000
Total contract value		60,000
Cost incurred up to 31 March 20X5:		
Attributable to work completed	21,000	
Inventory purchased for use in 20X5/6	3,000	24,000
Progress payments received		25,000
Other information:		
Expected further costs to completion		19,000

At 31 March 20X5, the contract was certified as 50% complete.

Required

Prepare the statement of comprehensive income and statement of financial position extracts showing the balances relating to this contract, as required by IAS 11 *Construction contracts*. **(5 marks)**

P7 5/05

(d) A five year finance lease commenced on 1 April 20X3. The annual payments are $30,000 in arrears. The fair value of the asset at 1 April 20X3 was $116,000. Use the sum of digits method for interest allocations and assume that the asset has no residual value at the end of the lease term.

Required

In accordance with IAS 17 *Leases*:

(i) Calculate the amount of finance cost that would be charged to the statement of comprehensive income for the year ended 31 March 20X5

(ii) Prepare statement of financial position extracts for the lease at 31 March 20X5. **(5 marks)**

P7 5/05

(e) CD is a manufacturing entity that runs a number of operations including a bottling plant that bottles carbonated soft drinks. CD has been developing a new bottling process that will allow the bottles to be filled and sealed more efficiently.

The new process took a year to develop. At the start of development, CD estimated that the new process would increase output by 15% with no additional cost (other than the extra bottles and their contents).

Development work commenced on 1 May 20X5 and was completed on 20 April 20X6. Testing at the end of the development confirmed CD's original estimates.

CD incurred expenditure of $180,000 on the above development in 20X5/X6.

CD plans to install the new process in its bottling plant and start operating the new process from 1 May 20X6.

CD's year end is 30 April.

Required

(i) Explain the requirements of IAS 38 *Intangible Assets* for the treatment of development costs.

(3 marks)

(ii) Explain how CD should treat its development costs in its financial statements for the year ended 30 April 20X6.
(2 marks)

(Total = 5 marks)

P7 5/06

(f) On 1 April 20X5, DX acquired plant and machinery with a fair value of $900,000 on a finance lease. The lease is for five years with the annual lease payments of $228,000 being paid in advance on 1 April each year. The interest rate implicit in the lease is 13.44%. The first payment was made on 1 April 20X5.

Required

(i) Calculate the finance charge in respect of the lease that will be shown in DX's income statement for the year ended 31 March 20X7.

(ii) Calculate the amount to be shown as a current liability and a non-current liability in DX's balance sheet at 31 March 20X7.

(All workings should be to the nearest $'000.)
(5 marks)

P7 5/07

(g) The objective of IAS 24 *Related Party Disclosures* is to ensure that financial statements disclose the effect of the existence of related parties.

Required

With reference to IAS 24, explain the meaning of the terms 'related party' and 'related party transaction'.
(5 marks)

P7 11/07

(h) EJ publishes trade magazines and sells them to retailers. EJ has just concluded negotiations with a large supermarket chain for the supply of a large quantity of several of its trade magazines on a regular basis.

EJ has agreed a substantial discount on the following terms:

- The same quantity of each trade magazine will be supplied each month;
- Quantities can only be changed at the end of each six month period;
- Payment must be made six monthly in advance.

The supermarket paid $150,000 on 1 September 20X7 for six months supply of trade magazines to 29 February 20X8. At 31 October 20X7, EJ had supplied two months of trade magazines.

EJ estimates that the cost of supplying the supermarket each month is $20,000.

Required

(i) State the criteria in IAS 18 *Revenue* for income recognition. **(2 marks)**

(ii) Explain, with reasons, how EJ should treat the above in its financial statements for the year ended 31 October 20X7.
(3 marks)

P7 11/07

(Total = 5 marks)

(Total = 40 marks)

26 AZ (FATP Pilot paper/amended) — 45 mins

AZ is a quoted manufacturing entity. Its finished products are stored in a nearby warehouse until ordered by customers. AZ has been re-organising the business to improve performance.

The trial balance for AZ at 31 March 20X3 was as follows:

	$'000	$'000
7% Loan Notes (redeemable 20X7)		18,250
Retained earnings at 31 March 20X2		14,677
Administrative expenses	16,020	
Bank and Cash	25,820	
Cost of goods manufactured in the year to 31 March 20X3 (excluding depreciation)	94,000	
Distribution costs	9,060	
Dividends received		1,200
Equity shares $1 each, fully paid		19,000
Interest paid	639	
Inventory at 31 March 20X2	4,852	
Plant and Equipment	30,315	
Allowance for depreciation at 31 March 20X2:		
Plant and Equipment		6,060
Vehicles		1,670
Allowance for doubtful trade receivables		600
Restructuring costs	121	
Sales revenue		124,900
Trade payables		8,120
Trade receivables	9,930	
Vehicles	3,720	
	194,477	194,477

Additional information provided

(a) Non-current assets are being depreciated as follows:

    Plant & Equipment   20% per annum straight line
    Vehicles   25% per annum reducing balance

Depreciation of plant and equipment is considered to be part of cost of sales, while depreciation of vehicles should be included under distribution costs.

(b) Tax due for the year to 31 March 20X3 is estimated at $15,000.

(c) The closing inventory at 31 March 20X3 was $5,180,000.

(d) The 7% loan notes are 10-year loans due for repayment by 31 March 20X7. AZ incurred no other interest charges in the year to 31 March 20X3.

(e) The restructuring costs in the trial balance represent the cost of the final phase of a major fundamental restructuring of the entity to improve competitiveness and future profitability.

(f) The auditors have drawn attention to the following issues not reflected in the trial balance:

   (i) Inventory brought forward at the beginning of the year had been understated by $500,000.

   (ii) Items included in closing inventory at cost of $1.2m were damaged in transit. They will require remedial work costing $250,000 and can then be sold for $1.35m.

   (iii) Administrative expenses include $600,000 paid on leasing a machine from 1 April 20X2. This should not have been treated as an operating lease. It is actually a finance lease. The original cost of the machine was $2m and the agreement provides for four annual payments in arrears of $600,000. The interest rate implicit in the lease is 7.7%.

Required

Prepare AZ's statement of comprehensive income for the year to 31 March 20X3, a statement of financial position at that date, and a statement of changes in equity for the year. These should be in a form suitable for presentation to the shareholders, in accordance with the requirements of International Accounting Standards.

Notes to the financial statements are NOT required, but all workings must be clearly shown. DO NOT prepare a statement of accounting policies.

(25 marks)

27 AF (FATP 5/05/amended) — 45 mins

AF is a furniture manufacturing entity. The trial balance for AF at 31 March 20X5 was as follows:

	$'000	$'000
6% loan notes (redeemable 20Y0)		1,500
Retained earnings at 31 March 20X4		388
Administrative expenses	1,540	
Available for sale investments at market value 31 March 20X4	1,640	
Bank and cash	822	
Cost of sales	3,463	
Distribution costs	1,590	
Dividend paid 1 December 20X4	275	
Interest paid on loan notes – half year to 30 September 20X4	45	
Inventory at 31 March 20X5	1,320	
Investment income received		68
Land and buildings at cost	5,190	
Ordinary shares of $1 each, fully paid		4,500
Plant and equipment at cost	3,400	
Provision for deferred tax		710
Accumulated depreciation at 31 March 20X4: Buildings		1,500
Accumulated depreciation at 31 March 20X4: Plant and equipment		1,659
Revaluation surplus		330
Sales revenue		8,210
Share premium		1,380
Trade payables		520
Trade receivables	1,480	
	20,765	20,765

Additional information provided

(a) Available for sale investments are carried in the financial statements at market value. The market value of the available for sale investments at 31 March 20X5 was $1,750,000.

(b) There were no sales or purchases of non-current assets or available for sale investments during the year ended 31 March 20X5.

(c) Income tax due for the year ended 31 March 20X5 is estimated at $250,000. The tax rate is 30%. There is no balance outstanding in relation to previous years' corporate income tax. At 31 March 20X5 capital allowances exceed depreciation by $2,700,000.

(d) Depreciation is charged on buildings using the straight-line basis at 3% each year. The cost of land included in land and buildings is $2,000,000. Plant and equipment is depreciated using the reducing balance method at 20%. Depreciation is regarded as a cost of sales.

(e) AF entered into a non-cancellable five year operating lease on 1 April 20X4 to acquire machinery to manufacture a new range of kitchen units. Under the terms of the lease, AF will receive the first year rent free, then $62,500 is payable for four years commencing in year two of the lease. The machine is estimated to have a useful economic life of 20 years.

(f) The 6% loan notes are 10 year loans due for repayment in March 20Y0. AF incurred no other finance costs in the year to 31 March 20X5.

Required

Prepare the statement of comprehensive income of AF for the year to 31 March 20X5, a statement of changes in equity and a statement of financial position at that date, in a form suitable for presentation to the shareholders and in accordance with the requirements of International Financial Reporting Standards.

Notes to the financial statements are **not** required, but all workings must be clearly shown. **(25 marks)**

28 Murdoch Co   45 mins

Murdoch Co compiles its financial statements to 30 June annually. At 30 June 20X9, the company's trial balance was as follows.

	$'000	$'000
Sales revenue		14,800
Purchases	8,280	
Inventory at 1 July 20X8	1,390	
Distribution costs	1,080	
Administration expenses	1,460	
Land at valuation	10,500	
Building: cost	8,000	
accumulated depreciation at 1 July 20X8		2,130
Plant and equipment: cost	12,800	
accumulated depreciation at 1 July 20X8		2,480
Trade receivables and payables	4,120	2,240
Cash at bank	160	
Ordinary shares of 50c each: as at 1 July 20X8		10,000
issued during year		4,000
Share premium account: as at 1 July 20X8		2,000
arising on shares issued during year		2,000
Revaluation surplus as at 1 July 20X8		3,000
Retained earnings		3,140
10% loan notes (redeemable 20Y8)		
(issued 1 April 20X9 with interest payable 31 March and 30 September each year)		2,000
	47,790	47,790

The following matters remain to be adjusted for in preparing the financial statements for the year ended 30 June 20X9:

(a) During May 20X9 the company announced the closure of one of its factories. The factory is a single cash-generating unit. Its carrying value before the announcement was $1.8m. After the announcement its fair value less costs to sell was $1.5m. This value relates entirely to the building as all the plant was fully depreciated, and has already been scrapped. The factory building is included in the trial balance at its original carrying value of $1.8m ($2m less depreciation). A buyer has been found and the factory building will be sold in 3 months time. It should now be re-classified under current assets as a 'non-current asset classified as held for sale'.

The factory has now ceased operation and during the year to 30 June 20X9 it made a loss of $0.5m and ran up a corresponding overdraft of $0.5m. This will be paid off when the building is sold. The trading loss, the overdraft and the impairment loss on the building are **not** included in the trial balance, but should be included in the financial statements in accordance with IFRS 5 *Non-current Assets Held for Sale and Discontinued Operations*.

(b) Depreciation is to be provided as follows.

    Buildings   2% per year on cost
    Plant and equipment   20% per year on cost

80% of the depreciation is to be charged in cost of sales, and 10% each in distribution costs and administrative expenses.

(c) The land is to be revalued to $12,000,000. No change was required to the value of the buildings apart from the factory as noted above.

(e) Accruals and prepayments were:

	Accruals $'000	Prepayments $'000
Distribution costs	190	120
Administrative expenses	70	60

(f) Inventory at 30 June 20X9 amounted to $1,560,000.

Required

Prepare the company's statement of comprehensive income for the year ended 30 June 20X9 and statement of financial position as at that date for publication, complying as far as possible with the provisions of accounting standards. Ignore taxation.

(25 marks)

29 BG (FATP 11/05/amended) — 45 mins

BG provides office cleaning services to a range of organisations in its local area. BG operates through a small network of depots that are rented spaces situated in out-of-town industrial developments. BG has a policy to lease all vehicles on operating leases.

The trial balance for BG at 30 September 20X5 was as follows:

	$'000	$'000
10% bonds (redeemable 20Y0)		150
Administrative expenses	239	
Bank and cash	147	
Bond interest paid – half year to 31 March 20X5	8	
Cost of cleaning materials consumed	101	
Direct operating expenses (including cleaning staff)	548	
Dividend paid	60	
Equipment and fixtures, cost at 30 September 20X5	752	
Equity shares $1 each, fully paid		200
Income tax	9	
Inventory of cleaning materials at 30 September 20X5	37	
Investment income received		11
Provision for deferred tax		50
Accumulated depreciation at 30 September 20X4:		
Equipment and fixtures		370
Provision for legal claim balance at 30 September 20X4		190
Retained earnings at 30 September 20X4		256
Revenue		1,017
Share premium		40
Trade payables		24
Trade receivables	346	
Vehicle operating lease rentals paid	61	
	2,308	2,308

Additional information

(a) The income tax balance in the trial balance is a result of the underprovision of tax for the year ended 30 September 20X4.

(b) The taxation due for the year ended 30 September 20X5 is estimated at $64,000 and the deferred tax provision needs to be increased by $15,000.

(c) Equipment and fixtures are depreciated at 20% per annum straight line. Depreciation of equipment and fixtures is considered to be part of direct cost of sales. BG's policy is to charge a full year's depreciation in the year of acquisition and no depreciation in the year of disposal.

(d) The 10% bonds were issued in 20X0.

(e) BG paid an interim dividend during the year, but does not propose to pay a final dividend as profit for the year is well below expectations.

(f) At 30 September 20X4, BG had an outstanding legal claim from a customer alleging that BG had caused a major fire in the customer's premises. BG was advised that it would very probably lose the case, so a provision of $190,000 was set up at 30 September 20X4. During 20X5, new evidence was discovered and the case against BG was dropped. As there is no further liability, the directors have decided that the provision is no longer required.

Required

(a) Prepare the statement of comprehensive for BG for the year to 30 September 20X5 and a statement of financial position at that date, in a form suitable for presentation to the shareholders and in accordance with the requirements of International Financial Reporting Standards. Do NOT prepare a statement of changes in equity. **(15 marks)**

BG currently has 9 vans leased on operating leases. All of the leases were taken out on 1 October 20X3 when the vans were new and priced at $20,000 each. At that time BG could have acquired them under finance leases, paying 3 annual instalments of $8,000 for each van on 1 October 20X3, 20X4 and 20X5. The directors are wondering whether this would have been a better option.

Required

(b) Redraft the retained earnings balance at 30 September 20X5 of BG as it would be if the vans had been acquired as above under finance leases and depreciated at 20% per annum. Assume an interest rate of 21.53% pa. **(10 marks)**

(Total = 25 marks)

30 DM (FATP 11/06/amended) — 45 mins

The trial balance for DM, a trading entity, at 30 September 20X6 was as follows:

	$'000	$'000
6% Loan (repayable 20Z5)		140
Administrative expenses	91	
Cash and cash equivalents	43	
Distribution costs	46	
Dividend paid 1 June 20X6 (interim)	25	
Inventory at 30 September 20X5 (opening)	84	
Inventory purchases	285	
Land and buildings at cost	500	
Equity shares $1 each, fully paid		300
Plant and equipment at cost	211	
Provision for deferred tax at 30 September 20X5		40
Provision for depreciation at 30 September 20X5 – Buildings		45
Provision for depreciation at 30 September 20X5 – Plant and equipment		80
Retained earnings at 30 September 20X5		32
Sales revenue		602
Share premium		50
Trade payables		29
Trade receivables	6	
Vehicle lease rental paid	27	
	1,318	1,318

Additional information

(a) Inventory at 30 September 20X6 was $93,000. (Closing)

(b) There were no sales of non-current assets during the year ended 30 September 20X6.

(c) The income tax due for the year ended 30 September 20X6 is estimated at $24,000. The deferred tax provision needs to be increased by $15,000.

(d) Depreciation is charged on buildings using the straight line method at 3% per annum. The cost of land included in land and buildings is $200,000. Buildings depreciation is treated as an administration expense.

(e) Plant and equipment is depreciated using the reducing balance method at 20%. Plant and equipment depreciation is regarded as a cost of sales.

(f) Vehicles are depreciated using the straight line method at 20% per year. Vehicles depreciation is regarded as a distribution cost.

(g) During the year DM issued 100,000 new $1 equity shares at a premium of 50%. The proceeds were all received before 30 September 20X6 and are included in the trial balance figures.

(h) DM entered into a non-cancellable five-year finance lease on 1 October 20X5 to acquire a number of vehicles for use in the entity. The vehicles had a fair value of $100,000 and the annual lease payment is $27,000 per year in arrears. The finance charge is to be allocated using the actuarial method. The interest rate implicit in the lease is 10.92%. All the vehicles have economic useful lives of five years. The only entry in the accounting system is the lease payments made to date of $27,000.

(i) The 6% loan was taken out on 1 December 20X5.

Required

Prepare the statement of comprehensive income and a statement of changes in equity for the year ended 30 September 20X6 and a statement of financial position at that date, in a form suitable for presentation to the shareholders and in accordance with the requirements of International Financial Reporting Standards.

(Notes to the financial statements are NOT required, but all workings must be clearly shown and should be to the nearest $'000. Do not prepare a statement of accounting policies.) **(25 marks)**

31 DZ (FATP 5/07/amended) — 45 mins

DZ is a manufacturing entity and produces one group of products, known as product Y.

DZ's trial balance at 31 March 20X7 is shown below.

	$'000	$'000
Administration expenses	891	
Bank and cash	208	
Cash received on disposal of land		1,500
Cash received on disposal of plant		5
Cost of raw materials purchased in year	2,020	
Direct production labour costs	912	
Distribution costs	462	
Equity shares $1 each, fully paid		1,000
Inventory of finished goods at 31 March 20X6	240	
Inventory of raw materials at 31 March 20X6	132	
Land at valuation at 31 March 20X6	1,250	
Plant and equipment at cost at 31 March 20X6	4,180	
Production overheads (excluding depreciation)	633	
Property at cost at 31 March 20X6	11,200	
Provision for depreciation at 31 March 20X6 (see notes (d) and (e))		
Property		1,900
Plant and equipment		2,840
Research and development (see note (f))	500	
Retained earnings at 31 March 20X6		4,797
Revaluation surplus at 31 March 20X6		2,100
Revenue		8,772
Trade payables		748
Trade receivables	1,059	
Accruals		25
	23,687	23,687

Further information

(a) The property cost of $11,200,000 consisted of land $3,500,000 and buildings $7,700,000.

(b) During the year, DZ disposed of non-current assets as follows.

- A piece of surplus land was sold on 1 March 20X7 for $1,500,000
- Obsolete plant was sold for $5,000 scrap value on the same date
- All the cash received is included in the trial balance

Details of the assets sold were:

Asset type	Cost	Revalued amount	Accumulated dep'n
Land	$500,000	$1,250,000	$0
Plant and equipment	$620,000		$600,000

(c) On 31 March 20X7, DZ revalued its properties to $9,800,000 (land $4,100,000 and buildings $5,700,000).

(d) Buildings are depreciated at 5% per annum on the straight line basis. Buildings depreciation is treated as 80% production overhead and 20% administration.

(e) Plant and equipment is depreciated at 25% per annum using the reducing balance method, the depreciation being treated as a production overhead

(f) Product Y was developed in-house. Research and development is carried out on a continuous basis to ensure that the product range continues to meet customer demands. The research and development figure in the trial balance is made up as follows.

	$'000
Development costs capitalised in previous years	867
Less amortisation to 31 March 20X6	534
	333
Research costs incurred in the year to 31 March 20X7	119
Development costs (all meet IAS 38 *Intangible Assets* criteria) incurred in the year to 31 March 20X7	48
Total	500

(g) Development costs are amortised on a straight line basis at 20% per annum.

(h) Research and development costs are treated as cost of sales when charged to the income statement.

(i) DZ charges a full year's amortisation and depreciation in the year of acquisition and none in the year of disposal.

(j) Inventory of raw materials at 31 March 20X7 was $165,000. Inventory of finished goods at 31 March 20X7 was $270,000.

(k) The directors estimate the income tax charge on the year's profits at $811,000.

(l) No interim dividend was paid during the year.

Required

(a) Prepare DZ's property, plant and equipment note to the accounts for the year ended 31 March 20X7.

(6 marks)

(b) Prepare the statement of comprehensive income and a statement of changes in equity for the year to 31 March 20X7 and a statement of financial position at that date, in a form suitable for presentation to the shareholders and in accordance with the requirements of International Financial Reporting Standards.

(All workings should be to the nearest $'000).

(19 marks)

Notes to the financial statements are NOT required (except as specified in part (a) of the question) but ALL workings must be clearly shown. Do NOT prepare a statement of accounting policies.

(Total = 25 marks)

32 EY (FATP 11/07/amended) — 45 mins

EY is an office and industrial furniture manufacturing entity that specialises in developing and using new materials and manufacturing processes in the production of its furniture.

The statement of financial position below relates to the previous year, 31 October 20X6, which is followed by a summary of EY's cash book for the year to 31 October 20X7.

EY
STATEMENT OF FINANCIAL POSITION AT 31 OCTOBER 20X6

	$'000	$'000
Assets		
Non-current assets		
Property, plant and equipment – cost	7,300	
– depreciation	1,110	
		6,190
Current assets		
Inventory	1,200	
Trade receivables	753	
Cash and cash equivalents	82	
		2,035
		8,225
Equity and liabilities		
Equity		
Share capital	3,000	
Revaluation surplus	600	
Retained earnings	825	
		4,425
Non-current liabilities		
Loan notes	2,260	
Deferred tax	180	
		2,440
Current liabilities		
Trade and other payables	573	
Tax payable	670	
Interest payable	117	
		1,360
Total equity and liabilities		8,225

EY
SUMMARISED CASH BOOK FOR THE YEAR ENDED 31 OCTOBER 20X7

	Note	Receipts/(Payments) $'000
Cash book balance at 1 November 20X6		82
Expenditure incurred on government contract	(i)	(600)
Interest paid during the year	(ii)	(160)
Administration expenses paid		(500)
Income tax	(iii)	(690)
Purchase cost of property, plant and equipment	(iv)	(3,460)
Receipt for disposal of land	(v)	1,200
Cash received from customers		7,500
Payments to suppliers of production materials, wages and other production costs		(3,000)
Distribution and selling costs		(730)
Cash received from increase in loan notes		2,500
Cash book balance at 31 October 20X7		2,142

Notes

(i) The government contract is a long-term project for the supply of a new type of seating for government offices involving the development of new materials. The total contract value is $1,400,000. The expenditure includes all costs incurred during the first year of the contract. The project leader is confident that the remainder of the work will cost no more than $400,000. The contract provides that EY can charge for the proportion of work completed by 31 October each year. The percentage of cost incurred to total cost should be used to apportion profit/losses on the contract.

(ii) Interest outstanding at 31 October 20X7 was $130,000.

(iii) Income tax due for the year was estimated by EY at $420,000.

(iv) The property, plant and equipment balance at 31 October 20X6 was made up as follows.

	Land	Premises	Plant & equipment	Total
	$'000	$'000	$'000	$'000
Cost/valuation	2,000	1,500	3,800	7,300
Depreciation	0	350	760	1,110
Carrying value	2,000	1,150	3,040	6,190

During the year EY purchased new premises at a cost of $1,600,000, and new plant and equipment for $1,860,000. Premises are depreciated on the straight line basis at 6% per year, and plant and machinery are depreciated on the reducing balance at 15% per year and are treated as a cost of sale. EY charges a full year's depreciation in the year of acquisition. No assets were fully depreciated at 31 October 20X6.

(v) Land originally costing $600,000, which had previously been revalued to $1,000,000 was sold during the year for $1,200,000.

(vi) A bonus issue of shares was made on the basis of one new share for every six shares held.

(vii) Balances at 31 October 20X7 included.

Trade receivables	$620,000
Outstanding trade payables	$670,000
Inventory	$985,000

Required

Prepare the statement of comprehensive income and a statement of changes in equity for the year to 31 October 20X7 and a statement of financial position at that date, in a form suitable for presentation to the shareholders and in accordance with the requirements of International Financial Reporting Standards. (All workings should be to the nearest $000)

Notes to the financial statements are NOT required, but all workings must be clearly shown. Do NOT prepare a statement of accounting policies.

(25 marks)

33 FZ (FATP 5/08 amended) — 45 mins

FZ is an entity which owns a number of factories that specialise in packaging and selling fresh dairy products in bulk to wholesale entities and large supermarkets. FZ also own a chain of small newsagents' shops.

At its meeting on 1 January 20X8, the Board of FZ decided that, to maximise its strategic opportunities, it would sell the newsagents' shops and concentrate on its dairy product business.

FZ's trial balance at 31 March 20X8 is shown below.

	Notes	$'000	$'000
5% Loan notes (redeemable 20Z0)			1,000
Administrative expenses		440	
Cash and cash equivalents		853	
Cash received on disposal of vehicles			15
Cost of goods sold		4,120	
Distribution costs		432	
Equity dividend paid		500	
Factory buildings at valuation		12,000	
Goodwill		300	
Inventory at 31 March 20X8		900	
Newsagents shops at cost		6,200	
Ordinary shares $1 each, fully paid at 31 March 20X8			5,000
Plant and equipment		2,313	
Provision for deferred tax at 31 March 20X7			197
Provision for property, plant and equipment depreciation at 31 March 20X7	(c)		3,337
Retained earnings at 31 March 20X7			5,808
Revaluation surplus			190
Sales revenue			10,170
Share premium at 31 March 20X8			3,000
Trade payables			417
Trade receivables		929	
Vehicles at cost		147	
		29,134	29,134

Additional information

(a) The newsagents' shops were valued at $5,000,000 by an external valuer on 1 January 20X8. On the same date, a prospective buyer expressed an interest at that price. At 31 March 20X8, detailed negotiations were continuing, with the sale expected to be concluded by 31 July 20X8, for the full valuation of $5,000,000.

The net book values (all included in the relevant figures in the trial balance) of the assets relating to the newsagents' shops at 1 January 20X8, before revaluation, were:

	$'000
Goodwill	300
Newsagents' shops	4,960
	5,260

The newsagents' shops are regarded as a cash generating unit. The cost of selling the shops is estimated at $200,000.

The revenue and expenses of the newsagents' shops for the year ended 31 March 20X8, all included in the trial balance figures, were as follows.

	$'000
Revenue	772
Cost of sales	580
Administrative expenses	96
Distribution costs	57

The sales agreement provides for all employee contracts to be transferred to the new owners of the shops.

Loan note interest does not relate to newsagents shops.

(b) At their meeting on 1 February 20X8, the directors of FZ agreed a $2,000,000 reorganisation package for all of FZ, excluding the newsagents' shops. The restructuring was announced to the staff on 16 February 20X8. it was scheduled to begin implementation on 1 July 20X8 and to be completed by 31 December 20X8. The reorganisation package covered staff retraining, staff relocation and development of new computer systems.

(c) Property, plant and equipment depreciation at 31 March 20X7 comprised:

	$'000
Factory buildings	720
Plant and equipment	1,310
Vehicles	67
Newsagents' shops	1,240

(d) On 1 May 20X8, FZ was informed that one of its customers, X, had ceased trading. The liquidators advised FZ that it was very unlikely to receive payment of any of the $62,000 due from X at 31 March 20X8.

(e) The taxation due for the year ended 31 March 20X8 is estimated at $920,000 (net of tax credit for newsagents' shops of $120,000) and the deferred tax provision needs to be increased to $237,000 (all relating to continuing activities).

(f) Depreciation is to be charged on non-current assets as follows.

- Factory buildings, straight line basis at 3%
- Plant and equipment, straight line basis at 20%
- Newsagents' shops, straight line basis at 10%

These items of depreciation are regarded as a cost of sales.

- Vehicles, reducing balance at 25%

This depreciation is regarded as a distribution cost.

FZ provides a full year's depreciation in the year of purchase and no depreciation in the year of sale.

(g) During the year, FZ disposed of old vehicles for $15,000. The original cost of these vehicles was $57,000 and accumulated depreciation at 31 March 20X7 was $52,000.

(h) The revaluation surplus arose when the factory buildings were revalued in 20X5.

(i) During the year, FZ raised new capital by making a rights issue of 1,000,000 $1 equity shares at $1.50 each. All rights were taken up and all amounts are included in the trial balance.

(j) The 5% loan notes were issued in 20X0.

(k) FZ want to disclose the minimum information allowed by IFRS in its primary financial statements.

Required

(a) Explain, with reasons, how items (a) and (b) above should be treated in FZ's financial statements for the year ended 31 March 20X8. **(5 marks)**

(b) Prepare FZ's statement of comprehensive income for the year to 31 March 20X8 and a statement of financial position at that date, in a form suitable for presentation to the shareholders and in accordance with the requirements of International Financial Reporting Standards.

(20 marks)

Notes to the financial statements are not required, but all workings must be clearly shown. Do not prepare a statement of accounting policies.

(Total = 25 marks)

34 GZ (FATP 11/08 amended) — 45 mins

GZ is a small mining entity which operated a single gold mine for many years. The gold mine ceased operations on 31 October 20X7 and was closed on 1 January 20X8.

On 1 November 20X7, GZ commenced operating a new silver mine.

The trial balance for GZ at 31 October 20X8 was as follows:

	$'000	$'000
Administrative expenses	1,131	
Bank & cash	1,240	
Decommissioning and landscaping expenses of gold mine (see note (c))	1,008	
Direct operating expenses (excluding depreciation)	5,245	
Distribution costs	719	
Dividend paid 1 March 20X8	550	
Equity shares $1 each, fully paid		5,000
Finance lease payable at 1 November 20X7 (see note (g))		900
Government operating license, silver mine at cost (see note (b))	100	
Income tax	13	
Inventory at 31 October 20X8	2,410	
Investment income received		218
Mine properties at cost (see note (d))	6,719	
Plant (finance lease) at 1 November 20X7 (see note (g))	900	
Plant and equipment at 31 October 20X7 (excluding finance lease)	3,025	
Plant lease rentals paid in year	160	
Provision for decommissioning gold mine at 31 October 20X7		950
Provision for deferred tax at 31 October 20X7		731
Provision for depreciation at 31 October 20X7:		
Mine properties (see note (d))		2,123
Plant and equipment		370
Receipt from sale of plant (see note (c))		2
Retained earnings at 31 October 20X7		1,790
Revenue		9,600
Suspense account (see note (g))		1,820
Trade payables		2,431
Trade receivables	2,715	
	25,935	25,935

Additional information provided:

(a) Each mine requires a government operating licence for 20 years and is expected to be productive for that time. After 20 years, the mine will be closed and decommissioned.

(b) On 1 November 20X7, GZ received a government operating licence to operate the new silver mine. The licence cost $100,000 and is for 20 years. Included in the licence is a condition that, on closure of the mine, all above-ground structures must be removed and the ground landscaped. GZ has estimated this cost and discounted it to a present value of $3,230,000 at 31 October 20X8. The trial balance excludes this decommissioning provision.

(c) On 1 January 20X8, GZ closed its gold mine. The $950,000 shown in the trial balance provision as "provision for decommissioning gold mine" has been charged against profits in the previous year. The removal of buildings and other above ground structures, landscaping and other decommissioning costs was complete at 31 October 20X8; the actual cost incurred was $1,008,000. GZ sold old plant and equipment from the gold mine for $2,000 (original cost $200,000, net book value $5,000). The gold mine property is now surplus to GZ's requirements. At 31 October 20X8, the gold mine property had a market value of $520,000 with estimated selling and legal costs of $27,000.

(d) The mine property balances in the trial balance comprised:

Mine property	Gold mine $'000	Silver mine $'000	Total $'000
Cost	2,623	4,096	6,719
Provision for depreciation	2,123	0	2,123
	500	4,096	4,596

(e) Income tax due for the year ended 31 October 20X8 is estimated at $375,000. The deferred tax provision needs to be reduced by $60,000.

(f) Depreciation is charged on mining property using the straight-line basis at 5% per annum. Plant and equipment is depreciated using the reducing balance method at 25%. The depreciation policy is to charge a full year's depreciation in the year of acquisition and no depreciation in the year of disposal. Depreciation is regarded as a cost of production.

(g) GZ entered into a non-cancellable seven-year finance lease on 1 November 20X7 to acquire mining machinery. Under the terms of the lease, GZ will make annual payments of $160,000 in arrears, the first payment being made on 31 October 2008. The machinery is estimated to have a useful economic life of seven years. The fair value of the machinery at 1 November 20X7 was $900,000. GZ allocates finance charges using the sum of digits method.

(h) The final dividend for the year to 31 October 20X7 was paid on 1 March 20X8.

(i) GZ made a new issue of 1,400 equity shares on 31 October 20X8 at a premium of 30%. The cash received was debited to the bank account and credited to the suspense account.

Required

(a) Prepare GZ's Property, Plant and Equipment note to the financial statements for the year to 31 October 20X8. **(6 marks)**

(b) Prepare GZ's statement of comprehensive income and a statement of changes in equity for the year to 31 October 20X8 and a statement of financial position at that date, in a form suitable for presentation to the shareholders and in accordance with the requirements of International Financial Reporting Standards. (All workings should be to the nearest $'000).

Notes to the financial statements, except as indicated in part (a) above, are NOT required, but all workings must be clearly shown. Do NOT prepare a statement of accounting policies. **(19 marks)**

(Total = 25 marks)

Part C: Group Financial Statements

Questions 35 to 39 cover Group Financial Statements, the subject of Part C of the BPP Study Text for Paper F1.

35 Objective test questions: Consolidated financial statements

38 mins

1 Fanta acquired 100% of the ordinary share capital of Tizer on 1 October 20X7.

On 31 December 20X7 the share capital and retained earnings of Tizer were as follows:

	$'000
Ordinary shares of $1 each	400
Retained earnings at 1 January 20X7	100
Retained profit for the year ended 31 December 20X7	80
	580

The profits of Tizer have accrued evenly throughout 20X1. Goodwill arising on the acquisition of Tizer was $30,000.

What was the cost of the investment in Tizer?

A $400,000
B $580,000
C $610,000
D $590,000

(2 marks)

2 Mercedes has owned 100% of Benz for many years. At 31 March 20X9 the retained earnings of Mercedes were $450,000 and the consolidated retained earnings of the group were $560,000. Mercedes has no other subsidiaries.

During the year ended 31 March 20X9, Benz had sold goods to Mercedes for $50,000. Mercedes still had these goods in inventory at the year end. Benz uses a 25% mark up on all goods.

What were the retained earnings of Benz at 31 March 20X9?

A $110,000
B $60,000
C $170,000
D $120,000

(2 marks)

3 Oldsmobile, a company with subsidiaries, purchased 35% of the ordinary share capital of Chevrolet for $50,000 on 1 April 20X8.

Chevrolet's statement of financial position at 31 March 20X9 was as follows:

	$'000
Net assets	55
Ordinary share capital ($1 shares)	15
Retained earnings at 1 April 20X8	20
Net profit for the year ended 31 March 20X9	20
	55

During the year to 31 March 20X9 Chevrolet paid out a total dividend to its shareholders of $10,000. Oldsmobile considers that its investment in Chevrolet has been impaired by $6,000.

At what amount should Oldsmobile's investment in Chevrolet be shown in its consolidated statement of financial position as at 31 March 20X9?

A $57,000
B $50,500
C $47,500
D $44,000

(2 marks)

4   Ruby owns 30% of Emerald. During the year to 31 December 20X8 Emerald sold goods to Ruby for $160,000. Emerald applies a one-third mark up on cost. Ruby still had 25% of these goods in inventory at the year end.

What amount should be deducted from consolidated retained earnings in respect of this transaction?

A $40,000
B $3,000
C $10,000
D $4,000

(2 marks)

5   Colossal acquired 100% of the $100,000 ordinary share capital of Enormous for $300,000 on 1 January 20X9 when the retained earnings of Enormous were $156,000. At the date of acquisition the fair value of plant held by Enormous was $20,000 higher than its carrying value. This plant had a remaining life of 4 years at the acquisition date.

At 31 December 20X9 retained earnings are as follows:

	$
Colossal	275,000
Enormous	177,000

Colossal considers that goodwill on acquisition is impaired by 50%.

What are group retained earnings at 31 December 20X9?

A $279,000
B $284,000
C $296,000
D $291,000

(3 marks)

6   On 1 April 20X7 Rhino acquired 40% of the share capital of Hippo for $120,000, when the retained earnings of Hippo were $80,000. During the year Rhino sold goods to Hippo for $30,000, including a profit margin of 25%. These goods were still in inventory at the year end.

At 31 March 20X8 the retained earnings of Hippo were $140,000.

At what amount should Rhino's interest in Hippo be shown in the consolidated statement of financial position at 31 March 20X8?

A $173,000
B $144,000
C $141,000
D $105,000

(2 marks)

The following information is relevant for questions 7 and 8

On 1 January 20X6 A purchased 100,000 ordinary shares in B for $210,000. At that date B's retained earnings amounted to $90,000 and the fair value of its assets was equal to their book values.

Four years later, on 31 December 20X9, the statements of financial position of the two companies were:

	A $	B $
Sundry net assets	200,000	260,000
Shares in B	210,000	-
	410,000	260,000
Ordinary shares of $1	200,000	100,000
Retained earnings	210,000	160,000
	410,000	260,000

The share capital of B has remained unchanged since 1 January 20X6. Goodwill is impaired by 50%.

7   What amount should appear in the group consolidated statement of financial position at 31 December 20X9 for goodwill?

    A $25,000
    B $20,000
    C $10,000
    D $14,000

    (2 marks)

8   What amount should appear in the consolidated statement of financial position at 31 December 20X9 for group retained earnings?

    A $270,000
    B $338,000
    C $370,000
    D $280,000

    (2 marks)

The following information is relevant for questions 9 and 10

H acquired 100% of the share capital of S on 1 January 20X9 for $350,000.

The statements of financial position of the two companies at 31 December 20X9 were as follows:

	H $	S $
Sundry assets	590,000	290,000
Investment in S	350,000	-
	940,000	290,000
Issued share capital - $1 shares	400,000	140,000
Share premium account	320,000	50,000
Retained earnings at 1 January 20X9	140,000	60,000
Profit for year to 31 December 20X9	80,000	40,000
	940,000	290,000

There have been no changes in the share capital or share premium account of either company since 1 January 20X9. There was no impairment of goodwill.

9   What figure for goodwill should appear in the consolidated statement of financial position of the H group at 31 December 20X9?

    A $60,000
    B $100,000
    C $150,000
    D $160,000

    (2 marks)

10 What figure for group retained earnings should appear in the consolidated statement of financial position of the H group at 31 December 20X9?

    A $260,000
    B $220,000
    C $320,000
    D $200,000

    (2 marks)

(Total = 21 marks)

36 Goose and Gander — 45 mins

You are provided with the draft accounts of Goose and Gander at 31 December 20X8.

STATEMENTS OF COMPREHENSIVE INCOME FOR THE YEAR ENDED 31 DECEMBER 20X8

	Goose $'000	Gander $'000
Revenue	5,000	1,000
Cost of sales	2,900	600
Gross profit	2,100	400
Other expenses	1,700	320
Net profit	400	80
Tax	130	25
Profit for the year	270	55

STATEMENTS OF FINANCIAL POSITION AT 31 DECEMBER 20X8

	$'000	$'000
Non-current assets		
Property, plant and equipment	2,000	200
Current assets		
Inventory	500	120
Trade receivables	650	40
Bank and cash	390	35
	1,540	195
	3,540	395
Equity and liabilities		
Equity		
Share capital	500	100
Share premium	1500	–
Revaluation surplus	50	–
Retained earnings	350	200
	2,400	300
Current liabilities		
Trade payables	1,010	70
Tax	130	25
	1,140	95
	3,540	395

The following information is also available:

(a) Goose acquired 100% of the issued share capital of Gander (100,000 $1 shares) on 1 January 20X8 by issuing 4 new $1 shares in Goose in exchange for every 5 shares in Gander. The fair value of Goose's shares on the date of exchange was $5.50. The retained earnings of Gander were $185,000 on the date of acquisition. The acquisition of Gander has not been reflected in the draft accounts of Goose at 31 December 20X8.

(b) On 31 December 20X8 Goose despatched goods which cost $80,000 to Gander, at an invoiced cost of $100,000. Gander received the goods on 2 January 20X9 and recorded the transaction then.

(c) Included in the draft accounts of Goose at 31 December 20X8 is a property with a carrying value of $100,000. Due to recent urban development, the fair value of the property increased to $200,000 at 31 December 20X8. Goose has a policy of revaluing properties, but has yet to reflect this increase in its draft accounts.

Required

(a) Prepare a draft consolidated statement of comprehensive income and a draft consolidated statement of financial position for the Goose Group at 31 December 20X8. **(20 marks)**

(b) Explain why consolidated financial statements are useful to the users of financial statements (as opposed to just the parent company's separate (entity) financial statements). **(5 marks)**

(Total = 25 marks)

37 Parsley — 45 mins

You are provided with the following financial statements for Parsley, a limited liability company, and its subsidiary Sage

STATEMENT OF COMPREHENSIVE INCOME FOR THE YEAR ENDED 31 DECEMBER 20X9

	Parsley $'000	Sage $'000
Sales revenue	135,000	74,000
Cost of sales	(70,000)	(30,000)
Gross profit	65,000	44,000
Distribution costs	(7,500)	(6,200)
Administrative expenses	(19,000)	(7,784)
Income from Sage: loan note interest	4	–
dividends	8,000	–
Interest payable	–	(16)
Profit before tax	46,504	30,000
Income tax expense	(10,000)	(9,000)
Profit for the year	36,504	21,000

STATEMENTS OF FINANCIAL POSITION AS AT 31 DECEMBER 20X9

	Parsley $'000	Parsley $'000	Sage $'000	Sage $'000
Assets				
Non-current assets				
Property, plant and equipment		74,000		39,050
Investments:				
$1 ordinary shares in Sage at cost		30,000		–
Sage loan notes		50		–
		104,050		39,050
Current assets				
Inventory	10,630		4,498	
Receivables	18,460		12,230	
Bank	13,400		1,344	
		42,490		18,072
Total assets		146,540		57,122
Equity and liabilities				
Equity				
$1 ordinary shares		80,000		25,000
Retained earnings		37,540		15,000
		117,540		40,000
Non-current liabilities				
8% Loan note		–		200
Current liabilities				
Payables	6,000		1,922	
Tax	11,000		7,000	
Dividends payable	12,000		8,000	
		29,000		16,922
Total equity and liabilities		136,540		57,122

The following information is also available:

(a) Parsley purchased 100% of the $1 ordinary shares in Sage on 1 January 20X8. At that date Sage's retained earnings were $2,000,000.

(b) Parsley's annual impairment review of goodwill on acquisition of Sage valued it at $2,250,000 at 31 December 20X9.

(c) During the year ended 31 December 20X9 Parsley sold goods which originally cost $8,000,000 to Sage for $12,000,000. Sage still had 25% of these goods in inventory at 31 December 20X9.

(d) Sage owed Parsley $1,800,000 at 31 December 20X9 for some of the goods Parsley supplied during the year.

(e) Parsley owns $50,000 of Sage's loan notes. The interest is paid annually in arrears at 31 December. Interest for the year ended 31 December 20X9 is included in Sage's payables. Parsley has also included the interest in its receivables.

(f) All dividends were declared but not paid prior to the year end.

Required

(a) Calculate the goodwill arising on the acquisition of Sage. **(2 marks)**

(b) Prepare the following financial statements for Parsley:

  (i) The consolidated statement of comprehensive income for the year ended 31 December 20X9.
  (6 marks)

  (ii) The consolidated statement of financial position as at 31 December 20X9.

  Note. A working should be included for the retained earnings. Disclosure notes are not required.
  (14 marks)

(c) Explain the accounting treatment of intra-group trading in consolidated accounts. **(3 marks)**

(Total = 25 marks)

38 Molecule — 45 mins

Molecule is the parent company of Atom and owns 30% of Electron. The following are the statements of financial position for all three companies as at 31 October 20X7.

	Molecule $'000	Atom $'000	Electron $'000
Assets			
Non-current assets			
Property, plant and equipment	3,000	3,300	2,000
Investments: shares in Atom at cost	4,545	–	–
shares in Electron at cost	800	–	–
Current assets			
Inventory	1,500	800	400
Receivables	1,800	750	300
Bank	600	350	150
	3,900	1,900	850
Total assets	12,245	5,200	2,850
Equity and liabilities			
Equity			
$1 ordinary shares	9,000	4,000	2,000
Retained earnings	1,325	200	600
	10,325	4,200	2,600
Current liabilities			
Payables	1,220	200	150
Tax	700	800	100
Total equity and liabilities	12,245	5,200	2,800

The following information is also available.

(a) Molecule purchased all of the shares in Atom some years ago when Atom had retained earnings of $60,000. All goodwill on acquisition has been fully written off as impaired in prior years. Molecule purchased its shares in Electron on 1 November 20X6 when Electron had retained earnings of $300,000.

(b) During the year Molecule sold goods with an invoice value of $240,000 to Atom. These goods were invoiced at cost plus 20%. Half of the goods are still in Atom's inventory at the year end.

(c) Atom owes Molecule $30,000 at 31 October 20X7 for goods it purchased during the year.

(d) Molecule wants to recognise an impairment of $100,000 in respect of its investment in Electron.

(e) Molecule has identified that a receivable of $450,000 from a customer who went bankrupt in August 20X5 was included in its accounts at 31 October 20X6. This balance was known to be irrecoverable at the previous year end, but no adjustments were made. Molecule wishes to correct this error, but has not yet made any adjustments to the 31 October 20X7 accounts.

Required

(a) Calculate the goodwill on acquisition of Atom. **(2 marks)**

(b) Prepare the consolidated statement of financial position for the Molecule group as at 31 October 20X7.

Note. A working should be included for group retained earnings. Disclosure notes are not required.

(20 marks)

(c) A company that owns less than 50% of the shares of another company will regard it as an 'associate' if it is able to exert 'significant influence'. Identify three circumstances that might demonstrate 'significant influence'. **(3 marks)**

(Total = 25 marks)

39 Tom, Dick and Harry 45 mins

The following statements of financial position have been prepared as at 31 October 20X9.

	Tom $'000	Tom $'000	Dick $'000	Dick $'000	Harry $'000	Harry $'000
Non-current assets						
Property, plant and equipment		205		120		220
Investments						
100,000 shares in Dick Ltd at cost		200		–		–
60,000 shares in Harry Ltd at cost		115		–		–
Current assets						
Inventory	100		70		90	
Receivables	170		40		70	
Bank	190		30		50	
		460		140		210
		980		260		430
Equity and liabilities						
$1 ordinary shares	500		100		200	
Retained earnings	370		130		150	
		870		230		350
Current liabilities						
Trade payables		110		30		80
		980		260		430

Additional information

(a) Tom purchased all the share capital of Dick on 1 November 20X8 for $200,000. The previous owners of Dick needed to sell quickly as they were in financial difficulty. The book value of Dick's net assets on the date of acquisition was $190,000. A valuation exercise performed by a reputable firm showed that the fair value of Dick's property, plant and equipment at that date was $50,000 greater than book value. The increase in fair value was not accounted for in the books of Dick. If Dick had re-valued its non-current assets at 31 October 20X8, an addition of $2,000 would have been made to the depreciation charged for 20X8/20X9.

(b) Tom sold goods for $25,000 to Dick during the year. The price included a 25% mark up. 40% of them are still held in inventory by Dick.

(c) Tom's investment in Harry was acquired on 31 October 20X5 when the retained earnings of Harry were $130,000. The fair value of Harry's assets were the same as their net book value at the date of acquisition. At 31 October 20X9, the investment in Harry is impaired by $4,000.

Required

(a) (i) Calculate the goodwill on acquisition of Dick.

(ii) Explain the treatment required by IFRS 3 for a bargain purchase that creates negative goodwill.

(6 marks)

(b) Prepare the consolidated statement of financial position for the Tom Group as at 31 October 20X9.

(19 marks)

(Total = 25 marks)

Part D: Principles of business taxation

Questions 40 to 47 cover Principles of business taxation, the subject of Part D of the BPP Study Text for Paper F1.

40 Objective test questions: General principles of taxation — 88 mins

1. Country X uses a Pay-As-You-Earn (PAYE) system for collecting taxes from employees. Each employer is provided with information about each employee's tax position and tables showing the amount of tax to deduct each period. Employers are required to deduct tax from employees and pay it to the revenue authorities on a monthly basis

   From the perspective of the government, list THREE advantages of the PAYE system. **(3 marks)**

2. Where is employee tax recorded in a set of financial accounts?

   A   Charged to employee costs in the income statement
   B   Charged to cost of sales in the income statement
   C   Included as a payable in the balance sheet
   D   Included as a receivable in the balance sheet **(2 marks)**

3. Which of the following powers is *not* available to tax authorities.

   A   Power to review and query filed returns
   B   Power to detain company officials
   C   Power to request special returns
   D   Power to enter and search premises **(2 marks)**

4. Complete the blanks:

   Direct taxation is charged directly on the .... or .... that is intended to pay the tax. **(2 marks)**

5. Complete the following equation.

   Accounting profit + ? – non-taxable income – tax allowable expenditure = ? **(2 marks)**

6. In 1776, Adam Smith proposed that an acceptable tax should meet four characteristics. Three of these characteristics were certainty, convenience and efficiency.

   Identify the FOURTH characteristic.

   A   Neutrality
   B   Transparency
   C   Equity
   D   Simplicity **(2 marks)**

7. Define tax evasion. **(2 marks)**

8. List (using no more than five words per item) the four main sources of tax rules in a country. **(4 marks)**

9. A withholding tax is

   A   tax withheld from payment to the tax authorities.
   B   tax paid less an amount withheld from payment.
   C   tax deducted at source before payment of interest or dividends.
   D   tax paid on increases in value of investment holdings. **(2 marks)**

Questions | 75

10 The effective incidence of a tax is

   A   the date the tax is actually paid.
   B   the person or entity that finally bears the cost of the tax.
   C   the date the tax assessment is issued.
   D   the person or entity receiving the tax assessment.   (2 marks)

11 In no more than 15 words, define the meaning of 'competent jurisdiction'.   (2 marks)

12 Which **one** of the following powers is a tax authority least likely to have granted to them?

   A   Power of arrest.
   B   Power to examine records.
   C   Power of entry and search.
   D   Power to give information to other country's tax authorities.   (2 marks)

13 An entity sells furniture and adds a sales tax to the selling price of all products sold. A customer purchasing furniture from the entity has to pay the cost of the furniture plus the sales tax. The customer therefore bears the cost of the sales tax.

   This is referred to as

   A   Formal incidence
   B   Indirect incidence
   C   Effective incidence
   D   Direct incidence   (2 marks)

14 BM has a taxable profit of $30,000 and receives a tax assessment of $3,000.

   BV has a taxable profit of $60,000 and receives a tax assessment of $7,500.

   BM and BV are resident in the same tax jurisdiction.

   This tax could be said to be

   A   A progressive tax
   B   A regressive tax
   C   A direct tax
   D   A proportional tax   (2 marks)

15 List three possible reasons why governments set deadlines for filing returns and/or paying taxes. (3 marks)

16 What is 'hypothecation'?

   A   Process of earmarking tax revenues for specific types of expenditure
   B   Estimation of tax revenue made by the tax authorities for budget purposes
   C   Refund made by tax authorities for tax paid in other countries
   D   Payment of taxes due to tax authorities, net of tax refunds due from tax authorities   (2 marks)

17 State two reasons why a group of entities might want to claim group loss relief rather than use the loss in the entity to which it relates. (Group loss relief is where, for tax purposes the loss for the year of one entity in the group is offset against the profit of the year of one or more other entities in the group.)   (2 marks)

18 Explain briefly THREE major principles of modern taxation.   (3 marks)

19 Which ONE of the following is NOT an advantage for the tax authority of deduction of tax at source?

   A   The total amount of tax due for the period is easier to calculate
   B   Tax is collected earlier
   C   Administration costs are borne by the entity deducting tax
   D   Tax is deducted before income is paid to the taxpayer

   (2 marks)

20 HD sells office stationery and adds a sales tax to the selling price of all products sold. A customer purchasing goods from HD has to pay the cost of the goods plus the sales tax.

HD pays the sales tax collected to the tax authorities.

From the perspective of HD the sales tax would be said to have

- A formal incidence.
- B effective incidence.
- C informal incidence.
- D ineffective incidence.

(2 marks)

21 DR makes a taxable profit of $400,000 and pays an equity dividend of $250,000. Income tax on DR's profit is at a rate of 25%.

Equity shareholders pay tax on their dividend income at a rate of 30%.

If DR and its equity shareholders pay a total of $175,000 tax between them, what method of corporate income tax is being used in that country?

- A The classical system
- B The imputation system
- C The partial imputation system
- D The split rate system

(2 marks)

22 The 'tax gap' is the difference between:

- A When a tax payment is due and the date it is actually paid
- B The tax due calculated by the entity and the tax demanded by the tax authority
- C The amount of tax due to be paid and the amount actually collected
- D The date when the entity was notified by the tax authority of the tax due and the date the tax should be paid

(2 marks)

(Total = 49 marks)

41 Objective test questions: International tax — 59 mins

1 Company Z has a factory in Malaysia with retail outlets in Hong Kong. The company's registered office is in London but the head office is located in the Cayman Islands. All board meetings take place in the Cayman Islands. Where is Company Z's country of residence?

- A Malaysia
- B Hong Kong
- C England
- D Cayman Islands

(2 marks)

2 Which of the following is a source of tax rules?

- A International accounting standards
- B Local company legislation
- C International tax treaties
- D Domestic accounting practice

(2 marks)

3 The European Union (EU) is an example of a supranational body. In not more than 20 words, describe the effect the EU has on its member states' tax rules. (2 marks)

4 In countries such as the UK, different types of income are taxed according to different rules. What is the name of this system? (2 marks)

5 Name four payments that are usually affected by withholding tax. (2 marks)

6 Name three methods of giving double taxation relief. (2 marks)

Questions

7   Double tax relief is used to:

    A   Ensure that you do not pay tax twice on any of your income.
    B   Mitigate taxing overseas income twice.
    C   Avoid taxing dividends received from subsidiaries in the same country twice.
    D   Provide relief where a company pays tax at double the normal rate. **(2 marks)**

8   The OECD model tax convention defines a permanent establishment to include a number of different types of establishments:

    1   A place of management
    2   A warehouse
    3   A workshop
    4   A quarry
    5   A building site that was used for 9 months

Which of the above are included in the OECD's list of permanent establishments?

    A   1, 2 and 3 only
    B   1, 3 and 4 only
    C   2, 3 and 4 only
    D   3, 4 and 5 only **(2 marks)**

9   Corporate residence for tax purposes can be determined in a number of ways, depending on the country concerned.

Which ONE of the following is NOT normally used to determine corporate residence for tax purposes?

    A   The country from which control of the entity is exercised.
    B   The country of incorporation of the entity.
    C   The country where management of the entity hold their meetings.
    D   The country where most of the entity's products are sold **(2 marks)**

10 An entity, DP, in Country A receives a dividend from an entity in Country B. The gross dividend of $50,000 is subject to a withholding tax of $5,000 and $45,000 is paid to DP.

Country A levies a tax of 12% on overseas dividends.

Country A and Country B have both signed a double taxation treaty based on the OECD model convention and both apply the credit method when relieving double taxation.

How much tax would DP be expected to pay in Country A on the dividend received from the entity in Country B?

    A $400
    B $1,000
    C $5,400
    D $6,000 **(2 marks)**

11 Where a resident entity runs an overseas operation as a branch of the entity, certain tax implications arise.

Which one of the following does not usually apply in relation to an overseas branch?

    A   Assets can be transferred to the branch without triggering a capital gain
    B   Corporate income tax is paid on profits remitted by the branch
    C   Tax depreciation can be claimed on any qualifying assets used in the trade of the branch
    D   Losses sustained by the branch are immediately deductible against the resident entity's income. **(2 marks)**

12   The following details relate to EA:

- Incorporated in Country A.
- Carries out its main business activities in Country B.
- Its senior management operate from Country C and effective control is exercised from Country C.

Assume countries A, B and C have all signed double tax treaties with each other, based on the OECD model tax convention.

Which country will EA be deemed to be resident in for tax purposes?

A   Country A
B   Country B
C   Country C
D   Both Countries B and C   (2 marks)

---

13   The OECD Model tax convention defines a permanent establishment.

Which ONE of the following is not specifically listed as a "permanent establishment" by the OECD Model tax convention?

A   An office.
B   A factory.
C   An oil well.
D   A site of an 11 month construction project.   (2 marks)

---

14   Developed countries generally use three tax bases. One tax base widely used is income.

List the other TWO widely used bases.   (2 marks)

---

15   The following details are relevant:

- HC carries out its main business activities in Country A;
- HC is incorporated in Country B;
- HC's senior management exercise control from Country C, but there are no sales or purchases made in Country C;
- HC raises its finance and is quoted on the stock exchange in Country D.

Assume Countries A, B, C and D have all signed double taxation treaties with each other, based on the OECD model tax convention.

Which country will HC be deemed to be resident in for tax purposes?

A   Country A
B   Country B
C   Country C
D   Country D   (2 marks)

---

16   EB has an investment of 25% of the equity shares in XY, an entity resident in a foreign country.

EB receives a dividend of $90,000 from XY, the amount being after the deduction of withholding tax of 10%.

XY had profits before tax for the year of $1,200,000 and paid corporate income tax of $200,000.

How much underlying tax can EB claim for double taxation relief?   (3 marks)

(Total = 33 marks)

… | Questions | 79

42 Objective test questions: Indirect taxes — 52 mins

1. Excise duties are deemed to be most suitable for commodities that have certain specific characteristics.

   List THREE characteristics of a commodity that, from a revenue authority's point of view, would make that commodity suitable for an excise duty to be imposed. **(3 marks)**

2. Which of the following is an indirect tax?

   A Withholding tax
   B Employee tax
   C Sales tax
   D Company income tax **(2 marks)**

3. The cost of a sales tax is borne by which person?

   A The supplier of raw materials
   B The end consumer
   C The retailer
   D The wholesaler **(2 marks)**

   The following data are given for sub-questions 4 and 5 below

   Country D uses a value added tax (VAT) system whereby VAT is charged on all goods and services at a rate of 15%. Registered VAT entities are allowed to recover input VAT paid on their purchases.

   Country E uses a multi-stage sales tax system, where a cumulative tax is levied every time a sale is made. The tax rate is 7% and tax paid on purchases is not recoverable.

   DA is a manufacturer and sells products to DB, a retailer, for $500 excluding tax. DB sells the products to customers for a total of $1,000 excluding tax.

   DA paid $200 plus VAT/sales tax for the manufacturing cost of its products.

4. Assume DA operates in Country D and sells products to DB in the same country.

   Calculate the net VAT due to be paid by DA and DB for the products. **(2 marks)**

5. Assume DA operates in Country E and sells products to DB in the same country.

   Calculate the total sales tax due to be paid on all of the sales of the products. **(2 marks)**

6. Which of the following types of taxes is regarded as an indirect tax?

   A Taxes on income.
   B Taxes on capital gains.
   C Taxes on inherited wealth.
   D Sales tax (Value added tax). **(2 marks)**

7. AE purchases products from a foreign entity and imports them into a country A. On import, the products are subject to an excise duty of $5 per item and Value Added Tax (VAT) of 15% on cost plus excise duty.

   AE purchased 200 items for $30 each and after importing them sold all of the items for $50 each plus VAT at 15%.

   How much is due to be paid to the tax authorities for these transactions?

   A $450
   B $1,450
   C $2,050
   D $2,500 **(3 marks)**

8   Country OS has a value added tax (VAT) system where VAT is charged on all goods and services. Registered VAT entities are allowed to recover input VAT paid on their purchases.

VAT operates at different levels in OS:

- Standard rate   10%
- Luxury rate   20%
- Zero rate   0%

During the last VAT period, an entity, BZ, purchased materials and services costing $100,000, excluding VAT. All materials and services were at standard rate VAT.

BZ converted the materials into two products Z and L; product Z is zero rated and product L is luxury rated for VAT purposes.

During the VAT period, BZ made the following sales, excluding VAT:

	$
Z	60,000
L	120,000

At the end of the period, BZ paid the net VAT due to the tax authorities.

Assuming BZ had no other VAT-related transactions, how much VAT did BZ pay?   **(2 marks)**

9   CU manufactures clothing and operates in a country that has a Value Added Tax system (VAT). The VAT system allows entities to reclaim input tax that they have paid on taxable supplies. VAT is at 15% of the selling price at all stages of the manufacturing and distribution chain.

CU manufactures a batch of clothing and pays expenses (taxable inputs) of $100 plus VAT. CU sells the batch of clothing to a retailer CZ for $250 plus VAT. CZ unpacks the clothing and sells the items separately to various customers for a total of $600 plus VAT.

How much VAT do CU and CZ each have to pay in respect of this one batch of clothing?   **(2 marks)**

10 Country Z has a VAT system where VAT is charged on all goods and services. Registered VAT entities are allowed to recover input VAT paid on their purchases.

VAT operates at three different levels in Z:

- Standard rate   15%
- Luxury rate   22%
- Zero rate   0%

During the last VAT period, an entity, GW, purchased materials and services costing $138,000, including VAT. All materials and services were at standard rate VAT.

GW converted the materials into two products A and B; product A is zero-rated and product B is luxury-rated for VAT purposes.

During the VAT period, GW made the following sales, including VAT:

	$
A	70,000
B	183,000

At the end of the period, GW paid the net VAT due to the tax authorities.

Assume no opening or closing inventory balances.

Assuming GW had no other VAT-related transactions, calculate GW's profit and the amount of VAT that GW paid?

(4 marks)

11 HN purchases products from a foreign country. The products cost $14 each and are subject to excise duty of $3 per item and VAT at 15%.

If HN imports 1,000 items, how much does it pay to the tax authorities for this transaction?

A $2,100
B $5,100
C $5,550
D $19,550

(2 marks)

12 Country Z has a VAT system which allows entities to reclaim input tax paid.

In Country Z, the VAT rates are:

Zero rated   0%
Standard rated   15%

FE owns and runs a small retail store. The store's sales include items that are zero rated, standard rated and exempt. FE's electronic cash register provides an analysis of sales. The figures for the three months to 30 April 20X8 were:

	Sales value, including VAT where appropriate $
Zero rated	13,000
Standard rated	18,400
Exempt	11,000
Total	42,400

FE's analysis of expenditure for the same period provided the following:

	Expenditure, excluding VAT $
Zero rated purchases	6,000
Standard rated purchases relating to standard rate outputs	10,000
Standard rated purchases relating to zero rate outputs	4,000
Standard rated purchases relating to exempt outputs	5,000
	25,000

Calculate the VAT due to/from FE for the three months ended 30 April 20X8.   (3 marks)

(Total = 29 marks)

43 Objective test questions: Company taxation   67 mins

1   Company G makes an accounting profit of $350,000 during the year. This includes non-taxable income of $25,000 and depreciation of $30,000. In addition, $15,000 of the expenses are disallowable for tax purposes. If the tax allowable depreciation totals $32,000, what is the taxable profit?

A $323,000
B $338,000
C $352,000
D $362,000

(2 marks)

2   Company G makes a taxable profit of $350,000 during the year. This includes adjustments for non-taxable income of $25,000, depreciation of $30,000 and $15,000 disallowed expenses. If the tax allowable depreciation totals $32,000, what is the accounting profit?

A $323,000
B $338,000
C $352,000
D $362,000

(2 marks)

3   Company G makes an accounting loss of $350,000 during the year. This includes non-taxable income of $25,000 and depreciation of $30,000. In addition, $400,000 of the expenses are disallowable for tax purposes. If the tax allowable depreciation totals $32,000, what is the taxable amount?

   A $23,000 profit
   B $23,000 loss
   C $123,000 profit
   D $123,000 profit   (2 marks)

4   Company W makes a taxable profit of $50m during the year. This is after adjustments for non-taxable income of $3m, depreciation of $15m and $1m disallowed expenses. If the tax allowable depreciation totals $4m, what is the accounting profit?

   A $38m
   B $41m
   C $58m
   D $59m   (2 marks)

5   Company M makes an accounting profit of $250,000 during the year. This includes depreciation of $45,000 and disallowable expenses of $20,000. If the tax allowable depreciation totals $30,000 and the tax rate is 30%, what is the tax payable?

   A $64,500
   B $75,000
   C $79,500
   D $85,500   (2 marks)

6   Company B makes an accounting profit of $360,000 during the year. This includes non-taxable income of $35,000 and depreciation of $40,000. In addition, $10,000 of the expenses are disallowable for tax purposes. If the tax allowable depreciation totals $30,000 and the tax rate is 20%, what is the tax payable?

   A $60,000
   B $65,000
   C $69,000
   D $72,000   (2 marks)

7   Company X makes an accounting profit of $500,000 during the year. This includes non-taxable income of $25,000 and depreciation of $50,000.

   The finance director finds that $5,000 of the expenses are disallowable for tax purposes. If the tax allowable depreciation totals $60,000 and the tax rate is 25%, what is the tax payable?

   A $116,250
   B $117,500
   C $123,750
   D $132,500   (2 marks)

8   Company G makes an accounting profit of $250,000 during the year. This is after charging depreciation of $40,000 and tax disallowable expenses of $2,000. If the tax allowable depreciation totals $30,000 and the tax rate is 30%, what is the tax payable?

   A $71,400
   B $72,000
   C $77,400
   D $78,600   (2 marks)

9   Tax on an entity's trading profits could be referred to as:

    1   Income tax
    2   Profits tax
    3   Indirect tax
    4   Direct tax
    5   Earnings tax

    Which TWO of the above would most accurately describe tax on an entity's trading profits:

    A   1 and 3
    B   1 and 4
    C   2 and 3
    D   4 and 5   (2 marks)

10 E has an accounting profit before tax of $95,000. The tax rate on trading profits applicable to E for the year is 25%. The accounting profit included non-taxable income from government grants of $15,000 and non-tax allowable expenditure of $10,000 on entertaining expenses.

    How much tax is E due to pay for the year?   (2 marks)

11 AC made the following payment during the year ended 30 April 20X5:

	$'000
Operating costs (excluding depreciation)	23
Finance costs	4
Capital repayment of loans	10
Payments for the purchase of new computer equipment for use in AC's business	20

    AC's revenue for the period was $45,000 and the corporate income tax rate applicable to AC's profits was 25%. The computer equipment qualifies for tax allowances of 10% per year on a straight line basis.

    Calculate AC's tax payable for the year ended 30 April 20X5.   (3 marks)

12 Country B has a corporate income tax system that treats capital gains/losses separately from trading profits/losses. Capital gains/losses cannot be offset against trading profits/losses. All losses can be carried forward indefinitely, but cannot be carried back to previous years. Trading profits and capital gains are both taxed at 20%.

    BD had no brought forward losses on 1 October 20X2. BD's results for 20X3 to 20X5 were as follows:

	Trading profit/(loss) $'000	Capital gains/(loss) $'000
Year to September 20X3	200	(100)
Year to September 20X4	(120)	0
Year to September 20X5	150	130

    Calculate BD's corporate income tax due for each of the years ended 30 September 20X3 to 20X5.
                                                                                                   (3 marks)

13 A full imputation system of corporate income tax is one where an entity is taxable on

    A   all of its income and gains whether they are distributed or not. The shareholder is liable for taxation on all dividends received.

    B   all of its income and gains whether they are distributed or not, but all the underlying corporation tax is passed to the shareholder as a tax credit.

    C   all of its income and gains whether they are distributed or not, but only part of the underlying corporation tax is passed to the shareholder as a tax credit.

    D   its retained profits at one rate and on its distributed profits at another (usually lower) rate of tax.
                                                                                                   (2 marks)

14 DZ recognised a tax liability of $290,000 in its financial statements for the year ended 30 September 20X5. This was subsequently agreed with and paid to the tax authorities as $280,000 on 1 March 20X6. The directors of DZ estimate that the tax due on the profits for the year to 30 September 20X6 will be $320,000. DZ has no deferred tax liability.

What is DZ's tax charge in its statement of comprehensive income for the year ended 30 September 20X6?

    A $310,000
    B $320,000
    C $330,000
    D $600,000   (2 marks)

15 DD purchased an item of plant and machinery costing $500,000 on 1 April 20X4, which qualified for 50% capital allowances in the first year, and 20% each year thereafter on the reducing balance basis.

DD's policy in respect of plant and machinery is to charge depreciation on a straight line basis over five years, with no residual value. On 1 April 20X6, DD decides to revalue the item of plant and machinery upwards, from its net book value, by $120,000.

Assuming there are no other capital transactions in the three year period and a tax rate of 30% throughout, calculate the amount of deferred tax to be shown in DD's statement of comprehensive income for the year ended 31 March 20X7, and the deferred tax provision to be included in its statement of financial position at 31 March 20X7.   (4 marks)

16 EG purchased a property for $630,000 on 1 September 20X0. EG incurred additional costs for the purchase of $3,500 surveyors' fees and $6,500 legal fees. EG then spent $100,000 renovating the property prior to letting it. All of EG's expenditure was classified as capital expenditure according to the local tax regulations.

Indexation of the purchase and renovation costs is allowed on EE's property. The index increased by 50% between September 20X0 and October 20X7. Assume that acquisition and renovation costs were incurred in September 20X0. EG sold the property on 1 October 20X7 for $1,250,000, incurring tax allowable costs on disposal of $2,000.

Calculate EG's tax due on disposal assuming a tax rate of 30%.   (3 marks)

(Total = 37 marks)

44 Objective test questions: Deferred tax — 74 mins

1. A company had a credit balance brought forward on current tax of $20,000. During the year it paid tax of $18,000 and it has a provision for the current year of $50,000. It has increased the deferred tax provision by $5,000. What is the total charge to tax for the year in the statement of comprehensive income?

    A $53,000
    B $55,000
    C $57,000
    D $68,000

    (2 marks)

2. A company had a debit balance brought forward on current tax of $2,000. During the year it has paid no tax and received a tax refund of $1,800. It has a provision for the current year of $30,000. It has decreased the deferred tax provision by $5,000. What is the total charge to tax for the year in the statement of comprehensive income?

    A $23,200
    B $24,800
    C $25,200
    D $35,200

    (2 marks)

3. In accounting for deferred tax, which of the following items can give rise to temporary differences?

    1   Differences between accounting depreciation and tax allowances for capital expenditure
    2   Expenses charged in the income statement but disallowed for tax
    3   Revaluation of a non-current asset
    4   Unrelieved tax losses

    A   1, 3 and 4 only
    B   1 and 2 only
    C   3 and 4 only
    D   All four items

    (2 marks)

4. Which of the following are examples of assets or liabilities whose carrying amount is always equal to their tax base?

    1   Accrued expenses that will never be deductible for tax purposes
    2   Accrued expenses that have already been deducted in determining the current tax liability for current or earlier periods
    3   Accrued income that will never be taxable
    4   A loan payable in the statement of financial position at the amount originally received, which is also the amount eventually repayable

    A   1 and 3 only
    B   1 and 2 only
    C   2 and 4 only
    D   All four items

    (2 marks)

5. Which of the following statements about IAS 12 *Income taxes* are correct?

    1   Companies may discount deferred tax assets and liabilities if the effect would be material.
    2   The financial statements must disclose an explanation of the relationship between tax expense and accounting profit.
    3   Deferred tax may not be recognised in respect of goodwill unless any impairment of that goodwill is deductible for tax purposes.
    4   The tax base of an asset or liability is the amount attributed to that asset or liability for tax purposes.

A	All the statements are correct	
B	2, 3 and 4 only are correct	
C	1 and 4 only are correct	
D	None of the statements is correct.	(2 marks)

6 The following information relates to an entity.

- At 1 January 20X8, the net book value of non-current assets exceeded their tax written down value by $850,000.

- For the year ended 31 December 20X8, the entity claimed depreciation for tax purposes of $500,000 and charged depreciation of $450,000 in the financial statements.

- During the year ended 31 December 20X8, the entity revalued a freehold property. The revaluation surplus was $250,000. The entity has no plans to sell the property and realise the gain in the foreseeable future.

- The tax rate was 30% throughout the year.

What is the provision for deferred tax required by IAS 12 *Income taxes* at 31 December 20X8?

A	$240,000	
B	$270,000	
C	$315,000	
D	$345,000	(2 marks)

7 A company had a credit balance brought forward on current tax of $25,000. During the year it has paid no tax and received a tax refund of $2,500. It has a provision for the current year of $30,000. It has decreased the deferred tax provision by $10,000. What is the total charge to tax for the year in the statement of comprehensive income?

A	$5,000 debit	
B	$5,000 credit	
C	$7,500 debit	
D	$7,500 credit	(2 marks)

8 A country had a current tax regime whereby relief is given for tax paid on dividends. What system of tax is this? (2 marks)

9 A company had a credit balance brought forward on current tax of $25,000. During the year it paid tax of $27,800. It has a provision for the current year of $28,000. It has increased the deferred tax provision by $5,000. What is the total charge to tax for the year in the statement of comprehensive income?

A	$31,200	
B	$33,000	
C	$33,800	
D	$35,800	(2 marks)

10 BC, a small entity, purchased its only non-current tangible asset on 1 October 20X3. The asset cost $900,000, all of which qualified for tax depreciation.

BC's asset qualified for an accelerated first year tax allowance of 50%. The second and subsequent years qualified for tax depreciation at 25% per year on the reducing balance method.

BC's accounting depreciation policy is to depreciate the asset over its useful economic life of five years, assuming a residual value of $50,000.

Assume that BC pays tax on its income at the rate of 30%.

Calculate BC's deferred tax balance required in the statement of financial position as at 30 September 20X5 according to IAS 12 *Income taxes*. (4 marks)

11 On 31 March 20X6, CH had a credit balance brought forward on its deferred tax account of $642,000. There was also a credit balance on its corporate income tax account of $31,000, representing an over-estimate of the tax charge for the year ended 31 March 20X5.

CH's taxable profit for the year ended 31 March 20X6 was $946,000. CH's directors estimated the deferred tax provision required at 31 March 20X6 to be $759,000 and the applicable income tax rate for the year to 31 March 20X6 as 22%.

Calculate the income tax expense that CH will charge in its statement of comprehensive income for the year ended 31 March 20X6, as required by IAS 12 *Income taxes*. **(3 marks)**

12 FD purchased an item of plant and machinery costing $600,000 on 1 April 20X5, which qualified for 50% capital allowances in the first year and 25% per year thereafter, on the reducing balance basis.

FD's policy in respect of plant and machinery is to charge depreciation on a straight line basis over five years, with no residual value.

On 1 April 20X7, FD carried out an impairment review of all its non-current assets. This item of plant and machinery was found to have a value in use of $240,000. FD adjusted its financial records and wrote the plant and machinery down to its value in use on 1 April 20X7.

Assuming there are no other temporary differences in the period and a tax rate of 25% per annum over the five years, calculate the amount of any deferred tax balances outstanding at 31 March 20X7 and 31 March 20X8. (Work to the nearest $1,000.) **(4 marks)**

13 EE reported accounting profits of $822,000 for the period ended 30 November 20X7. This was after deducting entertaining expenses of $32,000 and a donation to a political party of $50,000, both of which are disallowable for tax purposes.

EE's reported profit also included $103,000 government grant income that was exempt from taxation. EE paid dividends of $240,000 in the period.

Assume EE had no temporary differences between accounting profits and taxable profits.

Assume that a classical tax system applies to EE's profits and that the tax rate is 25%.

What would EE's tax payable be on its profits for the year to 30 November 20X7? **(2 marks)**

14 A government wanted to encourage investment in new non-current assets by entities and decided to change tax allowances for non-current assets to give a 100% first year allowance on all new non-current assets purchased after 1 January 20X5.

ED purchased new machinery for $400,000 on 1 October 20X5 and claimed the 100% first year allowance. For accounting purposes ED depreciated the machinery on the reducing balance basis at 25% per year. The rate of corporate income tax to be applied to ED's taxable profits was 22%.

Assume ED had no other temporary differences.

Calculate the amount of deferred tax that ED would show in its statement of financial position at 30 September 20X7.

(3 marks)

15 HF purchased an asset on 1 April 20X7 for $220,000. HF claimed a first year tax allowance of 30% and then an annual 20% writing down allowance, using the reducing balance method. HF depreciates the asset over eight years using straight line depreciation, assuming no residual value. On 1 April 20X8, HF revalued the asset and increased the net book value by $50,000. The asset's useful life was not affected. Assume there are no other temporary differences in the period and a tax rate of 25% per annum.

Calculate the amount of deferred tax movement in the year ended 31 March 20X9 and the deferred tax balance at 31 March 20X9, in accordance with IAS 12 *Income taxes*.

(4 marks)

16   CY had the following amounts for 20X3 to 20X5:

Year ended 31 December:	20X3 $	20X4 $	20X5 $
Accounting depreciation for the year	1,630	1,590	1,530
Tax depreciation allowance for the year	2,120	1,860	1,320

At 31 December 20X2, CY had the following balances brought forward:

	$
Cost of property, plant and equipment qualifying for tax depreciation	20,000
Accounting depreciation	5,000
Tax depreciation	12,500

CY had no non-current asset acquisitions or disposals during the period 20X3 to 20X5.
Assume the corporate income tax rate is 25% for all years.
Calculate the deferred tax provision required by IAS 12 *Income taxes* at 31 December 20X5. **(3 marks)**

(Total = 41 marks)

45 Section B questions: Taxation I   45 mins

(a) Define a taxable person and give three examples. What is a competent jurisdiction for tax purposes?
(5 marks)

(b) (i) Give a definition of an indirect tax and explain how it works. **(3 marks)**
    (ii) There are two types of indirect taxes. State what these are and give two examples of each. **(2 marks)**

(Total = 5 marks)

(c) On 1 January 20X3, SPJ had an opening credit balance of $5,000 on its tax account, which represented the balance on the account after settling its tax liability for the previous year. SPJ had a credit balance on its deferred tax account of $1·6 million at the same date.

SPJ has been advised that it should expect to pay $1 million tax on its trading profits for the year ended 31 December 20X3 and increase its deferred tax account balance by $150,000.

Required

Prepare extracts from the statement of comprehensive income for the year ended 31 December 20X3, statement of financial position at that date and notes to the accounts showing the tax entries required.
(5 marks)

P7 Pilot paper

(d) CW owns 40% of the equity shares in Z, an entity resident in a foreign country. CW receives a dividend of $45,000 from Z; the amount received is after deduction of withholding tax of 10%. Z had before tax profits for the year of $500,000 and paid corporate income tax of $100,000.

Required

(i) Explain the meaning of 'withholding tax' and 'underlying tax.' **(2 marks)**
(ii) Calculate the amount of withholding tax paid by CW. **(1 mark)**
(iii) Calculate the amount of underlying tax that relates to CW's dividend. **(2 marks)**

(Total = 5 marks)

P7 5/06

(e) EF is an importer and imports perfumes and similar products in bulk. EF repackages the products and sells them to retailers. EF is registered for Value Added Tax (VAT).

EF imports a consignment of perfume priced at $10,000 (excluding excise duty and VAT) and pays excise duty of 20% and VAT on the total (including duty) at 15%.

EF pays $6,900 repackaging costs, including VAT at 15% and then sells all the perfume for $40,250 including VAT at 15%.

EF has not paid or received any VAT payments to/from the VAT authorities for this consignment.

Required

(i) Calculate EF's net profit on the perfume consignment.
(ii) Calculate the net VAT due to be paid by EF on the perfume consignment. **(Total = 5 marks)**

P7 11/07

(Total = 25 marks)

46 Section B questions: Taxation II   45 mins

(a) Governments use a range of specific excise duties as well as general sales taxes on goods.

Required

(i) Explain the reasons why a government might apply a specific excise duty to a category of goods. **(3 marks)**

(ii) Explain the difference between a single stage and a multi-stage sales tax. **(2 marks)**

(Total = 5 marks)

P7 5/09

(b) Tax authorities have various powers to enforce compliance with the tax rules.

State what these powers are and give examples of each. **(5 marks)**

(c) What is withholding tax and why do tax authorities use it? Give two examples of payments affected by withholding tax. **(5 marks)**

(d) Why do countries need to enter into double taxation agreements? What are the three main methods of giving double taxation relief? **(5 marks)**

(e) *Required*

(i) Explain the difference between tax avoidance and tax evasion. **(2 marks)**
(ii) Briefly explain the methods that governments can use to reduce tax avoidance and tax evasion. **(3 marks)**

(Total = 5 marks)

(Total = 25 marks)

47 Section B questions: Taxation III   45 mins

(a) H is a major manufacturing entity. According to the entity's records, temporary differences of $2.00 million had arisen at 30 April 20X4 because of differences between the carrying amount of non-current assets and their tax base, due to H claiming accelerated tax relief in the earlier years of the asset lives.

At 30 April 20X3, the temporary differences attributable to non-current assets were $2.30 million.

H's tax rate has been 30% in the past. On 30 April 20X4, the directors of H were advised that the rate of taxation would decrease to 28% by the time that the temporary differences on the non-current assets reversed.

Required

Prepare the note in respect of deferred tax as it would appear in the financial statements of H for the year ended 30 April 20X4. (Your answer should be expressed in $ million and you should work to two decimal places.) **(5 marks)**

(b) B is a retail entity. Its tax rate is 30%. It has a current tax payable brought forward from the year ended 30 April 20X3 of $750,000 and a deferred tax payable of $250,000.

On 30 April 20X4, the estimated tax charge for the year ended 30 April 20X4 was $1,400,000. The actual tax charge for the year ended 30 April 20X3 was agreed with the tax authority and settled with a payment of $720,000. The deferred tax payable needs to be increased to $300,000 as at 30 April 20X4.

Required

Prepare the notes in respect of current and deferred tax as they would appear in the financial statements of B for the year ended 30 April 20X4. (Your answer should be expressed in $ million and you should work to two decimal places.) **(5 marks)**

(c) DG purchased its only non-current tangible asset on 1 October 20X2. The asset cost $200,000, all of which qualified for tax depreciation. DG's accounting depreciation policy is to depreciate the asset over its useful economic life of five years, assuming no residual value, charging a full year's depreciation in the year of acquisition and no depreciation in the year of disposal.

The asset qualified for tax depreciation at a rate of 30% per year on the reducing balance method. DG sold the asset on 30 September 20X6 for $60,000.

The rate of income tax to apply to DG's profit is 20%. DG's accounting period is 1 October to 30 September.

Required

(i) Calculate DG's deferred tax balance at 30 September 20X5.
(ii) Calculate DG's accounting profit/loss that will be recognised in its statement of comprehensive income on the disposal of the asset, in accordance with IAS 16 *Property, Plant and Equipment*.
(iii) Calculate DG's tax balancing allowance/charge arising on the disposal of the asset. **(5 marks)**

P7 11/06

(d) AB acquired non-current assets on 1 April 20X3 costing $250,000. The assets qualified for accelerated first year tax allowance at the rate of 50% for the first year. The second and subsequent years were at a tax depreciation rate of 25% per year on the reducing balance method.

AB depreciates all non-current assets at 20% a year on the straight line basis.

The rate of corporate tax applying to AB for 20X3/X4 and 20X4/X5 was 30%. Assume AB has no other qualifying non-current assets.

Required

Apply IAS 12 *Income taxes* and calculate:

(i) the deferred tax balance required at 31 March 20X4
(ii) the deferred tax balance required at 31 March 20X5
(iii) the charge to the income statement for the year ended 31 March 20X5 **(5 marks)**

P7 5/05

(e) Country X has the following tax regulations in force.

- The tax year is 1 May to 30 April
- All corporate profits are taxed at 20%
- When calculating corporate taxable income, depreciation of non-current assets cannot be charged against taxable income.
- Tax depreciation is allowed at the following rates.
  - Buildings at 5% per annum on a straight line basis
  - All other non-current tangible assets are allowed tax depreciation at 25% per annum on a reducing balance basis
- No tax allowances are allowed on land or furniture and fittings.

FB commenced trading on 1 May 20X5 when it purchased all its non-current assets.

FB's non-current asset balances were:

	Cost 1 May 20X5 $	Net book value 1 May 20X7 $	Tax written down value 1 May 20X7 $
Land	20,000	20,000	–
Buildings	80,000	73,600	72,000
Plant and equipment	21,000	1,000	11,812
Furniture and fittings	15,000	5,000	–

FB did not purchase any non-current assets between 1 May 20X5 and 30 April 20X7. On 2 May 20X7, FB disposed of all its plant and equipment for $5,000 and purchased new plant and equipment for $30,000. The new plant and equipment qualified for a first year tax allowance of 50%.

FB STATEMENT OF COMPREHENSIVE INCOME FOR THE YEAR ENDED 30 APRIL 20X8

	$
Gross profit	210,000
Administrative expenses	(114,000)
Gain on disposal of plant and equipment	4,000
Depreciation – furniture and fittings	(5,000)
Depreciation – buildings	(3,200)
Depreciation – plant and equipment	(6,000)
Distribution costs	(49,000)
	36,800
Finance cost	(7,000)
Profit before tax	29,800

Required

Calculate FB's corporate income tax due for the year ended 30 April 20X8. **(5 marks)**

(Total = 25 marks)

ANSWERS

1 Objective test answers: The regulatory framework

1	C	Guidance on application and interpretation of IASs/IFRSs is provided by the International Financial Reporting Interpretations Committee (IFRIC).
2	A	The priority given to different user groups in different countries (eg investor groups in the US and employees in Europe) is actually a **barrier** to harmonisation.
3	B	Many of the older IASs permitted **two** accounting treatments for like transactions or events – the benchmark treatment and the allowed alternative. As these are revised allowed alternative treatments are being eliminated. This gives preparers of accounts **less** choice.
4		Expense and equity
5	C	The *Framework* cites two underlying assumptions: The accounts have been prepared on an accruals basis (accruals). The business is expected to continue in operation for the foreseeable future (going concern).
6	B	The elements of financial statements are assets, liabilities and equity in the statement of financial position and income and expenses in the statement of comprehensive income. Profits and losses are not elements.
7	B	The income statement measures **performance**. Financial position is measured in the statement of financial position and financial adaptability in the statement of cash flows
8	D	Accruals and going concern.
9		An asset is a resource controlled by an entity as a result of past transactions or events and from which future economic benefits are expected to flow to the entity.
10	D	Generally accepted accounting practice
11	C	International Accounting Standards Committee (IASC) Foundation Trustees
12	C	IFRIC reports to the IASB. SAC advises the IASB.
13		Decreases in economic benefits during the accounting period in the form of outflows or depletions of assets or incurrences of liabilities that result in decreases in equity, other than those relating to distributions to equity participants.
		[This is the IASB definition, which contains **36** words. You can choose which words to leave out.]
14		To provide information about the financial position, performance and changes in financial position of an entity that is useful to a wide range of users in making economic decisions.
15	D	Going concern and accruals
16	D	The IASC Foundation oversees and directs the work of the IASB.
17		Reliability and understandability.
18		Going concern and accruals based accounting
19		The three stages are:
		1 Establishment of Advisory Committee
		2 Discussion Draft issued
		3 Exposure Draft issued

2 Objective test answers: External audit

1 These matters can be subdivided into:
   - Qualified opinion
   - Adverse opinion
   - Disclaimer of opinion

2 B The auditor has been prevented from obtaining sufficient appropriate audit evidence.

3 C No qualification is needed as the directors have made full disclosure.

4 D The auditors report covers all of these matters.

5 B This is a limitation on scope.

6 C The auditors will be unable to give an opinion in this case.

7 A This will be an 'except for' qualification.

8 A In order to state that the financial statements show a true and fair view the auditor must satisfy himself that the other three matters are valid.

9 D The auditors will begin by trying to persuade the directors.

10 Power to require access to all books and records
    Power to require information and explanations from officers of the company
    Power to attend meetings and address shareholders

11 C If the auditor believes that the financial statements do not show a true and fair view this should first be discussed with management. If management refuse to adjust the accounts, the auditor would give an adverse opinion in the audit report.

12 A ISA 700 describes the different audit opinions.

13 A The auditor does not report on items that are not material.

14 To enable the auditor to express an opinion as to whether the financial statements give a true and fair presentation of the entity's affairs.

3 Objective test answers: Ethics

1 B The audit of the financial statements will be carried out by an accountant in practice.

2 B Reliability, Morality and Efficiency are not fundamental principles.

3 D The accountant should respect confidentiality unless there is a legal or professional right or duty to disclose.

4 B Rotation of audit partners is a safeguard to prevent self-interest threats.

5 C A and D are familiarity threats, B is an intimidation threat.

6 A The other options are different threats: B is intimidation, C is familiarity and D is self-review.

7 C A, B and D are all threats to the fundamental principles but are not strictly conflicts of interest.

8 C A, B and D all describe the features of a rules-based code.

9 A B describes integrity; C describes objectivity and D describes professional competence and due care.

10 B Disclosure of information to advance the interests of a new client would not be permitted under the Code.

11 D HMRC is not a source of ethical codes for accountants.

_# 4 Section B answers: Regulation

(a) The IASB *Framework* lays out the elements of financial statements as follows.

(i) Asset

A resource controlled by an entity as a result of past events and from which future economic benefits are expected to flow to the entity.

An example of an asset is an item of machinery used in the business.

(ii) Liability

A present obligation of the entity arising from past events, the settlement of which is expected to result in an outflow of resources from the entity.

An example of a liability is an amount due to a supplier for goods received.

(iii) Equity

The residual interest in the assets of the entity after deducting all its liabilities.

Ordinary share capital is an example of equity.

(iv) Income

Increases in economic benefits during the accounting period in the form of inflows or enhancements of assets or decreases of liabilities that result in increases in equity, other than those relating to contributions from equity participants.

An example of income is income recognised on the sale of goods.

(v) Expenses

Decreases in economic benefits during the accounting period in the form of outflows or depletions of assets that result in decreases in equity, other than those relating to distributions to equity participants.

Depreciation is an example of an expense.

(b)

> **Examiner's comments.** Candidates failed to include enough detail in their answers. Many answers identified a characteristic and then the explanation added nothing to it, for example, 'Relevance – information needs to be relevant'.

The four principal qualitative characteristics of financial information are as follows.

Relevance

Information is said to be relevant when it influences the economic decisions of users by helping them to evaluate past, present and future events or by confirming, or correcting their past evaluations. So relevant information has both a predictive and confirmatory role.

Reliability

Information is reliable when it is free from material error and bias, and can be depended upon by users to represent faithfully that which it either purports to represent or could reasonably be expected to represent.

Comparability

The importance of comparability is that users must be able to compare the financial statements of an entity over time and to compare the financial statements of different entities. For this to be possible users must be informed of the accounting policies employed in the preparation of the financial statements and any changes in those policies and their effects. The financial statements must also show corresponding amounts for the previous period.

Understandability

The financial statement information should be readily understandable to users. For this purpose users are assumed to have a reasonable knowledge of business and economic activities and accounting and a willingness to study the information with reasonable diligence.

(c)

> **Examiner's comments.** Most candidates did well on this question, although some could not think of three alternatives. A common error was using bullet points or short notes to answer the question and as a result not providing sufficient detail for 5 marks.

C could pursue any of the following options:

(i) **Develop its own standards without reference to the IASB.** This would produce standards which reflected trading conditions in the country but, when it developed to the point of needing to attract foreign investment, investors may not be drawn to companies whose financial statements are not prepared under generally recognised standards.

(ii) **Adopt IFRS.** This would mean that C had adopted high-quality, generally recognised standards from the outset, and would have no future harmonisation process to undergo. However, it may find that time and expense has gone into implementing standards which may not be that relevant to its current economic situation.

(iii) **Adopt those IFRSs which are currently applicable**, such as IAS 41 *Agriculture*, and **develop additional standards of its own based on IFRS**. This would produce a set of standards which were theoretically high-quality and relevant to its own economy. However, the judgement and expertise required to carry this out may not be available and C will be resolving issues between local standards and IFRS on an ongoing basis.

(d)

> **Top tips.** We have only given five answers here as this is all that is required for five marks.
>
> **Examiner's comments.** The answers provided for this question were very weak. Many candidates did not know what the purpose of the Framework was and tried explaining the purpose of financial statements.

The purposes of the *Framework* are:

(i) To assist in the **review of existing IASs and IFRSs** and the **development of new IFRSs**
(ii) To promote **harmonisation** of accounting standards by reducing the number of allowed alternative accounting treatments
(iii) To **assist national standard-setting bodies** in developing national standards
(iv) To assist preparers of financial statements in **applying IFRSs** and dealing with topics not yet covered by an IFRS
(v) To **assist auditors** in determining whether financial statements comply with IFRS

> **Alternative answers**
> You would also have scored marks if you had identified any of the following purposes.
> - To **assist users** of financial statements prepared under IFRS in interpreting the information contained in them
> - To provide **general information on the approach** used in formulating IFRSs

(e)

> **Examiner's comments.** This question was very badly answered. Those candidates that did identify the correct IAS and the correct accounting treatment often omitted to explain why the items should be treated that way, as a consequence only partial marks could be awarded.

In order to decide how to treat these items of expenditure in its financial statements, EK must decide whether the expenditure gives rise to an asset or intangible asset which can be recognised in the statement of financial position. Asset recognition criteria are dealt with in the IASB *Framework*. Intangible assets are covered by IAS 38 *Intangible assets*.

The IASB *Framework* defines an asset as **a resource controlled by an entity as a result of past events** and from which **further economic benefits are expected to flow** to the entity.

Both assets and intangible assets can only be recognised if both the following apply.

- It is probable that future economic benefits will flow to the entity.
- The cost of the asset can be measured reliably.

  (i) <u>Book publishing and film rights</u>

  These rights give access to future economic benefits and could even be resold, so the $1m cost can be recognised as an intangible asset. No amortisation is necessary until the book is actually published.

  (ii) <u>Trade fair</u>

  Since no new orders were taken as a direct result of the event and no estimate can be made of additional revenue, the cost of the trade fair cannot be recognised as an asset. Future economic benefits may not be probable. The cost of the trade fair does not meet the recognition criteria for an asset and should therefore be treated as an expense in the year incurred.

  (iii) <u>Consultant</u>

  Although the cost of the consultancy itself is known, it is virtually impossible to quantify any change in the value of the image of EK. Since the cost of the corporate image cannot be measured reliably, the consultancy fees should not be recognised as an asset and should be expensed in the year incurred.

5 Section B answers: External audit

(a)

> **Examiner's comments.** Common errors made by candidates in this question were:
>
> – incorrectly concluding that item 1 was material by incorrectly calculating the percentage of revenue as 500/15,000 instead of 500/15,000,000 and the percentage of profit as 500/1,500 instead of 500/1,500,000.
>
> – suggesting that item 2 (development costs) should be written off against the previous year's profit, which is incorrect as the circumstances existing at that balance sheet date met the criteria required by IAS 38.
>
> – not recognising that item 3 required immediate full provision as per IAS 37.

(i) <u>Item 1</u> – the obsolete inventory is not material as $500 is 0·003% of revenue and is 0·03% of profit, therefore management's decision is acceptable. The inventory can be written off in the current year.

<u>Item 2</u> – the deferred development expenditure must be charged to profit or loss as soon as it ceases to meet the IAS 38 criteria for deferral. As the project has now been abandoned, the expenditure ceases to meet the IAS 38 criteria for deferral. Therefore the $600,000 should be charged to profit or loss in the current year.

(ii) <u>Item 3 – decommissioning costs</u>

IAS 37 *Provisions, contingent liabilities and contingent assets* requires decommissioning costs to be recognised as soon as the liability arises, which is usually when the facility starts to operate. HF should create a provision for the full $5,000,000 decommissioning costs, discounted to present value, and add it to the cost of the asset (debit asset, credit provision). This will be a material increase in the net asset value and will increase the depreciation charged to profit or loss.

<u>Audit report</u>

If the directors do not agree to change the treatment of the decommissioning costs to recognise the full provision in the financial statements, an "except for" qualified audit report will need to be issued as all matters are correct except for the treatment of the decommissioning costs.

Answers

(b) (i) **Qualified opinion** – an auditor will be unable to issue an unqualified audit report if he has disagreements with management regarding the treatment of one or more items in the accounts, or if the scope of his audit has been limited in some way, for instance certain records may not have been made available to him. When the auditor concludes that he cannot issue an unqualified report for one of these reasons, but that the effect of the disagreement or limitation of scope is not so material or pervasive as to require an adverse opinion or a disclaimer of opinion, then he will express a qualified opinion. The opinion will be expressed as being 'except for the effects of the matter to which the qualification relates'.

(ii) **Disclaimer of opinion** – where the possible effect of a limitation on scope is so material or pervasive that the auditor has not been able to obtain sufficient appropriate audit evidence and is therefore unable to express an opinion on the financial statements, a disclaimer of opinion will be expressed. This limitation may have arisen through circumstances, or may have been imposed by the client or may have arisen due to the inadequate nature of the company's accounting records. The auditor's report should give an explanation of the nature of the limitation of scope and quantify the effects on the financial statements where possible.

(iii) **Adverse opinion** – where the effect of a disagreement is so material or pervasive that the auditor concludes that a qualified opinion is insufficient to disclose the misleading or incomplete nature of the financial statements an adverse opinion will be expressed. Such a disagreement may concern the selection of accounting policies, the application of accounting standards or the inadequacy of disclosures. The report must fully describe the circumstances leading to the adverse opinion. The opinion will state that, because of the effect of these circumstances, the financial statements do not present fairly the financial position of the company and its results.

(c) <u>Right of access to records</u>

The auditor has a right of access at all times to the books, accounts and vouchers of the company.

<u>Right to require information</u>

The auditor has a right to require from the company's officers such information and explanations as he thinks necessary for the performance of his duties as auditor. It is an offence for a company's officer to make a statement to the auditor which is materially misleading, false or deceptive.

These rights make it possible for the auditor to carry out an audit. If these rights are violated, the auditor will qualify his report. If the situation is serious, for instance if the auditor believes the directors to be involved in a fraud, he has the following rights which enable him to communicate directly to the shareholders:

<u>Right to attend/receive notice of general meetings</u>

The directors cannot keep the auditor away from the AGMs by not informing him of when they are taking place.

<u>Right to speak at general meetings</u>

The auditor has a right to be heard at general meetings which he attends, on any part of the business that concerns him as auditor.

<u>Right in relation to written resolutions</u>

The auditor has the right to receive a copy of any written resolution proposed. This means that he must receive a copy of any resolution which is proposed to terminate his engagement.

In practice, an auditor would not expect to have to invoke these rights very often, but the fact that they exist establishes his status in relation to the directors and makes it possible for him to get the co-operation that he needs in order to carry out his engagement.

(d)

> **Examiner's comments.** Many answers to this question were of low quality. Many candidates clearly did not understand the objective of an audit and a large proportion of answers were unable to correctly identify the type of report or the information required.

(i) **The objective of an external audit** is to enable the auditor to express an opinion on whether the financial statements give a true and fair view (or present fairly) the financial position of the company and the results of its operations and its cash flows, in accordance with applicable Accounting Standards.

(ii) **EA & Co should issue a qualified opinion** based on disagreement on accounting policies under ISA 700. We have not been told that this issue is so material or pervasive that the financial statements are misleading or incomplete, so an adverse opinion is not indicated.

They will include in their report:

'Profit on long-term contracts has not been accounted for in accordance with IAS 11. Per the standard, a foreseeable loss on a long-term contract should be recognised immediately. In the financial statements for the year to 30 September 2006, only that portion of the loss which has been incurred to date has been included. $3.7m has been included in the statement of comprehensive income in respect of long-term contracts. This should be amended to $1.3m in order to recognise in full the expected loss.

In our opinion, except for the effect on the financial statements of the matter referred to in the preceding paragraph, the financial statements give a true and fair view...'

6 Section B answers: Ethics

(a) The CIMA Code requires the professional accountant to comply with five fundamental principles:

- Integrity
- Objectivity
- Professional Competence and Due Care
- Confidentiality
- Professional Behaviour

Compliance with these principles is required in order for the accountant to discharge his duty to act in the public interest.

Specific threats to his compliance with these principles can arise during the course of his work. The conceptual framework requires the accountant to identify, evaluate and address threats to compliance with the fundamental principles.

The framework sets out five categories of threat:

- Self-interest threats
- Self-review threats
- Advocacy threats
- Familiarity threats
- Intimidation threats

The accountant must recognise the threat when it arises, evaluate whether or not it is significant and put in place safeguards to deal with it. The Code gives examples of how the categories of threat can arise and examples of relevant safeguards.

There are major differences between this approach and a rules-based approach. The conceptual framework approach puts the responsibility on the accountant to ensure compliance with the principles. In this way, whatever threat arises, the accountant has to consider it. A list of rules could not encompass every possible threat and could even lead to attempts to circumvent them. Any situation not explicitly covered would be deemed to be not a threat and situations would then arise which would require the rules to be continually updated. The application of a conceptual framework avoids this.

(b) Conflicts of interest can arise for the accountant in public practice when he has business interests of his own which put him in competition with a client. This may threaten his objectivity when dealing with the affairs of that client. Or he may find himself acting for two clients whose interests are in conflict, which threatens his impartiality. A situation can arise where a client is in dispute with a company in which the accountant has a substantial shareholding. This can be a self-interest threat to compliance with the principles. The principle of confidentiality must be strictly maintained and may also be threatened by a conflict of interest situation.

The accountant in public practice must evaluate the significance of any such threats. Before accepting or continuing with a client engagement he should consider whether there are any conflicts of interest which could give rise to threats. If so, safeguards are needed.

A number of safeguards can be put in place to deal with threats arising from conflicts of interest:

- The client should be notified of any conflict of interest arising from the activities or business interests of the firm
- All parties concerned should be notified that the accountant is acting for two or more parties in respect of an issue where their interests are in conflict
- The client should be notified that the accountant acts for more than one client in a particular market sector

In all of these situations the client is then asked to give their consent to the accountant acting for them or continuing to act for them. If that consent is refused, the accountant must not continue to act for them, or for the other party involved.

Additional safeguards should also be considered in order to maintain confidentiality and security of data, such as separate engagement teams, strict security procedures and signed confidentiality agreements.

(c) It is in the public interest and required by the CIMA Code of Ethics that an accountant in public practice should be independent of the client.

The Code says that independence requires:

(a) Independence of mind. This means that conclusions are not affected by influences that compromise professional judgement. The individual is then able to act with integrity and exercise objectivity and professional scepticism.

(b) Independence in appearance. This means avoidance of facts and circumstances that would lead anybody to conclude that the integrity, objectivity or professional scepticism of the firm or one of its members had been compromised.

The accountant in public practice is responsible to the shareholders of the client company and in varying degrees to the wider public. He has to be independent of the client and he has to be seen to be independent, otherwise the perception will be that he cannot be trusted to give a correct and unbiased opinion. There have been a number of cases recently where audit firms have been implicated in the financial misdeeds of their clients, most notably Arthur Andersen, and this brings the profession into disrepute.

Professional firms take this issue very seriously. A common situation where independence must be safeguarded is when the firm also performs other services, such as consultancy or tax work, for an audit client. In this situation there must be a clear division between the accountants providing the consultancy or tax services and those working on the audit, with no exchange of information between them. In the case of an audit client, it is very important to ensure that no member of the audit team has any relationship with any member of the client company which could threaten their independence.

7 Objective test answers: Presentation

1 A Members do not inspect the accounting records – the auditors do this on their behalf.

2 A All of these items appear in the statement of changes in equity.

3 D Authorised share capital is disclosed in the notes to the balance sheet, the other disclosures are made in the income statement or notes.

4 C 2 is a change of accounting estimate, 4 is specifically mentioned in IAS 8 as not constituting a change of accounting policy.

5 D Material errors are treated in the same way as changes of accounting policy, by the application of retrospective restatement.

6 B IAS 8 requires that a change in accounting policy is accounted for by retrospective application.

7 B A change in the method of valuing inventory is a change of accounting policy

8	A	Changing the method of depreciation is a change of estimation technique not a change of accounting policy and therefore retrospective application is not required. However the current year figures must be changed to reflect the change in estimation technique and the change must be disclosed.
9	C	Provisions are covered by IAS 37.
10	D	Revenue and finance cost
11	B	This is the most commonly seen form of the statement of comprehensive income (income statement), which includes cost of sales and distribution costs.
12	D	A is a change in accounting policy, B is specifically mentioned in IAS 8 as a change in an accounting policy to be dealt with as a revaluation in accordance with IAS 16, C is an error per IAS 8.

8 Section B answers: Presentation

(a) Companies might be expected to publish accounts using standard formats so as to ensure **complete disclosure** of material and important items and to ensure **consistency between accounting periods and comparability between companies.**

In addition, in certain European and other countries where standard formats have been in use for many years their use provides governments with **consistent information for the preparation of national accounts** and other economic statistics.

The detail shown in each of the standard income statements would enable users of accounts to calculate certain key **ratios** such as gross margins, net margins, ratio of administration costs to sales or profit and to identify the proportion of the net income arising from operations separately to that arising from financing transactions.

This information would be of use to **shareholders** and stockholders' analysts who will wish to assess the **profitability** of a company and compare it with possible alternative investments.

(b)

> **Examiner's comments.** Candidates scored high marks on this question. This question was the most popular part of question 2 and was generally the best answer.
>
> The most common error was to incorrectly adjust for the change in inventory value and some candidates ignored the requirement to make a provision for compensation.

CE
STATEMENT OF COMPREHENSIVE INCOME FOR THE YEAR ENDED 31 MARCH 20X6

	$'000
Revenue	2,000
Cost of sales (W)	(688)
Gross profit	1,312
Distribution costs	(200)
Administrative expenses (260 + 500)	(760)
Finance costs	(190)
Profit before tax	162

Working: Cost of sales

Per trial balance	480
Inventory adjustment	16
Depreciation ((1,500 − 540) × 20%)	192
	688

104　Answers

9 Objective test answers: Statements of cash flows

1　A　It is important to know which way round the additions and subtractions go when preparing a cash flow statement.

2　D　Profit on disposal will be included in profit, so should be deducted.

3　C　These items do not affect cash flow.

4　D　The final figure in the cash flow statement is the increase or decrease in cash and cash equivalents.

5　A

PROPERTY, PLANT AND EQUIPMENT: CARRYING VALUE

	$m		$m
Balance 31.12.X3	30	Depreciation	6
Additions	16	Disposal (bal)	4
		Balance 31.12.X4	36
	46		56

As the carrying value of the asset disposed of is $4m and there was a loss on disposal of $1m, the proceeds were $3m.

6　B　Equity investments do not generally fulfil the description of cash equivalents

7　A　All of these items involve movements of cash

8　C　Depreciation and losses on disposal are added back.

9　A

	$'000
Cash from sales	
$3,600 + $600 – $700	3,500
Cash paid for purchases	
$2,400 + $300 – $450	(2,250)
Payments for expenses	(760)
	490

10　Property, plant and equipment purchases = $105,000

PROPERTY, PLANT AND EQUIPMENT

	$'000		$'000
Opening balance	180	Depreciation	40
Revaluation	20	Disposal (15 – 10)	5
Additions (bal fig)	105	Closing balance	260
	305		305

11　A　Interest paid = $38,000

INTEREST PAYABLE

	$		$
Cash paid (bal fig)	38,000	Opening balance	12,000
Closing balance	15,000	Statement of comprehensive income	41,000
	53,000		53,000

10 Section B answer: Statement of cash flows

> **Examiner's comments.** A very large proportion of candidates prepared a statement of cash flows according to IAS 7 indirect method rather than the direct method, thereby losing most of the marks.

FC
STATEMENT OF CASH FLOWS FOR THE YEAR ENDED 31 MARCH 20X8

	$'000	$'000
Cash flows from operating activities		
Cash received from customers (W1)	440	
Rents received	45	
Cash paid to suppliers (W2)	(225)	
Cash paid to and on behalf of employees	(70)	
Other operating expenses	(15)	
Cash generated from operations		175

Workings

1 Cash received from customers

	$'000
Opening trade receivables	45
Revenue	445
Closing trade receivables	(50)
Cash received from customers	440

2 Cash paid to suppliers

	$'000
Cost of sales	220
Opening inventory	(25)
Closing inventory	40
Purchases	235
Opening payables	20
Closing payables	(30)
Cash paid to suppliers	225

11 HZ (FATP 5/09/amended)

> **Text references.** Statements of cash flows are covered in Chapter 8. Redeemable preference shares are covered in Chapter 12.
>
> **Top tips.** In the exam write out your proformas and insert the numbers that don't require calculation first. There was quite a lot to do for the statement of cash flows, so work methodically and remember to tackle the parts you can confidently do before you deal with the more tricky areas.
>
> **Easy marks.** This statement of cash flows contained some tricky parts, such as calculating the property, plant and equipment additions and dealing with the adjustments made to profit before tax in part (a). However, there were some easy marks available in the cash flows from financing activities, such as dealing with the loan repayment and the share issues.

Marking scheme

	Marks	
Adjustments to suspense account	2	
Adjustments to profit before tax	3	
		5

Statement of cash flows

Cash flows from operating activities

Profit before tax	1	
Finance cost	1	
Depreciation	½	
Gain on disposal	1	
Development expenditure	1	
Impairment of goodwill	1	
Provision for legal claim	1	
Movement in: receivables	1	
Inventories	1	
Payables	1	
Interest paid	1½	
Tax paid	1½	
		12½

Cash flows from investing activities

Proceeds of disposal	½	
Cost of additions	1½	
Development expenditure	1	
		3

Cash flows from financing activities

Repayment of loan	1	
Proceeds of ordinary share issue	1	
Proceeds of preferred share issue	1	
Equity dividend paid	½	
		3½
Movement in cash and cash equivalents		1
		25

(a)

Top tips. Make sure you read the question carefully to identify all the requirements. In this part the question, the examiner is asking for *both* the entries required to remove the balance on the suspense account *and* for a revised profit before tax figure. The number of marks available for this part of the question should have helped you to see that there were a number of adjustments to make to profit before tax.

Examiners comments. Many candidates did not realise that the preferred shares should be classified as non-current liabilities according to IAS 32, and so very few answers adjusted the profit before tax figure for the required interest on the preferred shares.

The balance in the suspense account relates to the issue of the preferred shares. The preferred shares are classified as a non-current liability per IAS 32 as HZ must pay cash to redeem the shares on 1 April 20Y8. To clear the suspense account the entries required are:

	$'000
Debit suspense account	1,000
Credit non-current liabilities	1,000

Required adjustments to the draft income statement

The issue costs associated with the preferred shares can be deducted from the non-current liability balance and so should be added back to the income statement. The interest charge associated with the preferred shares is classified as a finance charge per IAS 32 and so should be charged to profit or loss for the year. The development expenditure relating to 20X6/20X7 should be written off to the income statement as it no longer meets the IAS 38 criteria to be deferred.

Revised profit before tax calculation:

	$'000
Per draft income statement	305
Less write off of development expenditure	(170)
Add back preferred share issue costs	70
Less preferred share finance cost (930 x 6.72%)	(62)
Revised profit before tax	143

(b)

> **Examiners comments.** Format marks were frequently lost in this part of the question as candidates included items in the wrong category in the statement of cash flows. Common mistakes made by candidates included:
>
> – not using the figure calculated in part (a) as the starting point for profit before tax
>
> – not deducting the gain on disposal
>
> – not adding back the goodwill impairment or the provision for legal claim
>
> – not including share premium in the funds raised from the new share issue

HZ
STATEMENT OF CASH FLOWS FOR THE YEAR ENDED 31 MARCH 20X9

	$'000	$'000
Cash flows from operating activities		
Profit before taxation	143	
Finance cost (W1)	122	
Depreciation	940	
Gain on disposal (98-128)	(30)	
Development expenditure	170	
Impairment of goodwill (350 – 217)	133	
Provision for legal claim	120	
Operating profit before working capital changes	1,598	
Increase in inventory (890 - 750)	(140)	
Increase in receivables (924 - 545)	(379)	
Increase in payables (744 – 565)	179	
Cash generated from operations	1,258	
Interest paid (W2)	(206)	
Income taxes paid (W3)	(250)	
Net cash from operating activities		802
Cash flows from investing activities		
Purchase of property, plant and equipment (W4)	(480)	
Proceeds of sale of property, plant and equipment	128	
Development expenditure (170 – 198)	(28)	
Net cash used in investing activities		(380)
Cash flows from financing activities		
Dividend paid	(290)	
Repayment of interest-bearing borrowings	(1,250)	
Proceeds from issue of equity shares (2,873-2,470) + (732 - 530)	605	
Proceeds from issue of preferred shares (1,000 – 70)	930	
Net cash used in financing activities		(5)
Net increase in cash and cash equivalents (717 - 300)		417
Cash and cash equivalents at 1 April 20X8		300
Cash and cash equivalents at 31 March 20X9		717

Workings

1   *Finance cost*

	$'000
Balance per draft income statement	60
Add preferred shares finance charge from part (a)	62
Total finance charge	122

2   *Interest paid*

INTEREST PAYABLE

	$'000		$'000
Interest paid per draft accounts (balance)	156	31.3.20X8 Balance b/d	113
31.3.20X9 Balance c/d	17	Finance cost per income statement	60
	173		173

	$'000
Interest paid per draft accounts	156
Add preferred shares dividend paid (classified as a finance charge per IAS 32)	50
Total interest paid	206

3   *Income taxes paid*

INCOME TAXES

	$'000		$'000
Tax paid (balance)	250	31.3.20X8 balance b/d current	247
31.3.X9 balance c/d current	117	31.3.20X8 balance b/d deferred	250
31.3.X9 balance c/d deferred	312	Income tax expenses	182
	679		679

4   *Property, plant and equipment*

PROPERTY, PLANT AND EQUIPMENT

	$'000		$'000
31.3.20X8 Balance b/d	6,250	Disposals	98
Revaluation (562 – 400)	162	Depreciation	940
Purchases (balance)	480	31.3.20X9 Balance c/d	5,854
	6,892		6,892

12   Tex (FATP Pilot paper/amended)

Text references. Statements of cash flows are covered in Chapter 8.

Top tips. The key to this type of question is familiarity with the format of the statements. The best way to achieve this is through practising your question technique. This question gives you practice on all three financial statements.

Easy marks. There was some calculation to do on taxes, but there were a lot of easy marks in the statement of cash flows. You should have been able to get most of the marks for the statement of cash flows and scored well on the statement of financial position as long as you proceeded methodically.

Marking scheme

		Marks	
(a)	**Statement of cash flows**	1	
	Finance cost	½	
	Depreciation	1	
	Working capital charges – each	3	
	Interest paid	½	
	Income tax paid	2	
	Purchase of PPE	1	
	Proceeds of sale of PPE	1	
	Dividend paid	½	
	Repayment of borrowings	1	
	Proceeds from share issue	1½	
			13
(b)	**Statement of financial position**		
	Property, plant and equipment	1½	
	Inventory	1	
	Trade receivables	1½	
	Bank	3	
	Share capital	½	
	Retained earnings	1	
	Interest-bearing borrowing	½	
	Deferred tax	½	
	Trade payables	1½	
	Taxation	½	
	Presentation	½	
			12
			25

(a) TEX
STATEMENT OF CASH FLOWS FOR THE YEAR ENDED 30 SEPTEMBER 20X1

	$'000	$'000
Cash flows from operating activities		
Profit before taxation	3,576	
Finance cost	124	
Depreciation	2,640	
Loss on disposal (2,600 – 900 – 730)	970	
Operating profit before working capital changes	7,310	
Increase in inventory (1,600 – 1,100)	(500)	
Increase in receivables (1,500 – 800)	(700)	
Decrease in payables (800 – 700)	(100)	
Cash generated from operations	6,010	
Interest paid	(124)	
Income taxes paid (W)	(485)	
Net cash from operating activities		5,401
Cash flows from investing activities		
Purchase of property, plant and equipment	(8,000)	
Proceeds of sale of property, plant and equipment	730	
Net cash used in investing activities		(7,270)
Cash flows from financing activities		
Dividend paid	(1,000)	
Repayment of interest-bearing borrowings	(1,200)	
Proceeds from issue of shares (10,834 – 7,815)	3,019	
Net cash from financing activities		819
Net decrease in cash and cash equivalents (1,200 – 150)		(1,050)
Cash and cash equivalents at 1 October 20X0		1,200
Cash and cash equivalents at 30 September 20X1		150

Working

Income taxes paid

INCOME TAXES

	$'000		$'000
Cash flow (bal fig)	485	Opening balance – current	685
Closing balance – current	1,040	Opening balance – deferred	400
Closing balance – deferred	600	Income statement	1,040
	2,125		2,125

(b) TEX
STATEMENT OF FINANCIAL POSITION AS AT 30 SEPTEMBER 20X2

	$'000	$'000
Non-current assets		
Property plant and equipment (18,160 – (5000 - 2000))		15,160
Current assets		
Inventory (W1)	1,700	
Trade receivables (W2)	2,800	
Bank (W4)	4,390	8,890
		24,050
Equity and liabilities		
Equity		
Share capital		10,834
Retained earnings (W5)		8,216
		19,050
Non-current liabilities		
Interest-bearing borrowing		1,700
Deferred tax		600
Current liabilities		
Trade payables (W3)	1,400	
Taxation	1,300	2,700
		24,050

Workings

1 INVENTORY

	$'000		$'000
Balance b/f	1,600	Cost of sales	8,900
Purchases	9,000	Balance c/f (bal figure)	1,700
	10,600		10,600

2 TRADE RECEIVABLES

	$'000		$'000
Balance b/f	1,500	Cash received	16,700
Sales	18,000	Balance c/f (bal figure)	2,800
	19,500		19,500

3 TRADE PAYABLES

	$'000		$'000
Cash paid	8,300	Balance b/f	700
Balance c/f (bal figure)	1,400	Purchases	9,000
	9,700		9,700

4   BANK

	$'000		$'000
Balance b/f	150	Payments to suppliers	8,300
Received from customers	16,700	Expenses paid	2,000
		Tax paid	1,040
		Loan interest paid	120
		Dividend paid	1,000
		Balance c/f (bal figure)	4,390
	16,850		16,850

5   RETAINED EARNINGS

	$'000		$'000
Dividend paid	1,000	Balance b/f	6,536
Balance c/f (bal figure)	8,216	Profit for year	2,680
	9,216		9,216

13 AG (FATP 5/05/amended)

Text references. Statements of cash flows are covered in Chapter 8. The issues you need to consider in redrafting the statement of financial position are covered in Chapters 4, 5 and 6.

Top tips. Make sure you read Section C questions carefully in your reading time before the examination begins, noting the proformas and any unusual items. In the exam write out your proformas and insert the easy numbers first. Remember to tackle the parts you can confidently do first and deal with the other areas at the end.

Easy marks. Cash flows from operating activities is simple and logical and you can get most of it right. The working capital adjustments are easy marks and you will always have to adjust for depreciation and interest and to deduct tax and interest paid. Look out for any other adjustments. Cash flows from investing activities will always have property, plant and equipment transactions, which you can get right. Then look for any figures you do not have to calculate and put them in. Proceeds of a share issue are easy to work out – just take the movement on share capital and share premium for ordinary shares.

Examiner's comments. Some candidates gained full marks on this question. Errors included not using the correct format, mistakes in the property, plant and equipment calculations and errors in calculating tax and accruals.

AG
STATEMENT OF CASH FLOWS FOR THE YEAR ENDED 31 MARCH 20X5

	$'000	$'000
Cash flows from operating activities		
Profit before taxation	135	
Depreciation	720	
Profit on sale of non-current assets (98 – 75)	(23)	
Development expenditure amortised	80	
Goodwill written-off	100	
Increase in accrued expenses (W1)	10	
Interest expense	65	
		1,087
Increase in receivables	(95)	
Increase in inventories	(110)	
Increase in payables	130	
		(75)
Cash generated from operations		1,012
Interest paid (W2)	(140)	
Income taxes paid (W3)	(150)	
		(290)
Net cash from operating activities		722

	$'000	$'000
Cash flows from investing activities		
Purchase of property, plant and equipment (W4)	(370)	
Sale of property, plant and equipment	98	
Development expenditure (W5)	(50)	
Net cash used in investing activities		(322)
Cash flows from financing activities		
Ordinary share issue (1.4m shares @ $0.75)	1,050	
Preference share issue (0.5m shares @ $1.00)	500	
Dividend paid	(100)	
Repurchase of loan notes	(1,000)	
Net cash used in financing activities		450
Net increase in cash and cash equivalents		850
Cash and cash equivalents at beginning of period		232
Cash and cash equivalents at end of period		1082

Workings

1   Accrued expenses

	$'000	$'000
Balance at 31.3.20X4	172	
Less accrued interest payable	(87)	
		85
Balance at 31.3.20X5	107	
less accrued interest payable	(12)	
		95
Increase in non-interest accruals		10

2   Interest paid

INTEREST PAYABLE

	$'000		$'000
Interest paid (balance)	140	31.3.20X4 Balance b/d	87
31.3.20X5 Balance c/d	12	Finance costs	65
	152		152

3   Income taxes paid

INCOME TAXES

	$'000		$'000
Deferred tax transfer	50	Balance b/d	190
Tax paid (balance)	150	Income tax expenses	90
31.3.20X5 Balance c/d	80		
	280		280

4   Property, plant and equipment

PROPERTY, PLANT AND EQUIPMENT

	$'000		$'000
31.3.20X4 Balance c/d	3,900	Disposals	75
Revaluation	125	Depreciation	720
Purchases (balance)	370	31.3.20X5 Balance c/d	3,600
	4,395		4,395

5   Development costs

DEVELOPMENT COSTS

	$'000		$'000
31.3.20X4 Balance b/d	400	Amortisation	80
Expenditure (balance)	50	31.3.20X5 Balance c/d	370
	450		450

6   Dividends paid

RETAINED EARNINGS

	$'000		$'000
Dividend paid	100	31.3.20X4 Balance b/d	1,415
31.3.20X5 Balance c/d (balance)	1,360	Profit for year	45
	1,460		1,460

14 CJ (FATP 5/06 amended)

Text references. Cash flow statements are covered in Chapter 8: *IAS 7 Statement of cash flows*. Construction contracts are in Chapter 10: *Inventories and construction contracts*.

Top tips. It would be a good idea to use the reading time before the exam to make a note of the proformas you need to produce and then analyse the additional information. Highlight any unusual items and try to decide on which order to tackle the adjustments. On tackling the question make sure you pick out the parts you can do first and deal with the other areas at the end. Always adopt a methodical approach as Section C questions can be quite time pressured.

Easy marks. 'Cash flows from operating activities' was easy apart from the tax and would have gained you a lot of marks. The only complication in the rest of the cash flow was the property, plant and equipment. The construction contract was easy if you knew how to deal with it. If nothing else, you could probably have arrived at attributable profit and added that to retained earnings.

Examiner's comments. This question was generally very well done, with many candidates obtaining full marks. Common errors included not using the correct IAS 7 format, mixing up sale proceeds and gain on disposal and failing to adjust for deferred tax.

(a)   CJ
STATEMENT OF CASH FLOWS FOR THE YEAR ENDED 31 MARCH 20X6

	$'000	$'000
Cash flows from operating activities		
Profit before tax	4,198	
Depreciation	4,055	
Finance cost	1,302	
Profit on sale of plant (118 – 95)	(23)	
Increase in inventory	(214)	
Increase in receivables	(306)	
Increase in payables (excluding interest)	420	
Cash generated from operations	9,432	
Interest paid (1,302 – 350 + 650)	(1,602)	
Income tax paid (1,810 + 1,900 – 1,914)	(1,796)	
Net cash from operating activities		6,034
Cash flows from investing activities		
Payment to acquire property, plant and equipment (W)	(2,310)	
Receipt on disposal of plant	118	
Net cash used in investing activities		(2,192)
Cash flow from financing activities		
Proceeds of share issue	10,000	
Dividends paid	(800)	
Net cash flow from financing activities		9,200
Increase in cash and cash equivalents		13,042
Cash and cash equivalents at 31.3.X5		(880)
Cash and cash equivalents at 31.3.X6		12,162

Workings

Property

PROPERTY

	$'000		$'000
Balance b/d	18,000	Depreciation	2,070
Revaluation	1,500	Balance c/d	19,160
Additions (balance)	1,730		
	21,230		21,230

Plant and equipment

PLANT AND EQUIPMENT

	$'000		$'000
Balance b/d	10,000	Disposal	95
Additions (balance)	580	Depreciation	1,985
		Balance c/d	8,500
	10,580		10,580

Additions

	$'000
Property additions	1,730
Plant additions	580
Total	2,310

(b) CJ
STATEMENT OF FINANCIAL POSITION AT 31 MARCH 20X6

	$'000	$'000
Non-current assets		
Property, plant and equipment	27,660	
Available for sale investments	2,100	
		29,760
Current assets		
Inventory and WIP (2,714 + 560(W))	3,274	
Trade receivables (2,106 + 500(W))	2,606	
Cash at bank	11,753	
Cash in hand	409	
		18,042
Total assets		47,802
Equity and liabilities		
Ordinary shares	12,000	
Share premium	10,000	
Revaluation surplus	4,200	
Retained earnings (2,809 + 360(W))	3,169	
		29,369
Non-current liabilities		
Interest bearing borrowings	7,000	
Provision for deferred tax	999	
		7,999
Current liabilities		
Trade and other payables (1,820 + 700)	2,520	
Income tax payable	1,914	
		4,434
Total equity and liabilities		47,802

Working

Long-term contract

	$'000
Total expected profit (5,000 – 2,500 – 700)	1,800
Profit to date (1,800 × 20%)	360

Adjustment to retained profit

	$'000
Revenue (5,000 × 20%)	1,000
Cost of sales	(640)
Profit	360

Adjustments to statement of financial position

	$'000
Inventory – WIP	
Gross amount due from customers	
Costs to date	700
Profit to date	360
	1,060
Progress billings	(500)
Due from customers	560
Receivables – progress billings	500
Payables – due to suppliers	700

15 DN (FATP 11/06/amended)

Top tips. You need to be well organised to get the statement of financial position done in this question. Make sure you know your proformas and can set them out accurately and quickly. As with all Section C questions, it is best to concentrate on the easy marks first and make an attempt at some of the harder workings at the end of the question time.

Easy marks. Nothing here was difficult, although part (b) was time pressured. If your workings were clear, there were plenty of easy marks available.

Examiner's comments. (part a) There were some excellent answers to this question. Common errors were:
- Not using the correct IAS 7 format
- Mixing up proceeds of sale and gain on disposal
- Not allowing for property revaluation
- Incorrectly calculating proceeds of share issue

Marking scheme

	Marks
Statement of cash flows	
Cash flows from operating activities	
Profit before tax	1
Depreciation	1
Interest expense	1
Profit on disposal	1
Movement in: receivables	1
Inventories	1
Payables	1
Interest paid	1½
Tax paid	½
	9
Cash flows from investing activities	
Proceeds of disposal	1
Cost of additions	2
	3

Cash flows from financing activities
Proceeds of new loan	1	
Proceeds of share issue	1	
		2
Movement in cash and cash equivalents		1
		15

Statement of financial position

Property, plant and equipment	½
Inventory	½
Receivables	1
Cash	2½
Share capital	½
Share premium	½
Revaluation surplus	½
Retained earnings	2½
Loan stock	½
Trade payables	1
	10

(a) DN
STATEMENT OF CASH FLOWS FOR THE YEAR ENDED 31 OCTOBER 20X6

	$'000	$'000
Cash flows from operating activities		
Profit before tax		790
Adjustments for:		
Depreciation (230 + 100)		330
Interest expense		110
Profit on sale of plant		(5)
		1,225
Increase in receivables		(110)
Increase in inventories		(50)
Increase in payables		20
Cash generated from operations		1,085
Interest paid (75 + 110 – 55)		(130)
Income taxes paid		(120)
Net cash from operating activities		835
Cash flows from investing activities		
Proceeds from sale of plant	15	
Cost of acquiring new plant (W)	(677)	
Net cash used in investing activities		(662)
Cash flows from financing activities		
Proceeds from new loan	1,500	
Proceeds of share issue (300 + 300)	600	
Net cash from financing activities		2,100
Net increase in cash and cash equivalents		2,273
Cash and cash equivalents at beginning of period		45
Cash and cash equivalents at end of period		2,318

Working: plant and equipment

PLANT AND EQUIPMENT

	$'000		$'000
Balance b/d	1,405	Disposal	10
Additions (balance)	677	Depreciation	230
		Balance c/d	1,842
	2,082		2,082

Note. There were no additions to properties, which is cost and revaluation surplus less depreciation.

(b) DN
STATEMENT OF FINANCIAL POSITION AT 31 OCTOBER 20X7

	$'000	$'000
Net current assets		
Property, plant and equipment (4,942 – 330)		4,612
Current assets		
Inventory	190	
Receivables (340 + 3,300 – 3,100)	540	
Cash (W1)	3,043	
		3,773
Total assets		8,385
Equity and liabilities		
Equity		
Share capital	1,300	
Share premium	300	
Revaluation surplus	400	
Retained earnings (W2)	2,680	
		4,280
Non-current liabilities		
Bank loans		3,500
Current liabilities		
Trade payables (105 + 1,700 – 1,600)		205
Total equity and liabilities		8,385

Workings

1 Cash

CASH

	$'000		$'000
Balance b/d	2,318		
Receipts from customers	3,100	Supplier payments	1,600
		Expenses	500
		Interest 20X6	55
		Interest 20X7 ($1,500 × 6%)	90
		Tax 20X6	70
		Tax 20X7	60
		Balance c/d	3,043
	5,418		5,418

2 Retained earnings

RETAINED EARNINGS

	$'000		$'000
Balance c/d	2,680	Balance b/d	2,060
		Profit for year (W3)	620
	2,680		2,680

3 Profit to 31 October 20X7

	$'000
Revenue	3,300
Cost of sales	(1,700)
Gross profit	1,600
Depreciation	(330)
Expenses	(500)
Finance cost	(90)
	680
Tax	(60)
Profit for year	620

16 Lemming Inc

> **Text references.** The statement of comprehensive income is covered in Chapter 3: *Presentation of published Statements of cash flows* are covered in Chapter 8: *IAS 7: Statement of cash flows*
>
> **Top tips.** Interest expense and interest paid are the same here, as all interest to date has been paid. This will not always be the case so watch out for any accrued interest amounts in other questions.

(a) LEMMING
STATEMENT OF COMPREHENSIVE INCOME FOR THE YEAR ENDED 31 AUGUST 20X9

	$'000
Revenue	14,050
Cost of sales (W1)	(10,490)
Gross profit	3,560
Profit on sale of plant (250 – (1000 – 800))	50
Operating expenses (700 + 1,200)	(1,900)
	1,710
Finance costs (1,500 × 10%)	(150)
Profit before tax	1,560
Income tax expense	(500)
Profit for the year	1,060
Other comprehensive income:	
Revaluation gain on land	1,000
Total comprehensive income for the year	2,060

Workings

1 Cost of sales

	$'000
Purchases	10,690
Opening inventory	1,200
Closing inventory	(1,400)
	10,490

(b) LEMMING
STATEMENT OF CASH FLOWS FOR THE YEAR ENDED 31 AUGUST 20X9

	$'000	$'000
Cash flows from operating activities		
Profit before taxation		1,560
Depreciation		1,200
Profit on sale of property, plant and equipment		(50)
Interest expense		150
Increase in inventory		(200)
Decrease in receivables		100
Decrease in payables		(100)
Cash generated from operations		2,660
Interest paid		(150)
Income taxes paid (500 + 400 – 500)		(400)
Net cash from operating activities		2,110
Cash flows from investing activities		
Purchase of property, plant and equipment	(2,500)	
Proceeds of sale of property, plant and equipment	250	
Net cash used in investing activities		(2,250)
Cash flows from financing activities		
Dividends paid (W1)	(500)	
Issue of share capital (400 x 0.5) + (400 x 0.5)	400	
Issue of loan notes	500	
Net cash from financing activities		400
Net increase in cash and cash equivalents		260
Cash and cash equivalents at beginning of period (200 – 360)		(160)
Cash and cash equivalents at end of period (300 – 200)		100

Workings

1   Retained earnings

RETAINED EARNINGS

	$'000		$'000
Dividend paid (balance)	500	Balance b/f	2,400
Balance c/f	2,960	Profit for year	1,060
	3,460		3,460

17 Objective test answers: Non-current assets, inventories and construction contracts I

1   C   780 + 117 + 30 + 28 + 100 = 1,055

2   D   They are all correct

3   D   Neither internally generated goodwill nor internally developed brands can be capitalised.

4   A   Goodwill on acquisition is retained in the statement of financial position and reviewed annually for impairment.

5   A   Carriage outwards is charged to distribution, abnormal costs are not included in inventory.

6   D   1   Production overheads should be included in cost on the basis of a company's normal level of activity.

    2   Trade discounts should be deducted but not settlement discounts.

    3   IAS 2 does not allow the use of LIFO.

7   C

	$
Contract revenue recognised (900 × 60%)	540,000
Costs	(840,000)
Expected loss (900 – 1,200)	(300,000)
Costs incurred	720,000
Recognised loss	(300,000)
Progress billings	(400,000)
Due from customer	20,000

8   C   Recoverable amount is the higher of value in use and net realisable value.

9
    Revenue = $40m × 45% = $18m
    Profit   = $6m × 45%   = $2.7m

	$m
Contract price	40
Total costs (16 + 18)	(34)
Anticipated profit	6

10

	$
Carrying value (100,000 × 0.75^4)	31,640
Recoverable amount	28,000
Impairment loss	3,640

11   The contract is 70% complete. Revenue earned = $90m × 70% = $63m.

12   CN should recognise a loss of $20m (90m – 77m – 33m).

13   D   An allocation of EW's administration costs would not be included as these do not relate specifically to the non-current asset.

18 Objective test answers: Non current-assets, inventories and construction contracts II

1   C

	$
Original purchase price	50,000
Depreciation 20X1: (50,000 – 5,000)/5	(9,000)
Depreciation 20X2	(9,000)
Upgrade	15,000
	47,000
Depreciation 20X3: (47,000 – 5,000)/5	(8,400)
Net book value 1 January 20X4	38,600
Disposal proceeds	(7,000)
Loss on disposal	31,600

2   B   The impairment loss is applied first against the goodwill and then against the other non-current assets on a pro-rata basis. It will be allocated as follows:

	$m
Building	10
Plant and equipment	5
Goodwill	5
	20

The carrying value of the building will then become $10m (20 – 10)

3   A fall in the value of an asset, so that its recoverable amount is now less than its carrying value in the statement of financial position.

4   B   Low production or idle plant does *not* lead to a higher fixed overhead allocation to each unit.

5   The amount for which an asset could be exchanged between knowledgeable, willing parties in an arm's length transaction.

6   The publishing rights cannot be recognised as they have no reliable monetary value as they were a gift and had no cost. The expected future value cannot be recognised as an asset as the event has not yet occurred.

7   Value of goodwill = $130,000

	$'000	$'000
Fair value of consideration – shares (10,000 × $20)		200,000
Cash		20,000
		220,000
Fair value of net assets acquired:		
Tangible non-current assets	25,000	
Patents	15,000	
Brand name	50,000	
		(90,000)
Goodwill		130,000

8

Year ended:	Cost/valuation	Depreciation	Acc depreciation	Carrying Value
March 20X2	100,000	10,000	10,000	90,000
March 20X3	100,000	10,000	20,000	80,000
March 20X4	95,000	(20,000)	–	95,000
March 20X4	95,000	11,875 (95,000/8)	11,875	83,125
March 20X5	**95,000**	**16,625** (83,125/5)	**28,500**	**66,500**

9   Depreciable amount is asset cost or valuation less residual value.

10   A   This is replacement of a significant part of the asset. The carrying amount of the existing furnace lining must be derecognised. B, C and D refer to repairs and maintenance.

11   Carrying value of machine at 30 September 20X5 = 10,500

Remaining useful life = 2 years

Depreciation for year ended 30 September 20X6 (10,500/2) = 5,250

12　This question appears to refer to the criteria for recognising development expenditure, which are:

1　Technical feasibility of completing the intangible asset
2　Intention to complete and use or sell the asset
3　Ability to use or sell the asset
4　The asset will generate future economic benefits
5　Adequate resources exist to complete the project
6　Expenditure on the asset can be reliably measured

The answer only requires four of these.

13
	$'000
Total contract value	3,000
Total costs (1,500 + 250 + 400)	(2,150)
Expected total profit	850

Percentage completed = 1,500/2,150 % = 70%

Statement of comprehensive income amounts:

	$'000
Revenue (3,000 × 70%)	2,100
Costs	(1,500)
Profit	600

19　Section B answers: Non-current assets, inventories and construction contracts

(a)　(i)　**Research costs**

IAS 38 does not allow the capitalisation of research costs.

Development costs

IAS 38 lays down strict **criteria** to determine when carry forward of development costs is permissible.

- The expenditure attributable to the intangible asset during its development must be measurable.
- The technical feasibility of completing the product or process so that it will be available for sale or use can be demonstrated.
- The entity intends to complete the intangible asset and use or sell it.
- It must be able to use or sell the intangible asset.
- There must be a market for the output of the intangible asset or, if it is to be used internally rather than sold, its usefulness to the entity, can be demonstrated.
- Adequate technical, financial and other resources must exist, or their availability must be demonstrated, to complete the development and use or sell the intangible asset.

(ii)　IAS 1 has three basic accounting assumptions: going concern, accruals and consistency.

Each of these concepts is relevant in considering the criteria discussed above for carrying forward development expenditure.

Going concern. The business must be in a position to continue its operations at least to the extent of generating resources sufficient to complete the development project and therefore to market the end product.

Accruals. The purpose of deferring development expenditure at all is to comply with the accruals concept by matching such expenditure with the income expected to arise from it.

Consistency. IAS 38 states that the criteria for deferral of expenditure should be consistently applied.

(b) The general principle underlying IAS 2 is that inventories should be shown in financial statements at the **lower of cost and net realisable value**. This principle accords with both the matching concept, which requires costs to be matched with the relevant revenues, and the prudence concept, which requires that profits are not anticipated and any probable losses are provided for.

The **cost** of an item of manufactured inventory can include both external and internal costs and it is important that only correctly attributable costs are included. These are direct acquisition costs, direct inventory holding costs and production overheads based on a **normal** level of activity. General overheads are excluded.

Production overheads are usually incurred on a time basis and not in relation to the quantities of inventory produced. Most businesses, however, are assumed to continue to exist in the medium term and production overheads are part of the inevitable cost of providing production facilities in the medium term. Thus, so long as the scale of the overheads is not distorted by unusual levels of activity, it is reasonable to include them in the 'cost' of inventory produced in the period to which they relate. Identifying a 'normal' level of activity is more difficult where business is seasonal.

The establishment of NRV also poses a number of practical problems. For many intermediate products, and even for finished items, there may be a limited market and the inventory volumes may represent a significant proportion of the market especially if disposed of under distress conditions. Where a well-developed and liquid market does not exist, it is usually appropriate to base NRV on an orderly disposal after allowing for the reasonable additional costs of marketing and distribution.

(c)
MEMO

To: Transport manager
From: Trainee management accountant
Subject: Useful life

IAS 16 *Property, plant and equipment* requires that the useful lives of non-current assets should be regularly reviewed and changed if appropriate.

By 31 March 20X2 the delivery vehicle will have been depreciated for two years out of the original estimate of its useful life of four years:

	$
Cost	20,000
Depreciation ($20,000 × $2/4$)	(10,000)
Carrying value at 31 March 20X2	10,000

The carrying value at the start of the year ending 31 March 20X3 should now be written off over the remaining, revised useful life of four years giving an annual depreciation charge of $2,500 ($10,000/4).

In the income statement for the year ended 31 March 20X3 therefore the depreciation charge will be $2,500. In the statement of financial position the delivery vehicle will appear at its carrying value of $7,500 ($10,000 – 2,500).

(d)

> **Examiner's comments.** Most candidates made a better attempt at the buildings part of the question then the brand name. Some candidates did not depreciate the buildings for enough years before revaluating. Despite the question saying that the brand name had been acquired for £500,000, many candidates treated it as internally generated.

Building

The building has previously been revalued upwards and the gain on revaluation taken to the revaluation surplus). Therefore IAS 36 *Impairment of assets* states that the impairment loss of $200,000 ($1.7m – 1.5m) should be charged against the previous revaluation surplus of $900,000 leaving a revaluation surplus of $700,000 and a carrying value for the building of $1,500,000. The building is reported under property, plant and equipment.

Revaluation surplus at 30 Sept 20X4 = $1.8m – ($1.0 – ($1.0 × 2/20))
= $900,000

Carrying value of building at 30 Sept 20X5 = $1.8m – ($1.8m/18)
= $1.7m

Market value at 30 Sept 20X5 = $1.5m

Brand name

IAS 36 requires the brand to be written down to its recoverable amount, which is the higher of its fair value less costs to sell and value in use. Therefore the recoverable amount is the market value of $200,000 as this is higher than its value in use of $150,000.

The impairment loss of $50,000 (250,000 – 200,000) is recognised immediately in the income statement. The brand is measured at $200,000 in the statement of financial position and reported as an intangible asset.

Carrying value = $500,000 – ($500,000 × 5/10)
= $250,000

Recoverable amount = higher of fair value and value in use
= $200,000

Impairment = $50,000 ($250,000 – 200,000) charged to the income statement

Brand in statement of financial position = $200,000

(e)

> **Examiner's comments.** The most common error made by those who understood the concept of revaluing non-current assets was to miscount the number of years' depreciation, either using 4 or 6 years before the first revaluation in 2007.

Building A

	$
Cost	200,000
Depreciation to 31.8.01 (200,000/20 × 5)	(50,000)
Carrying value	150,000
Revaluation 31.8.01 – to revaluation surplus	30,000
Carrying value	180,000
Depreciation to 31.8.06 (180,000/15 × 5)	(60,000)
	120,000
Valuation 31.8.06 – impairment loss	(20,000)
Carrying value	100,000

Building A has suffered an impairment loss of $7,500 at 31 August 2006 which can be debited to revaluation surplus reversing the previous revaluation gain.

Building B

	$
Cost	120,000
Depreciation to 31.8.01 (120,000/15 × 5)	(40,000)
Carrying value	80,000
Valuation 31.8.01 – impairment loss	(5,000)
Carrying value	75,000
Depreciation to 31.8.06 (75,000/10 × 5)	(37,500)
	37,500
Valuation 31.8.06 – impairment loss	(7,500)
Carrying value	30,000

Building B has suffered impairment losses totalling $7,500 at 31 August 2006, which will be charged to the statement of comprehensive income.

(f)

> **Examiner's comments.** This question caused problems for some candidates who ignored the details given and calculated the percentage complete using costs instead of using the value of work completed as specified in the question. Other common errors were not identifying clearly what each result represented and not identifying the amount due on the contract as an asset or a liability.

HS Construction contract

	$'000
Total revenue	300
Total costs to complete (170 + 100)	(270)
Total profit	30

State of completion of contract = 165/300 x 100% = 55%

Amounts recognised in the statement of comprehensive income for the year ended 31 March 20X9

	$'000
Revenue (value of work completed)	165.0
Profit (30 x 55%)	16.5

Amounts recognised in the statement of financial position at 31 March 20X9

	$'000
Costs incurred	170.0
Profit recognised	16.5
	186.5
Less progress billings	(130.0)
Amount recognised as an asset/(liability)	56.5

Recognise an asset in statement of financial position under current assets:

Gross amount due from customer $56,500

20 Geneva

Top tips. Begin by working out for each contract whether a profit or a loss is forecast. If it is a profit, calculate how much can be recognised. If it is a loss, it is all recognised immediately.

Easy marks. Note that all of these contacts started in the current year – so any attributable profit to date belongs to the current year. This makes the calculations easier.

Treatment of construction contracts in the statement of financial position

	$'000
Contract Lausanne	
Asset (1,000 + 240 – 1,080)	
Gross amount due from customers for contract work	160
Contract Bern	
Liability (1,100 – 200 – 950)	
Gross amount due to customers for contract work	50
Contract Zurich	
Liability (640 + 70 – 800)	
Gross amount due to customers for contract work	90

Treatment of construction contracts in the statement of comprehensive income

	Lausanne	Bern	Zurich
	$'000	$'000	$'000
Revenue	1,200	1,000	700
Cost of sales	960	1,200	630
Gross profit/(loss)	240	(200)	70

21 Objective test answers: Capital transactions and financial instruments

1	C	The premium is transferred from share capital to share premium
2	C	$500,000 + $11,000 (990,000 × 50c + 10,000 × $1.60)
		Note that the forfeited shares each brought in a total of $2.60
3	D	Share capital $500,000 + $250,000 + $300,000 + $350,000
		Share premium $800,000 – $250,000 + $900,000 + $910,000
4	A	The called-up value will be debited to share capital and credited to a forfeited shares account.
5	D	All four are permitted.
6	D	If a shareholder fails to pay a call his shares are forfeited and the company is not obliged to return his money.
7	C	Cumulative and redeemable preference shares are classified as financial liabilities under IAS 32.
8	B	As a deduction from equity.
9	A	Cash received on application and allotment

$1 × 5,000 = $5,000

Balance of share capital due = $2,500

Cash received on reissue of shares $1 × 5,000 = $5,000

Additional share premium:

INVESTMENT IN OWN SHARES ACCOUNT

	$		$
Call amount	2,500	Bank	5,000
Share premium	2,500		
	5,000		5,000

10 $3.8m

	$m
Receipt from issue ($10m - $0.5m)	9.5
Dividend payable over 4 years ($10m × 7% × 4)	(2.8)
Payable on redemption ($10m + 5%)	(10.5)
Total finance charge	(3.8)

11 $10.025m

	$m
Receipt from issue	9.5
Finance charge 10%	0.95
Dividend paid	(0.7)
Balance at 31 December 20X8	9.75
Finance charge 10%	0.975
Dividend paid	(0.7)
Balance at 31 December 20X9	10.025

12 B Treasury shares are an entity's own shares which it has repurchased and holds in 'treasury'. Treasury shares can be re-issued or issued as part of employee share schemes in the future.

22 Objective test answers: Accounting standards I

1	A	$3/10 \times \$3,000$
2	D	$2/6 \times \$3,000$
3	D	Adjusting events are shown in the financial statements, not the notes.
4	C	$\$1,800,000 - \$116,000 - \$20,000 = \$1,664,000$
5	B	Discovery of fraud, error or impairment, which will have existed at the end of the reporting period.
6	D	These have all occurred after the reporting period.
7	C	1 Contingent liability that is possible, therefore disclose. 2 Contingent liability but remote, therefore no disclosure. 3 Non-adjusting event after the reporting period, material therefore disclose.
8	B	IAS 37 excludes retraining and relocation of continuing staff from restructuring provisions.
9	A	All three criteria must be present.
10	D	This does not affect the position as at the year end.
11	D	The dividend will not be shown in the statement of comprehensive income or appear as a liability in the statement of financial position.
12	1	An entity has a present obligation as a result of a past event.
	2	It is probable that an outflow of resources embodying economic benefits will be required to settle the obligation.
	3	A reliable estimate can be made of the amount of the obligation.
13	C	
14		An **operating segment** is a component of an entity: (a) that engages in business activities from which it may earn revenues and incur expenses (b) whose operating results are regularly reviewed by the entity's chief operating decision maker to make decisions about resources to be allocated to the segment and assess its performance, and (c) for which discrete financial information is available
15	B	Revenue must be 10% or more of the total revenue of all segments.
16	B	This does not affect the position as at the year end.
17	D	

23 Objective test answers: Accounting standards II

1	C	Item 1 is not correct – if it is probable and the amount can be estimated reliably, then it must be provided for.
2	C	Customers, suppliers and providers of finance are not related parties.
3	C	In a finance lease, the risks and rewards of ownership are transferred.

4   A

	$
Deposit	30,000
Instalments (8 × $20,000)	160,000
	190,000
Fair value	154,000
Interest	36,000

Sum of the digits = $\dfrac{8 \times 9}{2} = 36$

6 months to			
June X1	$8/36 \times \$36,000$		
Dec X1	$7/36 \times \$36,000$		
June X2	$6/36 \times \$36,000$		
Dec X2	$5/36 \times \$36,000$		
June X3	$4/36 \times \$36,000$	=	$4,000
Dec X3	$3/36 \times \$36,000$	=	$3,000
			$7,000

5   D   The fire is non-adjusting as it does not clarify the 31 December value of the building. It is therefore only disclosed if it threatens the company's going concern status.

Again the customer is assumed to be insolvent at 31 December. We simply did not know this and therefore it is an adjusting event and it should be adjusted for.

The answer would be B if the customer had become insolvent after the year end.

6   C   1   As the board decision had not been communicated to customers and employees there is assumed to be no legal or constructive obligation therefore no provision should be made.

            2   As refunds have been made in the past to all customers there is a valid expectation from customers that the refunds will be made therefore the amount should be provided for.

            3   There is no present obligation to carry out the refurbishment therefore no provision should be made under IAS 37.

7   B   Members of the close family of any key management of an entity are presumed to be related parties.

8   An entity has a present obligation (legal or constructive) as a result of a past event.

         It is probable that an outflow of resources embodying economic benefits will be required to settle the obligation.

         A reliable estimate can be made of the amount of the obligation.

9   C   A provision should be made for the claim against AP.

10   B   Customers, suppliers and bankers are not normally related parties.

11   Finance cost = $2,160

	$
Total finance cost	
Total payments 12,000 × 5	60,000
Fair value	51,900
Finance cost	8,100

Payments being made over five year period:

To 30 Sept 20X4   5/15 × 8,100
To 30 Sept 20X5   4/15 × 8,100 $2,160

12   C   BW must provide for customer refunds.

13   Any four of the following:

- the seller has transferred to the buyer the significant risks and rewards of ownership
- the seller retains neither continuing managerial involvement to the degree usually associated with ownership nor effective control over the goods sold
- the amount of revenue can be measured reliably
- it is probable that the economic benefits associated with the transaction will flow to the seller
- the costs incurred or to be incurred in respect of the transaction can be measured reliably

14

	$
Cost 1.1.X4	80,000
Interest 7.93%	6,344
Instalment	(20,000)
Balance 31.12.X4	66,344
Interest 7.93%	5,261
Instalment	(20,000)
Balance 31.12.X5	51,605
Interest 7.93%	4,092
Instalment	(20,000)
Balance 31.12.X6	35,697
Current liability (51,605 – 35,697) =	15,908
Non-current liability	35,697
Total balance at 31.12.X5	51,605

15

	$
Original cost	80,000
Depreciation 2004/2005 (80,000/12,000 × (2,600 + 2,350))	(33,000)
Net book value	47,000

16 D No sale has taken place, so DT must show that it is holding $90,000 which belongs to XX.

17 D Fair value less costs to sell ($740,000 - $10,000) is lower than carrying value ($750,000).

Note that non-current assets held for sale are not depreciated.

18 B Non-current assets held for sale are shown separately under the 'current assets' heading.

19 C Share transactions after the reporting period do not require adjustment.

20 A Large customers are *not necessarily* related parties of the entity.

21 Operating lease – spread the rent-free period over the term of the lease

Total rent payable = 4 × $12,000 = $48,000

Over five years = $48,000/5 = $9,600 per annum

$9,600 charged to profit or loss in each of 30 April 20X8 and 30 April 20X9.

24 Section B answers: Accounting standards I

(a) Asset

IAS 17 is an example of economic substance triumphing over legal form. In legal terms, with a finance lease, the lessor may be the owner of the asset, but the lessee enjoys all the **risks and rewards** which ownership of the asset would convey. This is the key element to IAS 17. The lessee is deemed to have an asset as they must maintain and run the asset through its useful life.

Liability

The lessee enjoys the future economic benefits of the asset as a result of entering into the lease. There is a corresponding liability which is the obligation to pay the instalments on the lease until it expires. Assets and liabilities cannot be netted off. If finance leases were treated in a similar manner to the existing treatment of operating leases then no asset would be recognised and lease payments would be expensed through the statement of comprehensive income as they were incurred. This is '**off balance sheet finance**'. The company has assets in use and liabilities to lessors which are not recorded in the financial statements. This would be misleading to the user of the accounts and make it appear as though the assets which were recorded were more efficient in producing returns than was actually the case.

(b) **MEMO**

To: Production manager
From: Trainee management accountant
Subject: De-commissioning costs

Provision

The accounting question regarding the de-commissioning costs is whether or not a provision should now be set up in the accounts for the eventual costs. According to IAS 37 any future obligations arising out of past events should be recognised immediately. The de-commissioning costs are a future obligation and the past event is the granting of the licence and the drilling of the site.

Therefore a provision should be recognised immediately in the accounts for the year ended 31 March 20X3. This will be $20million discounted to present value.

Discounting

As this cost gives access to future economic benefits in terms of oil reserves for the next 20 years then the discounted present value of the de-commissioning costs can be capitalised and treated as part of the cost of the oil well in the balance sheet. However this total cost, including the discounted de-commissioning costs should be reviewed to ensure that the net book value does not exceed the recoverable amount. If there is no impairment then the total cost of the oil well and discounted de-commissioning costs should be depreciated for the next 20 years and a charge made to the statement of comprehensive income.

(c) Because the airline operation was sold before the year end and was a distinguishable component of the entity it is a **discontinued operation** as defined by IFRS 5 *Non-current assets held for sale and discontinued operations.* A separate line in the statement of comprehensive income for discontinued operations should be included after the profit after tax for continuing operations. IFRS 5 states that this should be made up of the post-tax profit or loss of the discontinued operation and the post-tax gain or loss on disposal of the airline assets. The loss on sale of the fleet of aircraft of $250m and the provision for severance payments of $20m will both be reported in this line.

	$m
Discontinued operations	(270)

IFRS 5 also requires an **analysis** of the amount into:

(i) the revenue, expenses and pre-tax profit of discontinued operations (to include the loss made by the airline for the year and the provision for the $20m severance payments); and

(ii) the gain or loss recognised on the disposal of the assets (the $250m loss on the sale of the fleet of aircraft).

This can be presented either on the face of the statement of comprehensive income or in the notes.

The **cash flows** attributable to the operating, investing and financing activities of the airline should also be disclosed, either in the notes to the financial statements or in the statement of cash flows itself.

As the restructuring has been agreed and active steps have been taken to implement it a **provision** is required for $10m (because the entity has a constructive obligation to carry out the plan). This will be reported as part of the continuing activities, probably as part of administrative expenses.

(d)

> **Examiner's comments.** Most candidates correctly identified that the customer was not a related party. Most candidates correctly identified that George was a related party but did not give sufficient explanation.
>
> Some candidates correctly identified the provider of finance as not being a related party, but did not go on to identify that Arnold was a related party.

XC

XC is not a related party of CB. The discount represents no more than a normal commercial arrangement with a favoured customer.

Property

George is one of the key management personnel of the company and thus a related party, and the sale of the property to him at a discount of $250,000 must be disclosed in the financial statements.

FC

As a provider of finance, FC is not itself a related party. However, Arnold is close family of George and therefore a related party to CB, and the loan does not appear to have been advanced at normal commercial terms. The loan and the involvement of Arnold will need to be disclosed.

(e)

> **Examiner's comments.** Few candidates did well on this question. Most candidates failed to include all three elements of the finance cost in the total cost. Some candidates used the straight line or sum of digits method to allocate the finance cost instead of the actuarial method, despite the discount rate of 10% being given.

(a)

		$
Receipt (2,000,000 – 192,800)		1,807,200
Costs:		
Dividends (100,000 × 5)		500,000
Redemption		2,300,000
		(2,800,000)
Finance cost		(992,800)

(b)

	Balance	Interest 10%	Dividend	Balance
20X6	1,807,200	180,720	(100,000)	1,887,920
20X7	1,887,920	188,792	(100,000)	1,976,712
20X8	1,976,712	197,671	(100,000)	2,074,383
20X9	2,074,383	207,438	(100,000)	2,181,821
20Y0	2,181,821	218,179	(100,000)	2,300,000

The balance at 31 March 20Y0 is $2,300,000, which is the amount needed to redeem the shares.

(f)

> **Examiner's comments.** A large proportion of candidates seemed to have problems with the dates in this question. They said that the 20X5 accounts should be changed, despite the fact that the fraud was discovered more than 6 months after the year end and the accounts had been signed off by the directors two months earlier.

Fraud

The discovery of the fraud in April 20X6 would be an adjusting event after the reporting period if it had occurred before the financial statements were authorised for issue. If the accounts were approved on 1 March, they would probably have been issued by April. So it is unlikely that this can be accounted for in the September 20X5 financial statements.

In the September 20X6 financial statements the overstatement of profit for the year ended 30 September 20X5 must be accounted for as a prior year adjustment. This will be shown in the Statement of Changes in Equity. The profit for the year ended 30 September will be reduced to $555,000. This will affect the retained earnings for the current year but not the current year profit.

Payment from new customer

The payment received in advance in September 20X6 cannot be treated as income because DF has not yet done anything to earn that income. It should be posted to current liabilities as 'deferred income' and released to the statement of comprehensive income when the goods are despatched.

(g)

> **Examiner's comments.** Most candidates correctly identified the factory closure as a discontinued activity but did not give sufficient explanation to gain more than a mark. Few candidates were able to explain how to deal with assets 'held for sale'.

The factory will be treated as a *discontinued operation* under IFRS 5 at 31 March 20X7, as all operations have ceased and sale of the land and buildings is 'highly probable'.

In the statement of comprehensive income **one figure** will be shown under *discontinued operations*, being the trading loss for the period from the discontinued operation (we are not told what this is), plus the loss on disposal of the plant and equipment ($70,000), plus the closure costs ($620,000), less any tax allowances. This single figure should then be analysed in the notes.

In the statement of financial position, the carrying value of the land and buildings ($750,000) should be moved out of non-current assets and shown under current assets as 'non-current assets held for sale'. The fair value less costs to sell would be higher, so the property is left at its carrying value. It is not depreciated.

(h) (i)

> **Examiner's comments**. A large proportion of answers did not refer to the asset values and costs given in the question. If a question asks for an explanation of the treatment in financial statements and provides figures it should be fairly obvious that the answer must include reference to costs and asset values given.

EK can treat the sale of its retailing division as a discontinued operation under IFRS 5 for the following reasons:

- It is classified as held for sale.
- It represents a separate major line of business, with clearly distinguishable cash flows.

The retailing division can be classified as 'held for sale' because it is available for immediate sale, the company expects to dispose of it within one year and negotiations are already proceeding with a buyer.

(ii) Statement of comprehensive income

EK should disclose a single amount on the face of the statement of comprehensive income comprising:

(a) The post-tax profit or loss of the retailing division up to 31 October 20X7; and
(b) The post tax gain or loss on measurement to fair value less costs to sell. A disposal group held for sale should be measured at the lower of its carrying amount and fair value less costs to sell. For EK this is the lower of $443,000 and $398,000 ($423,000 – $25,000). The impairment loss of $45,000 should be recognised.

Statement of financial position

The assets of the retailing division should be removed from non-current assets and shown at their fair value under current assets, classified as 'non-current assets held for sale'. The impairment should all be deducted from the goodwill balance.

25 Section B answers: Accounting standards II

(a) IAS 37 defines a provision as a liability of uncertain timing or amount. It goes on further to state that a provision should only be recognised when:

(a) There is a present obligation, either legal or constructive, arising as a result of a past event.
(b) It is probable that an outflow of resources embodying economic benefits will be required in order to settle the obligation.
(c) A reliable estimate of the amount of the obligation can be made.

This can be compared to the IASB's definition of a liability in its Framework for *Preparation and Presentation of Financial Statements:*

A liability is a present obligation of the entity arising from past events, the settlement of which is expected to result in an outflow of resources from the entity.

The key elements from the liability definition are all encompassed in the rules for recognising a provision.

(a) **Obligation.** A liability is a present obligation and a provision is only recognised if there is an obligation. This obligation can either be a legal or a constructive obligation. A constructive obligation arises out of past practice or as a result of actions which have previously taken place which have created an expectation that the organisation will act in such a way.

(b) **Past event.** A provision must arise out of a past event so the event must already have happened at the balance sheet date. If the event has not yet occurred then there is no provision as the entity may be able to avoid it.

(c) **Outflow of resources.** A provision will only be recognised if it is probably that there will be an outflow of resources to settle the obligation which ties in with the IASB's definition of a liability.

(b) STATEMENT OF COMPREHENSIVE INCOME (EXTRACTS)

	Year 1 $'000	Year 2 $'000
Finance charge (W1)	5,567	4,453
Depreciation charge (W3)	17,660	17,660

STATEMENT OF FINANCIAL POSITION (EXTRACTS)

	Year 1 $'000	Year 2 $'000
Non-current assets		
Property, plant and equipment (W3)	70,640	52,980
Non-current liabilities		
Amounts due under leases (W2)	56,320	38,660
Current liabilities		
Amounts due under leases		
(72,867 – 56,320) (W2)	16,547	
(56,320 – 38,660) (W2)		17,660

Workings

1 Finance charge

	$'000
Total lease payments (5 × $21,000)	105,000
Fair value of asset	(88,300)
Total finance charge	16,700

Finance charge allocation

		$
Year 1	5/15 × 16,700	5,567
Year 2	4/15 × 16,700	4,453
Year 3	3/15 × 16,700	3,340
Year 4	2/15 × 16,700	2,227
Year 5	1/15 × 16,700	1,113
		16,700

2 Lease liabilities

	$
Fair trade value	88,300
Finance charge	5,567
Repayment	(21,000)
Balance end year one	72,867
Finance charge	4,453
Repayment	(21,000)
Balance end year two	56,320
Finance charge	3,340
Repayment	(21,000)
Balance end year three	38,660

3   Non-current assets

$$\text{Annual depreciation charge} = \frac{\$88,300}{5} = \$17,660$$

	$
Year 1	
Cost	88,300
Depreciation	(17,660)
Carrying value	70,640
Year 2	
Depreciation	(17,660)
Carrying value	52,980

(c)

> **Examiner's comments.** Few candidate were able to produce a correct answer. Errors included:
> - Not calculating overall profitability of the contract
> - Ignoring the work in progress inventory

Income statement

	$'000
Sales revenue (W)	30,000
Cost of sales (balancing figure)	21,500
Recognised profit (W)	8,500

Statement of financial position

	$,000
Total costs to date	24,000
Recognised profit	8,500
Progress billings	(25,000)
Gross amount due from customer	7,500

Working

Revenue	60,000
Costs to date	(24,000)
Costs to completion	(19,000)
Total expected profit	17,000
Profit to date: 17,000 × 50%	8,500
Revenue to date: 60,000 × 50%	30,000

(d)

> **Examiner's comments.** Most candidates were able to calculate the finance cost and the outstanding balances at each year end, but many were unable to produce correct statement of comprehensive income and statement of financial position extracts.
>
> Common errors included:
> - Basing the calculation on 4 years instead of 5
> - Applying the digit weightings in reverse order
> - Applying the sum of the digits to the annual repayment instead of the finance charge

(i) The amount of finance cost charged to the income statement for the year ended 31 March 20X5 is $9,067.

Working

	$
Total lease payments	150,000
Fair value of asset	116,000
Finance charge	34,000

Using sum of the digits:

31.3.X4	34,000 ×5/15 =	11,333
31.3.X5	34,000 × 4/15 =	9,067
31.3.X6	34,000 × 3/15 =	6,800
31.3.X7	34,000 × 2/15 =	4,533
31.3.X8	34,000 × 1/15 =	2,267
		34,000

(ii) *Statement of financial position extracts*

Property, plant and equipment
Held under finance lease 116,000
Depreciation (2/5) 46,400
69,600

Non-current liabilities
Amounts due under finance leases 53,200

Current liabilities
Amounts due under finance leases (76,400 – 53,200) 23,200

Working

	$
1.4.X3 Fair value of asset	116,000
Finance charge	11,333
Repayment	(30,000)
Balance 31.3.X4	97,333
Finance charge	9,067
Repayment	(30,000)
Balance 31.3.X5	76,400
Finance charge	6,800
Repayment	(30,000)
Balance 31.3.X6	53,200

(e)

> **Examiner's comment.** Most candidates were able to score good marks on this question. Many had learnt a mnemonic to aid their recall of the six criteria. In Part (ii) some candidates failed to explain why the development costs should be treated as recommended.

(i) Under IAS 38 development costs will normally be recognised as an expense in the accounting period in which they are incurred. However, they may be capitalised if they meet *all* of the following criteria:

- It is **technically feasible** to complete the asset so that it is available for use or sale.
- The **intention** is to **complete** the asset so that it can be used or sold.
- The business is able to **use** or **sell** the asset
- It can be demonstrated that the asset will **generate future economic benefits**. For instance, a market must exist for the product.
- **Adequate technical, financial and other resources exist** to complete the development.
- The development expenditure can be **reliably measured**.

(ii) CD's development costs meet all of the above criteria. The development is complete, testing has confirmed the future economic benefits and the costs involved have been reliably measured. CD should capitalise $180,000 development costs at 30 April 20X6. Amortisation should begin on 1 May 20X6 and continue over the expected life of the process.

(f)

> **Examiner's comments.** Most candidates were able to correctly calculate the finance charges and balances for each of the three years, but many candidates could not select the correct figures from their workings to answer the question.

(i) Finance charge for the year ended 31 March 20X7: $72,000

(ii) Current liability: $228,000
Non-current liability: $378,000

Working

	$'000
Purchase price	900
Payment 1 April 20X5	(228)
	672
Interest 13.44%	90
Payment 1 April 20X6	(228)
	534
Interest 13.44%	72
Balance at 31 March 20X7	606
Payment due 1 April 20X7 (current liability)	228
Balance due (non-current liability)	378
	606

Note. As payments are made in advance, the payment due on 1 April 20X7 includes no interest relating to future periods.

(g) **Related party** – under the terms of IAS 24 a party is related to an entity if:

(i) directly or indirectly the party

- controls, is controlled by, or is under common control with, the entity
- has an interest in the entity that gives it significant interest over the entity; or
- has joint control over the entity

(ii) the party is a member of the key management personnel of the entity or its parent, such as a director

(iii) the party is a close member of the family of any individual referred to in (i) or (ii) above

(iv) the party is an entity that is controlled, jointly controlled or significantly influenced by, or a significant proportion of whose voting rights are held by, any individual referred to in (ii) or (iii)

Related party transaction – a transfer of resources, services or obligations between related parties, regardless of whether a price is charged.

(h)

> **Examiner's comments.** Most candidates were able to give most of the IAS 18 criteria but few were able to apply the criteria correctly to the scenario.

(i) The criteria in IAS 18 for income recognition are as follows.

- The **risks** and **rewards** of ownership of the goods have been **transferred to the buyer**.
- The entity **retains neither managerial involvement nor effective control** over the goods.
- The amount of **revenue** can be **measured reliably**.
- It is **probable** that the **economic benefits** associated with the transaction will **flow** to the entity.
- The **costs** incurred in respect of the transaction can be measured reliably.
- The **stage of completion** of the transaction at the balance sheet date can be measured reliably (rendering of services).

(ii) The $150,000 received on 1 September 20X7 cannot be recognised as income at that point because the risks and rewards of ownership have not yet been transferred.

The $150,000 should be credited to deferred income in the statement of financial position and $25,000 should be released to income each month as the magazines are supplied. The estimated $20,000 each month cost of making the supply will be recognised as it arises – at which point it can be measured reliably.

Therefore at 31 October two months revenue can be taken into account and two months costs will be set against that as follows:

	$
Revenue	50,000
Cost of sales	(40,000)
Gross profit	10,000

26 AZ (FATP Pilot paper/amended)

Text references. Leases are covered in Chapter 7: *IAS 17 Leases*. Prior year adjustments are covered in Chapter 4: *Reporting financial performance*.

Top tips. Make sure that you approach this type of question methodically. Numerical questions can be time pressured so get as much practice as you can to perfect your technique. Always read the question carefully and then set out your proformas. Tackle the parts you can do first to secure the easy marks before moving on to the more difficult areas. You can use the reading time at the start of the exam to decide in which order to attempt the adjustments.

Easy marks. A number of the adjustments will affect more than one figure. Once you have done the statement of financial position, the statement of changes in equity is very easy. The complications here are the lease and the prior year adjustments. Do the lease calculations first, but don't spend too long on them.

Marking scheme

	Marks
Statement of comprehensive income	
Revenue	½
Cost of sales	2
Administrative expenses	1
Distribution costs	1
Finance cost	2
Taxation expense	½
Loss for the year	1
	8
Statement of changes in equity	
Share capital	½
Retained earnings	2
Total	1
	3½
Statement of financial position	
Property, plant and equipment	2½
Inventory	1½
Receivables	½
Share capital	½
Retained earnings	2½
Loan stock	½
Amounts due under finance lease	3
Trade payables	½
Tax payable	½
Accruals	1½
	13½
	25

AZ
STATEMENT OF COMPREHENSIVE INCOME FOR THE YEAR ENDING 31 MARCH 20X3

	$'000	$'000
Revenue		124,900
Cost of sales (W1)		(100,835)
Gross profit		24,065
Distribution costs (9,060 + 513 (W2))	(9,573)	
Administrative expenses (W3)	(15,420)	
Other operating expenses	(121)	
		(25,114)
		(1,049)
Income from investments	1,200	
Finance cost (W8)	(1,432)	
		(232)
Loss before tax		(1,281)
Income tax expense		(15)
Net loss for the year		(1,296)

AZ
STATEMENT OF CHANGES IN EQUITY FOR THE YEAR ENDED 31 MARCH 20X3

	Share capital $'000	Retained earnings $'000	Total $'000
Balance at 1 April 20X2	19,000	14,677	33,677
Prior year adjustment	–	500	500
Total comprehensive income for the year	–	(1,296)	(1,296)
Balance at 31 March 20X3	19,000	13,881	32,881

AZ
STATEMENT OF FINANCIAL POSITION AS AT 31 MARCH 20X3

	$'000	$'000
Non-current assets		
Property, plant and equipment (W4)		21,229
Current assets		
Inventory (W6)	5,080	
Trade receivables (9,930 – 600)	9,330	
Bank and cash	25,820	
		40,230
		61,459
Equity		
Share capital		19,000
Retained earnings (W5)		13,881
		32,881
Non-current liabilities		
7% loan notes	18,250	
Amount due under finance lease (W7)	1,074	
		19,324
Current liabilities		
Trade payables	8,120	
Amount due under finance lease (W7)	480	
Tax payable	15	
Accruals (18,250 × 7% – 639)	639	
		9,254
		61,459

Workings

1   Cost of sales

	$'000
Opening inventory (4,852 + 500)	5,352
Manufacturing cost	94,000
Depreciation of plant and equipment (W2)	6,563
Less closing inventory (W6)	(5,080)
	100,835

2   Depreciation

	$'000
Plant and equipment (20% × 30,315)	6,063
Leased equipment (2m/4)	500
Vehicles ((3,720 – 1,670) × 25%)	513

3   Administrative expenses

	$'000
Per trial balance	16,020
Less leasing cost	(600)
	15,420

4   Property, plant and equipment

	Plant and equipment $'000	Vehicles $'000	Total $'000
Cost (30,315 + 2,000)	32,315	3,720	36,035
Accumulated depreciation			
(6,060 + 6,563) (W2)	(12,623)		
(1,670 + 513) (W2)		(2,183)	(14,806)
Carrying value	19,692	1,537	21,229

5   Retained earnings

	$'000
Per trial balance	14,677
Prior year adjustment – inventory	500
Net loss for the year	(1,296)
	13,881

6   Closing inventory

	$'000
As stated	5,180
Cost of damaged goods	(1,200)
NRV of damaged goods	1,100
	5,080

7   Finance lease

	$'000
Original cost	2,000
Interest 7.7%	154
Payment	(600)
Balance 31.3.X3	1,554
Interest 7.7%	120
Payment	(600)
Balance 31.3.X4	1,074
Due within 1 year (600 – 120)	480
Due after 1 year	1,074
	1,554

8   Finance cost

Interest payable on finance lease	154
Loan note interest (18,250 × 7%)	1,278
	1,432

27 AF (FATP 5/05/amended)

Text references. Operating leases are covered in Chapter 7: *IAS 7 Leases*.

Top tips. Begin by setting out the pro-formas for the statement of comprehensive income and statement of financial position, then go methodically through the workings, making sure they are neat and easy for the marker to read and understand. You must show workings.

Easy marks. The property, plant and equipment calculations were straightforward and would have been worth a few marks, especially if you charged the depreciation to cost of sales as instructed. You may not have known how to deal with the operating lease, but the statement of comprehensive income was otherwise relatively simple. With a correct statement of financial position format in place, you could have slotted in those figures which needed no calculation, plus your plant and equipment figure. The only tricky part was probably the accruals, for which you needed to have worked out the loan interest and the charge for the operating lease.

Examiner's comments. Many candidates achieved almost full marks on this question, but very few were able to correctly deal with the operating lease. Errors were also made in dealing with the investment, tax, loan interest, and dividends.

Marking scheme

		Marks
Statement of comprehensive income		
Revenue	½	
Cost of sales	1½	
Other income	½	
Administrative expenses	½	
Distribution costs	½	
Finance costs	1	
Taxation expenses	1½	
Other comprehensive income	2	
		8
Statement of changes in equity		
Share capital	1	
Share premium	1	
Retained earnings	1½	
Revaluation surplus	1½	
		5
Statement of financial position		
Property, plant and equipment	2	
Available – for sales investment	1	
Inventory	½	
Receivables	½	
Cash	½	
Share capital	½	
Share premium	½	
Revaluation surplus	1	
Retained earnings	1	
Loan stock	½	
Deferred tax	1	
Trade payables	½	
Accruals	1½	
Tax payable	½	
		12
		25

AF
STATEMENT OF COMPREHENSIVE INCOME FOR THE YEAR ENDED 31 MARCH 20X5

	$'000
Sales revenue	8,210
Cost of sales (W2)	(3,957)
Gross profit	4,253
Other income	68
Distribution costs	(1,590)
Administrative expenses	(1,540)
Finance costs (1,500 × 6%)	(90)
Profit before tax	1,101
Income tax expense (W4)	(350)
Profit for the year	751
Other comprehensive income:	
Gain on available-for-sale investments	110
Total comprehensive income for the year	861

AF
STATEMENT OF CHANGES IN EQUITY FOR THE YEAR ENDED 31 MARCH 20X5

	Share capital $'000	Share premium $'000	Retained earnings $'000	Revaluation surplus $'000	Total $'000
Balance at 1 April 20X4	4,500	1,380	388	330	6,598
Total comprehensive income for the year			751	110	861
Dividend paid			(275)		(275)
Balance at 31 March 20X5	4,500	1,380	864	440	7,184

AF: STATEMENT OF FINANCIAL POSITION AS AT 31 MARCH 20X5

	$'000	$'000
Non-current assets		
Property, plant and equipment (W1)		4,987
Available-for-sale investment		1,750
Current assets		
Inventory	1,320	
Receivables	1,480	
Bank and cash	822	
		3,622
Total assets		10,359
Equity and liabilities		
Equity		
Share capital		4,500
Share premium		1,380
Revaluation surplus (330 + 110)		440
Retained earnings		864
		7,184
Non-current liabilities		
6% loan notes	1,500	
Deferred tax (710 + 100)	810	
		2,310
Current liabilities		
Payables	520	
Accruals (W5)	95	
Taxation payable	250	
		865
Total equity and liabilities		10,359

Workings

1   Property, plant and equipment

	Property $'000	Plant and equipment $'000	Total $'000
Cost	5,190	3,400	8,590
Depreciation b/f	(1,500)	(1,659)	(3,159)
Charge for year:			
(5,190 – 2,000) × 3%	(96)		(96)
(3,400 – 1,659) × 20%		(348)	(348)
Carrying value	3,594	1,393	4,987

2   Cost of sales

	$'000
Per trial balance	3,463
Depreciation (96 + 348)	444
Operating lease (W3)	50
	3,957

3   Operating lease

Four years @ 62,500 = 250,000
Spread over five years = 50,000 pa

4   Income tax expense

	$'000
Tax charge for year	250
Transfer to deferred tax ((2,700 × 30%) – 710)	100
	350

5   Accruals

	$'000
Interest payable (90 – 45)	45
Operating lease (W3)	50
	95

28 Murdoch Co

Text references. Discontinued operations are covered in Chapter 4: *Reporting financial performance*.

Top tips. Make sure you read the question carefully so you are aware of all the information provided, circling or highlighting key points. Set out your proformas and complete the easier parts first.

Easy marks. This question was straightforward apart from the discontinued operation. Candidates should note that they can still earn full marks even if they present workings alongside the figures in the financial statements they produce. Problem areas in this question were:

- Treatment of the discontinued operation
- Accruals and prepayments

It is good exam technique to leave the more difficult areas to the end and concentrate on the areas you find easy first.

Marking scheme

	Marks
Statement of comprehensive income	
Revenue	½
Cost of sales	1
Distribution costs	1½
Administrative expenses	1½
Finance costs	1½
Profit from continuing operations	1
Discounted operation	2½
Other comprehensive income	1
	10½
Statement of financial position	
Property, plant and equipment	3
Inventory	½
Receivables	1½
Non-current assets held for sale	2½
Share capital	½
Share premium	½
Revaluation surplus	1½
Retained earnings	1½
Loan stock	½
Trade payables	½
Accruals	1
Overdraft	1
	14½
	25

MURDOCH CO
STATEMENT OF COMPREHENSIVE INCOME FOR THE YEAR ENDED 30 JUNE 20X9

Continuing operations

	$'000
Sales revenue	14,800
Cost of sales (W1)	(10,254)
Gross profit	4,546
Distribution costs (1,080 + 268(W2) + 190 – 120)	(1,418)
Administrative expenses (1,460 + 268(W2) + 70 – 60)	(1,738)
Finance cost (2,000 × 10% × 3/12)	(50)
Profit for the year from continuing operations	1,340
Discontinued operation	
Loss for the period from discontinued operation	(800)*
Profit for the year	540
Other comprehensive income:	
Gain on revaluation of land	1,500
Total comprehensive income for the year	2,040

*Note

	$'000
Loss on discontinued operation	500
Loss recognised on measurement to fair value less costs to sell of assets constituting discontinued operation	300
	800

MURDOCH CO
STATEMENT OF FINANCIAL POSITION AS AT 30 JUNE 20X9

	$'000	$'000
Non current assets		
Land and buildings (12,000 + 8,000 – 2,130 – 120(W2) – 1,800)		15,950
Plant and equipment (12,800 – 2,480 – 2,560(W2))		7,760
		23,710
Current assets		
Inventory	1,560	
Receivables (4,120 + 120 + 60)	4,300	
		5,860
Non-current assets classified as held for sale		1,500
		31,070
Equity		
Share capital		14,000
Share premium account		4,000
Revaluation surplus (3,000 + 1500)		4,500
Retained earnings (3,140 + 540)		3,680
		26,180
Non-current liabilities		
10% loan notes 20Y8		2,000
Current liabilities		
Payables	2,240	
Accruals (190 + 70 + 50)	310	
Bank overdraft	340	
		2,890
		31,070

Workings

1   Cost of sales

	$'000
Opening inventory	1,390
Purchases	8,280
	9,670
Closing inventories	(1,560)
	8,110
Depreciation (W2)	2,144
Cost of sales	10,254

2   Depreciation

	$'000
Buildings ((8,000 – 2,000) @ 2%)	120
Plant (12,800 @ 20%)	2,560
	2,680

80% to cost of sales: 2,144. 10% to distribution and 10% to administration: 268

29 BG (FATP 11/05/amended)

Text references. Deferred tax is covered in Chapter 14: *IAS 12 Income taxes*. Finance leases are covered in Chapter 7: *IAS 17 Leases*.

Top tips. This is a straightforward set of financial statements. Set out the proformas and then go through the workings tackling the parts that you find easy first. Part (b) is easier than it looks. Note that the first instalment is a deposit. You must be able to deal with deferred tax.

Easy marks. The statement of comprehensive income down to tax is easy marks. You should have included the reversal of the provision. The assets section of the statement of financial position should have been no problem.

144 Answers

> **Examiner's comments.** Few candidates could correctly deal with the release of the provision. Many candidates are still following the old UK format, including the dividend paid as a deduction from the statement of comprehensive income. Errors were made in calculating deferred and current tax.

Marking scheme

		Marks
(a)	**Statement of comprehensive income**	
	Revenue	½
	Cost of sales	1½
	Distribution costs	½
	Administrative expenses	½
	Reversal of provision	1
	Finance costs	½
	Taxation expenses	1½
		6
	Statement of financial position	
	Property, plant and equipment	1½
	Inventory	½
	Receivables	½
	Cash	½
	Share capital	½
	Share premium	½
	Retained earnings	1½
	Loan stock	½
	Deferred tax	1
	Trade payables	1
	Tax payable	½
		9
		15
(b)	**Redraft retained earnings**	
	Add back rental payments	2
	Deduct finance lease interest	4
	Deduct depreciation	3
	Restated retained equipment	1
		10
		25

(a) BG
STATEMENT OF COMPREHENSIVE INCOME FOR THE YEAR ENDED 30 SEPTEMBER 20X5

	$'000
Revenue	1,017
Cost of sales (W1)	(799)
Gross profit	218
Distribution costs	(61)
Administrative expenses	(239)
Reversal of provision	190
Finance costs (net) (15 – 11)	(4)
Profit before tax	104
Income tax expense (W2)	(88)
Profit for the year	16

BG
STATEMENT OF FINANCIAL POSITION AS AT 30 SEPTEMBER 20X5

	$'000	$'000
Assets		
Non-current assets		
Property, plant and equipment (W3)		232
Current assets		
Inventories	37	
Trade receivables	346	
Bank and cash	147	
		530
Total assets		762
Equity and liabilities		
Equity		
Share capital		200
Share premium		40
Retained earnings (W5)		212
		452
Non-current liabilities		
Long-term borrowings	150	
Deferred tax (50 + 15)	65	215
Current liabilities		
Trade and other payables (W4)	31	
Current tax payable	64	95
Total equity and liabilities		762

Workings

1 Cost of sales

	$'000
Cost of cleaning materials consumed	101
Direct operating expenses	548
Depreciation – equipment and fixtures (20% x 752)	150
	799

2 Income tax expense

	$'000
Tax due for year	64
Underprovision in previous year	9
Deferred tax	15
	88

3 Equipment and fittings

	$'000
Cost	752
Accumulated depreciation (370 + 150 (W1))	520
Carrying value	232

4 Trade and other payables

	$'000
Trade payables	24
Accrued bond interest (15 – 8)	7
	31

5 Retained earnings

	$'000
Opening balance at 30 September 20X4	256
Total comprehensive income for the year	16
Dividends paid	(60)
	212

(b)

	$'000
Retained earnings as stated	212
Add back rental payments (61 × 2)	122
Deduct finance lease interest (W)	(36)
Deduct depreciation (180,000 × 40%)	(72)
Retained earnings if finance lease option used	226

Working

	$
Original cost	180,000
Deposit (8,000 × 9) 1.10.X3	(72,000)
	108,000
Interest to 30.9.X4 @ 21.53%	23,252
Instalment 1.10.X4	(72,000)
	59,252
Interest to 30.9.X5 (rounded)	12,748
Instalment 1.10.X5	(72,000)
	–

30 DM (FATP 11/06/amended)

Text references. The financial statement formats are covered in Chapter 3. Finance leases are in Chapter 7: IAS 17 *Leases*.

Top tips. In the exam, you should always use your reading time wisely. Note the proformas you will need to produce and decide the best order to tackle the adjustments. In a time pressured question do the easy parts first to secure the most marks.

Easy marks. You should have been able to score good marks on tax, non-current assets and proper formats. You should know how to deal with a finance lease by this stage – it will probably crop up somewhere. But don't spend too long on it.

Examiner's comments. Very few candidates gained full marks as they were unable to correctly deal with the finance lease liability. Deferred and current tax were often wrongly calculated and the statement of changes in equity was not very well done by most candidates.

Marking scheme

	Marks
Statement of comprehensive income	
Revenue	½
Cost of sales	1½
Distribution costs	1
Administrative expenses	1
Finance costs	2
Taxation expense	1
	7
Statement of changes in equity	
Share capital	1
Share premium	1
Retained earnings	2
	1
Total	5

Statement of financial position		Marks	
Property, plant and equipment		2½	
Inventory		½	
Receivables		1	
Cash		½	
Share capital		½	
Share premium		½	
Retained earnings		½	
Loan stock		½	
Deferred Tax		1	
Trade payables		½	
Interest payable		2	
Tax payable		½	
Amounts due under finance lease		2½	13
			25

DM
STATEMENT OF COMPREHENSIVE INCOME FOR THE YEAR ENDED 30 SEPTEMBER 20X6

	$'000
Revenue	602
Cost of sales (W1)	(302)
Gross profit	300
Distribution costs (46 + 20 (W2))	(66)
Administrative expenses (91 + 9 (W2))	(100)
Finance costs (W3)	(18)
Profit before tax	116
Income tax expense (24 + 15)	(39)
Profit for the year	77

DM
STATEMENT OF CHANGES IN EQUITY FOR THE YEAR ENDED 30 SEPTEMBER 20X6

	Share capital $'000	Share Premium $'000	Retained earnings $'000	Total $'000
Balance at 1.10.20X5	200		32	232
Share issue	100	50		150
Total comprehensive income for the year			77	77
Dividend paid	–	–	(25)	(25)
Balance at 30.9.20X6	300	50	84	434

DM
STATEMENT OF FINANCIAL POSITION AS AT 30 SEPTEMBER 20X6

	$'000	$'000
Non-current assets		
Property, plant and equipment (W2)		631
Current assets		
Inventory	93	
Receivables	6	
Cash	43	
		142
Total assets		773

	$'000	$'000
LIABILITIES AND EQUITY		
Equity		
Share capital	300	
Share premium	50	
Retained earnings	84	
		434
Non-current liabilities		
Deferred tax (40 + 15)	55	
Amounts due under finance lease (W4)	66	
6% Loan	140	
		261
Current liabilities		
Payables	29	
Taxation	24	
Amounts due under finance lease (W4)	18	
Loan interest payable (W3)	7	
		78
		773

Workings

1 Cost of sales

	$'000
Opening inventory	84
Purchases	285
Depreciation (W2)	26
Closing inventory	(93)
	302

2 Non-current assets

	Land $'000	Buildings $'000	Plant $'000	Vehicles $'000	Total $'000
Cost	200	300	211	100	811
Accumulated depreciation b/f		(45)	(80)		(125)
Current year depreciation	–	(9)	(26)	(20)	(55)
Net book value	200	246	105	80	631

3 Finance costs

	$'000
Loan interest (140 × 6% × 10/12)	7
Interest on finance lease (W4)	11
	18

4 Finance lease

	$'000
Cost	100
Interest 10.92%	11
Instalment paid	(27)
Balance at 30.9.2006	84
Due within one year (27 – (84 × 10.92%))*	18
Due after one year	66
	84

* Note that because the instalments are paid *in arrears* the instalment due within one year contains interest applicable to a future period, which must be deducted from the liability.

31 DZ (FATP 5/07/amended)

> **Text references.** Chapter 3 and 5.
>
> **Top tips.** Non-current assets (tangible and intangible) figured heavily in this question and it was important to organise the material clearly. A good answer to part (a) makes part (b) much easier. But do not spend too long on part (a). Time management is vital. The best way to pass is to make a good attempt at all parts of the exam and not spend too long on certain parts of a question.
>
> **Easy marks.** There were quite a few marks available for the financial statements and any errors on non-current assets would only be penalised once, so if your workings were clear you could still have scored well.
>
> **Examiner's comments.** Very few gained full marks as they were unable to correctly prepare a property, plant and equipment note. A significant number still have problems calculating basic depreciation and dealing with development expenditure.

Marking scheme

		Marks
Property, plant and equipment		
Land	1½	
Buildings	2	
Plant	2½	
		6
Statement of comprehensive income		
Revenue	½	
Cost of sales	2½	
Distribution costs	½	
Administrative expenses	1	
Gain on disposal of land	1	
Taxation expense	½	
Other comprehensive income	2½	
		8½
Statement of changes in equity		
Share capital	½	
Retained earnings	1½	
Revaluation surplus	1½	
Total	½	
		4
Statement of financial position		
Capitalised development costs	2	
Inventory	½	
Receivables	½	
Cash	½	
Share capital	½	
Revaluation surplus	½	
Retained earnings	½	
Trade payables	½	
Accruals	½	
Tax payable	½	
		6½
		25

(a) Property, plant and equipment

Cost	Land at valuation $'000	Land at cost $'000	Buildings $'000	Plant $'000	Total $'000
Balance 1 April 20X6	1,250	3,500	7,700	4,180	16,630
Disposal	(1,250)			(620)	(1,870)
Revaluation	–	600	(2,000)	–	(1,400)
	–	4,100	5,700	3,560	13,360
Depreciation					
Balance at 1 April 20X6	–	–	1,900	2,840	4,740
Disposals	–	–	-	(600)	(600)
			1,900	2,240	4,140
Charge for year:	–	–	385 *	330**	715
			2,285	2,570	4,855
Revaluation adjustment	–	–	(2,285)	–	(2,285)
	–	–	–	2,570	2,570
Balance 31 March 20X7	–	4,100	5,700	990	10,790
Balance 31 March 20X6	1,250	3,500	5,800	1,340	11,890

* 7,700 × 5%
** 3,560 – 2,240 × 25%

Depreciation charge:

	Cost of sales	Admin
Buildings	308	77
Plant	330	
	638	

(b) DZ
STATEMENT OF COMPREHENSIVE INCOME FOR THE YEAR ENDED 31 MARCH 20X7

	$'000
Revenue	8,772
Cost of sales (W1)	(4,457)
Gross profit	4,315
Distribution costs	(462)
Administration costs (891 + 77)	(968)
Gain on disposal of land (1,500 – 1,250)	250
Profit before taxation	3,135
Income tax expense	(811)
Profit for the year	2,324
Other comprehensive income:	
Gain on property revaluation (9,800 – (11,200 – 1,900 – 385))	885
Total comprehensive income for the year	3,209

DZ
STATEMENT OF CHANGES IN EQUITY FOR THE YEAR ENDED 31 MARCH 20X7

	Share capital $'000	Retained earnings $'000	Revaluation surplus $'000	Total $'000
Balance at 1 April 20X6	1,000	4,797	2,100	7,897
Transfer to retained earnings*		750	(750)	–
Total comprehensive income for the year	–	2,324	885	3,209
Balance at 31 March 20X7	1,000	7,871	2,235	11,106

* The land which was sold had previously been revalued from $500,000 to $1,250,000. Upon sale, this revaluation gain can be recognised and so is transferred to retained earnings.

DZ
STATEMENT OF FINANCIAL POSITION AT 31 MARCH 20X7

	$'000	$'000
Non-current assets		
Capitalised development costs (W2)		198
Property, plant and equipment (see (a))		10,790
		10,988
Current assets		
Inventory	435	
Receivables	1,059	
Cash	208	
		1,702
Total assets		12,690
Equity and liabilities		
Equity		
Share capital		1,000
Revaluation surplus		2,235
Retained earnings		7,871
		11,106
Current liabilities		
Payables	748	
Accruals	25	
Tax payable	811	
		1,584
Total equity and liabilities		12,690

Workings

1   Cost of sales

	$'000
Opening inventory (240 + 132)	372
Purchases	2,020
Production labour cost	912
Production overheads	633
Depreciation	638
Research costs	119
Amortisation of development costs ((867 + 48) × 20%)	183
Loss on disposal of plant (5 - (620-600))	15
Closing inventory (165 + 270)	(435)
	4,457

2   Capitalised development costs

	$'000
Balance per trial balance	500
Deduct research costs	(119)
Less current year amortisation (W1)	(183)
Balance at 31 March 20X7	198

32 EY (FATP 11/07/amended)

Text references. Chapter 3

Top tips. You were given a lot of information to deal with here but the question was much easier than it looked. It was important to be very methodical. Start by getting down the formats, then go through the notes cross-referencing to the entries in the cash book. Remember to tackle the parts of the question that you find easiest first.

Easy marks. You had to calculate revenue and cost of sales using movement on receivables and payables, so there would have been easy marks for this. Property, plant and equipment and the construction contract were also quite straightforward.

Examiner's comments. Overall this question was reasonably well done but few gained full marks. The statement of changes in equity was not done very well by most candidates. Very few candidates showed the bonus issue, those that did usually only showed one entry under share capital. The transfer of the realised gain on disposal from revaluation surplus to retained earnings was nearly always omitted from the statement. The format of this part was often poor, with no total column and headings omitted.

Marking scheme

	Marks	
Statement of comprehensive income		
Revenue	2	
Cost of sales	1	
Profit on sale of land	1	
Distribution costs	½	
Administrative expenses	1	
Finance costs	1½	
Taxation expense	1	
		8
Statement of changes in equity		
Share capital	1½	
Retained earnings	1½	
Revaluation surplus	1½	
		4½
Statement of financial position		
Property, plant and equipment	2½	
Inventory	½	
Receivables	½	
Amount due on construction contract	3½	
Share capital	½	
Revaluation surplus	½	
Retained earnings	½	
Loan note	1	
Trade payables	½	
Interest payables	½	
Tax payable	½	
Overdraft	1	12½
		25

EY
STATEMENT OF COMPREHENSIVE INCOME FOR THE YEAR ENDED 31 OCTOBER 20X7

	$'000
Revenue (W3)	8,207
Cost of sales (W4)	(4,647)
Gross profit	3,560
Profit on sale of land (1,200 – 1,000)	200
Distribution costs	(730)
Administrative expenses (W6)	(686)
Finance costs (W8)	(173)
Profit before tax	2,171
Taxation (W7)	(440)
Profit for the year	1,731

EY
STATEMENT OF CHANGES IN EQUITY FOR THE YEAR ENDED 31 OCTOBER 20X7

	Share capital $'000	Retained earnings $'000	Revaluation surplus $'000	Total $'000
Balance 1 November 20X6	3,000	825	600	4,425
Bonus issue (1 / 6)	500	(500)		
Realisation of revaluation surplus on land (1,000 – 600)		400	(400)	
Total comprehensive income for the year		1,731		1,731
Balance 31 October 20X7	3,500	2,456	200	6,156

EY
STATEMENT OF FINANCIAL POSITION AT 31 OCTOBER 20X7

	$'000
Non current assets	
Property, plant and equipment (W2)	7,729
Current assets	
Inventory	985
Trade receivables	620
Amount due on construction contract (W1)	840
Cash and cash equivalents	2,142
	4,587
Total assets	12,316
Equity and liabilities	
Equity	
Share capital	3,500
Revaluation surplus	200
Retained earnings	2,456
	6,156
Non-current liabilities	
Loan notes (2,260 + 2,500)	4,760
Deferred tax	180
	4,940
Current liabilities	
Trade payables	670
Interest payable	130
Tax payable	420
	1,220
Total equity and liabilities	12,316

Workings

1 Construction contract

	$'000
Total value	1,400
Costs to date	(600)
Costs to complete	(400)
Expected profit	400

Costs incurred to date are 60% of total. Amounts recognised are:

Revenue (1,400 × 60%)	840
Cost of sales (1,000 × 60%)	(600)
Attributable profit	240

Gross amount due from customers:

Costs to date	600
Attributable profit	240
	840

2 Property, plant and equipment

	Land $'000	Premises $'000	Plant $'000	Total $'000
Cost				
B/f 1 November 20X6	2,000	1,500	3,800	7,300
Additions	–	1,600	1,860	3,460
Disposal	(1,000)	–	–	(1,000)
Balance at 31 October 20X7	1,000	3,100	5,660	9,760
Accumulated depreciation				
B/f 1 November 20X6		350	760	1,110
Charge for year: (3,100 x 6%)		186		186
(5,660 – 760) x 15%		–	735	735
		536	1,495	2,031
Carrying value	1,000	2,564	4,165	7,729

Note that the excess of the land disposal proceeds over the carrying value ($200,000) will be recognised as profit in the year. The balance held in revaluation surplus ($400,000) can now be treated as realised and so is transferred to retained earnings.

3 Revenue

	$'000
Cash received from customers	7,500
Opening receivables	(753)
Closing receivables	620
Revenue recognised on construction contract (W1)	840
	8,207

4 Cost of sales

	$'000
Opening inventory	1,200
Purchases (W6)	3,097
Closing inventory	(985)
Plant depreciation (W3)	735
Cost of sales – construction contract (W1)	600
	4,647

5 Purchases

Payments to suppliers	3,000
Opening payables	(573)
Closing payables	670
	3,097

6 Administrative expenses

	$'000
Per cash book	500
Premises depreciation (W3)	186
	686

7 Income tax charge

Prior year underprovision (690 – 670)	20
Charge for year	420
Income statement charge	440

8 Finance cost

Interest paid during the year	160
Less balance due at 31.10.X6	(117)
Outstanding at 31.10.X7	130
Charge for year	173

33 FZ (FATP 5/08/amended)

> **Text references.** Assets held for sale are dealt with in Chapter 4: *Reporting financial performance*. Provisions are covered in Chapter 9: *Miscellaneous standards*.
>
> **Top tips.** In this question it is important to recognise that you are required to present financial statements under IFRS 5 *Non-current assets held for sale and discontinued operations*. Always read the question carefully so that you do not miss anything important. Make sure you know how to show discontinued operations in the statement of comprehensive income.
>
> **Easy marks.** Write out the proforma statement of comprehensive income and statement of financial position and slot in figures from the trial balance for some easy marks.
>
> **Examiner's comments.** A disappointing number of candidates were unable to correctly identify the sale of shops as a discontinued operation. Most candidates that correctly identified the discontinued operation did not apply their answer in part (a) to their workings in part (b).
>
> A disappointing number of candidates wanted to create a provision for the reorganisation package, even though the items constituting the package were all disallowed by IAS 37.
>
> Very few students provided for a discontinued operation in calculating the profit for the year.

Marking scheme

			Marks
(a)		1	
	Newsagents' shops	3	
	Reorganisation costs	2	
			5
(b)	**Statement of comprehensive income**		
	Revenue	½	
	Cost of sales	1½	
	Distribution costs	2	
	Administrative expenses	1	
	Finance costs	1½	
	Income tax expense	1	
	Loss from discontinued operation	2	
			9½
	Statement of financial position		
	Property, plant and equipment	2	
	Trade receivables	1	
	Non-current assets held for sale	1½	
	Inventory	½	
	Cash and cash equivalents	½	
	Share capital	½	
	Share premium	½	
	Revaluation surplus	½	
	Retained earnings	½	
	5% loan notes	½	
	Deferred tax	½	
	Trade payables	½	
	Tax payable	½	
	Interest payable	1	
			10½
	Total		25

(a) (i) The newsagents' shops meet the criteria of an **asset held for sale** under IFRS 5 *Non-current assets held for sale and discontinued operations*.

- The shops are available for immediate sale in their present condition.
- The sale is highly probable.

Non-current assets held for sale should be **measured at the lower of carrying amount and fair value less costs to sell**. For the newsagents' shops this is the $5,000,000 fair value less $200,000 selling costs or $4,800,000. The carrying amount is the higher amount of $5,260,000.

Under IFRS 5, an **impairment loss** should be recognised when fair value less costs to sell is lower than carrying amount. Thus, the difference between the carrying amount and the fair value less costs to sell of $460,000 should be written off, with $300,000 being allocated to goodwill and the remaining $160,000 to the newsagents' shops.

The newsagents' shops should be **presented separately** from other assets in the balance sheet under the heading 'non-current assets classified as held for sale'. A single amount should be presented on the face of the statement of comprehensive income as 'loss for the year from discontinued operation'. This amount should be the total of:

- The post-tax profit or loss of discontinued operations and
- The post-tax gain or loss recognised on the measurement to fair value less costs to sell.

(ii) IAS 37 Provisions, contingent liabilities and contingent assets deals with the accounting treatment necessary for this item.

When a **restructuring** involves a sale of an operation, as is the case with the newsagents' shops, IAS 37 states that no obligation arises until the entity has entered into a binding sale agreement. Since at year-end the sale of the shops had not been concluded, a provision cannot be made.

It is worth noting that even if the sale was binding at year-end, a provision would still be prohibited under IAS 37. This is because staff retraining, staff relocation and development of new computer systems are **specifically excluded**.

(b) FZ: STATEMENT OF COMPREHENSIVE INCOME FOR THE YEAR ENDED 31 MARCH 20X8

Continuing operations

	$'000
Revenue (10,170 – 772)	9,398
Cost of sales (W1)	(4,363)
Gross profit	5,035
Distribution costs (W3)	(384)
Administrative expenses (W5)	(406)
Profit from operations	4,245
Finance cost (1,000 × 5%)	(50)
Profit before tax	4,195
Income tax expense (W6)	(1,080)
Profit for the year from continuing operations	3,115

Discontinued operation

Loss for the year from discontinued operation (W7)	(301)
Profit for the year	2,814

FZ
STATEMENT OF FINANCIAL POSITION AT 31 MARCH 20X8

	$'000	$000
Assets		
Non-current assets		
Property, plant and equipment (W8)		11,516
Current assets		
Inventory	900	
Trade receivables (929 – 62)	867	
Cash and cash equivalents	853	
		2,620
Non-current assets classified as held for sale		4,800
Total assets		18,936

	$'000	$'000
Equity and liabilities		
Equity		
Share capital (4,000 + 1,000)	5,000	
Share premium account (2,500 + 500)	3,000	
Revaluation surplus	190	
Retained earnings (5,808 + 2,814 – 500)	8,122	
		16,312
Non-current liabilities		
5% Loan notes		1,000
Deferred tax		237
Current liabilities		
Trade payables	417	
Tax payable	920	
Interest payable	50	
		1,387
Total equity and liabilities		18,936

Workings

1   Cost of sales continuing operations

	$'000
Cost of goods sold (4,120 – 580)	3,540
Depreciation (W2)	823
Cost of sales	4,363

2   Depreciation continuing operations

	$'000
Factory buildings (12,000 × 3%)	360
Plant and equipment (2,313 × 20%)	463
Depreciation	823

3   Distribution costs continuing operations

	$'000
Distribution costs (432 – 57)	375
Vehicles depreciation ((147 – 67 – 57 + 52) × 25%)	19
Gain on disposal vehicles (W4)	(10)
	384

4   Gain on disposal

	$'000
Disposed vehicle cost	(57)
Disposed vehicle depreciation	52
Cash received	15
Gain on disposal	10

5   Administrative expenses continuing operations

	$'000
Administrative expenses (440 – 96)	344
Bad debt from customer X	62
Administrative expenses	406

6   Income tax expense continuing operations

	$'000
Taxation due for year (920 + 120)	1,040
Increase in deferred tax provision (237 – 197)	40
Income tax expense	1,080

7   Loss for the year on discontinued operation

	$'000
Revenue	772
Cost of sales	(580)
Impairment of goodwill	(300)
Impairment of shops	(160)
Administrative expenses	(96)
Distribution costs	(57)
Tax credit	120
Loss for the year	(301)

Note that IFRS 5 allows the analysis of the discontinued operation to be provided in the statement of comprehensive income rather than in the notes. The answer did not take this approach as note (k) of the question stated that FZ wants to disclose the minimum information allowed by IFRSs.

8   Property, plant and equipment

	Buildings $'000	Plant and equipment $'000	Vehicles $'000	Total $'000
Cost (147 – 57)	12,000	2,313	147	14,460
Disposal			(57)	(57)
Accumulated depreciation b/f	(720)	(1,310)	(67)	(2,097)
Depreciation disposal			52	52
Depreciation charge for the year	(360)	(463)	(19)	(842)
Carrying value	10,920	540	56	11,516

34 GZ (FATP 11/08/amended)

Text references. Chapter 3, 5, 7 and 9.

Top tips. Write out your proformas first making sure you space these out. Next, slot the trial balance figures which are unaffected by any adjustments into your proforma. Then tackle the information in the order you find easiest to complete the requirements.

Examiner's comments. Few candidates realised that the question included a discontinued activity so there were few answers with discontinued activities correctly treated in the statement of comprehensive income or the non-current assets held for sale correctly treated in the statement of financial position.

Common mistakes made by candidates were:

- not including leased plant as a non-current asset
- not treating the government licence as an intangible non-current asset. Most candidates charged it as an expense during the year.
- not grouping the discontinued activities together as an item in the income statement

Marking scheme

	Marks
Property, plant and equipment	
Mine property	3
Plant	2
Leased plant	1
	6

Answers   159

Statement of comprehensive income				Marks	
Revenue				½	
Cost of sales				2	
Investment income				½	
Distribution costs				½	
Administrative expenses				½	
Finance costs				1	
Taxation expense				1½	
Loss from discounted operations				2	
					8½

Statement of changes in equity
Share capital   1
Retained earnings   1
              2

Statement of financial position

Intangible assets	1
Inventory	½
Receivables	½
Cash	½
Non-current asset held	1½
Deferred Tax	½
Provision	1
Trade payables	½
Tax payable	½
Amounts due under finance lease	2

                8½
                25

(a) Plant and equipment

	Mine property $'000	Plant $'000	Leased plant $'000	Total $'000
Cost				
Balance at 1 November 20X7	6,719	3,025	0	9,744
Leased plant			900	900
Disposal		(200)		(200)
Decommissioning costs	3,230			3,230
Transfer to non-current assets held for sale	(2,623)			(2,623)
	7,326	2,825	900	11,051
Depreciation				
Balance at 1 November 20X7	2,123	370	0	2,493
Disposal		(195)		(195)
Transfer to non-current assets held for sale	(2,123)			(2,123)
Charge for year (W2)	366	663	225	1,254
	366	838	225	1,429
Carrying value 31 October 20X8	6,960	1,987	675	9,622

(b) GZ
STATEMENT OF COMPREHENSIVE INCOME FOR THE PERIOD ENDING 31 OCTOBER 20X8

	$'000
Revenue	9,600
Cost of sales (W3)	(6,504)
Gross profit	3,096
Investment income	218
Distribution costs	(719)
Administrative expenses	(1,131)
Profit from operations	1,464
Finance cost	(55)
Profit before tax	1,409
Income tax expense (W5)	(328)
Profit for the year from continuing operations	1,081
Loss for the year from discontinued operations (W9)	(68)
Profit for the year	1,013

GZ
STATEMENT OF CHANGES IN EQUITY FOR THE PERIOD ENDED 31 OCTOBER 20X8

	Share capital $'000	Share premium $'000	Retained earnings $'000	Total $'000
Balance at 1 Nov 20X7	5,000	0	1,790	6,790
Total comprehensive income for the period			1,013	1,013
Dividends			(550)	(550)
Issue of share capital (W6)	1,400	420		,820
Balance at 31 Oct 20X8	6,400	420	2,253	9,073

GZ
STATEMENT OF FINANCIAL POSITION AT 31 OCTOBER 20X8

	$'000	$000
Assets		
Non-current assets		
Property, plant and equipment (see a)		9,622
Intangible assets (W7)		95
		9,717
Current assets		
Inventory	2,410	
Trade receivables	2,715	
Cash and cash equivalents	1,240	
Non-current assets classified as held for sale (W1)	493	
		6,858
Total assets		16,575
Equity and liabilities		
Equity		
Share capital (W6)		6,400
Share premium account (W6)		420
Retained earnings		2,253
		9,073
Non-current liabilities		
Deferred tax (731-60)	671	
Finance lease (W4)	682	
Provision (W8)	3,230	
		4,583
Current liabilities		
Trade payables	2,431	
Tax payable	375	
Finance lease (W4)	113	
		2,919
Total equity and liabilities		16,575

Workings

1 Non-current asset held for sale

	$'000
Carrying amount	500
Fair value less costs to sell (520-27)	(493)
Loss on revaluation	7

2 Depreciation

	$'000
Mines (7,326 × 5%)	366
Property, plant and equipment (2,825 – 370 + 195) × 25%	663
Leased plant (900 × 25%)	225
	1,254

3 Cost of sales

	$'000
Per trial balance	5,245
Amortisation operating licence (100/20)	5
Depreciation (W2)	1,254
	6,504

4 Finance lease

	$'000
Total lease payments (7 × 160)	1,120
Fair value of asset	(900)
Total finance charge	220

Using sum of digits method:

31.10.X8   220 × 7/28 = 55 (finance charge)

	$'000
1 November 20X7	900
Finance charge	55
Payment	(160)
Balance at 31 October 20X8	795
Finance charge	47
Payment	(160)
Balance at 31 October 20X9	682

	$'000
Due within one year (795 – 682)	113
Due after one year	682
	795

5 Income tax expense

	$'000
Per trial balance	13
Reduction in deferred tax provision	(60)
Charge for year	375
	328

6 Share issue

	$'000
Share capital (1,400 x 1)	1,400
Share premium ((1,400 x 1.3) -1400)	420
	1,820

Share capital after issue = 5,000 + 1,400 = 6,400

7   Intangible assets

	$'000
Licence	100
Amortisation – (100/20)	(5)
Total	95

8   Provision

	$'000
As per trial balance	950
Gold mine closed	(950)
Decommissioning costs	3,230
	3,230

9   Discontinued operation

	$'000
Decommissioning expenditure	1,008
Less provision	(950)
	58
Loss on non-current asset held for sale (W1)	7
Loss on disposal of non-current asset (5 – 2)	3
Loss on discontinued operation	68

35 Objective test answers: Group financial statements

1   D

	$'000
Fair value of net assets acquired:	
Ordinary shares	400
Retained earnings at 1 January 20X7	100
Retained for 9 months to acquisition date (80 × 9/12)	60
	560
Add goodwill	30
	590

2   D

	$
Consolidated retained earnings	560,000
Less Mercedes plc	(450,000)
Add back unrealised profit (50,000 × 25/125)	10,000
	120,000

3   C

	$
Cost of investment	50,000
Share of post-acquisition retained earnings (20 × 35%)	7,000
Less dividend received (10 × 35%)	(3,500)
Less impairment	(6,000)
	47,500

4   B

	$'000
Profit on sale (160,000/4)	40,000
Unrealised profit (40,000 × 25%)	10,000
Group share (10,000 × 30%)	3,000

Answers 163

5 A

	Colossal plc $	Enormous Ltd $
Retained earnings per question	275,000	177,000
Less pre-acquisition		(156,000)
Depreciation on FV adjustment (20,000/4)		(5,000)
		16,000
Goodwill impairment (W)	(12,000)	
Enormous Ltd	16,000	
Group retained earnings	279,000	

Working

	$	$
Consideration transferred		300,000
Share capital	100,000	
Retained earnings	156,000	
Fair value adjustment	20,000	
		(276,000)
Goodwill at acquisition		24,000
Impairment (50%)		12,000

6 C

	$
Consideration transferred	120,000
Share of post-acquisition retained earnings ((140 – 80) × 40%)	24,000
Unrealised profit (30,000 × 25% × 40%)	(3,000)
	141,000

7 C

	$	$
Consideration transferred		210,000
Net assets acquired:		
Share capital	100,000	
Retained earnings	90,000	
		(190,000)
Goodwill at acquisition		20,000
Impairment		(10,000)
Goodwill at 31 December 20X9		10,000

8 A

	$
A – Retained earnings	210,000
B – Post-acquisition retained earnings (160,000 – 90,000)	70,000
Goodwill impairment	(10,000)
Group retained earnings	270,000

9 B

	$	$
Consideration transferred		350,000
Net assets acquired:		
Share capital	140,000	
Share premium	50,000	
Retained earnings	60,000	
		(250,000)
Goodwill at 31 December 20X9		100,000

10 A $140,000 + $80,000 + $40,000 = $260,000

＃ 36 Goose and Gander

Text reference. Consolidated financial statements are covered in Chapters 13-16.

Top tips. Don't forget **Part (b)**. There are five marks here for explaining the purpose of consolidated financial statements. Do it first, before getting tied up with Part (a).

(a) GOOSE GROUP

DRAFT CONSOLIDATED STATEMENT OF COMPREHENSIVE INCOME
FOR THE YEAR ENDED 31 DECEMBER 20X8

	$'000
Revenue (5,000 + 1,000 − 100)	5,900
Cost of sales (2,900 + 600 − 80)	3,420
Gross profit	2,480
Other expenses (1,700 + 320)	2,020
Net profit	460
Tax (130 + 25)	155
Profit for the year	305
Other comprehensive income:	
Gain on property revaluation	100
Total comprehensive income	405

DRAFT CONSOLIDATED STATEMENT OF FINANCIAL POSITION AS AT 31 DECEMBER 20X8

	$'000	$'000
Non-current assets		
Property, plant and equipment (2,000 + 200 + 100)	2,300	
Goodwill (W2)	155	
		2,455
Current assets		
Inventory (500 + 120 + 80)	700	
Trade receivables (650 − 100 + 40)	590	
Bank and cash (390 + 35)	425	
		1,715
		4,170
Equity and liabilities		
Share capital (500 + 80)		580
Share premium (1500 + 360)		1,860
Revaluation surplus (50 + 100)		150
Retained earnings (W5)		345
		2,935
Current liabilities		
Trade payables (1,010 + 70)	1,080	
Tax (130 + 25)	155	
		1,235
Total equity and liabilities		4,170

Workings

1 Group structure

```
Goose
  │
  │  100%, 1 Jan 20X8
  │
Gander
```

2   *Investment in Gander*

		$
Share capital	100,000 x 4/5 x 1 =	80,000
Share premium	100,000 x 4/5 x 4.5 =	360,000
		440,000

3   *Goodwill*

	$
Consideration paid	440,000
Less net assets acquired:	
Retained earnings	(185,000)
Share capital	(100,000)
	155,000

4   *Unrealised profit*

	$
Sale price	100,000
Cost price	(80,000)
Unrealised profit	20,000

Dr retained earnings, Cr group inventory

5   *Group retained earnings*

	Goose $	Gander $	Total $
Per individual statements	350,000	200,000	
Less pre-acquisition reserves	–	(185,000)	
	350,000	15,000	365,000
Less unrealised profit			(20,000)
			345,000

(b)   *Usefulness of consolidated financial statements*

The main reason for preparing consolidated accounts is that groups operate as a single economic unit, and it is not possible to understand the affairs of the parent company without taking into account the financial position and performance of all the companies that it controls. The directors of the parent company should be held fully accountable for all the money they have invested on their shareholders behalf, whether that has been done directly by the parent or via a subsidiary.

There are also practical reasons why parent company accounts cannot show the full picture. The parent company's own financial statements only show the original cost of the investment and the dividends received from the subsidiary. As explained below, this hides the true value and nature of the investment in the subsidiary, and, without consolidation, could be used to manipulate the reported results of the parent.

- The cost of the investment will include a premium for goodwill, but this is only quantified and reported if consolidated accounts are prepared.
- Without consolidation, the assets and liabilities of the subsidiary are disguised.
    - A subsidiary could be very highly geared, making its liquidity and profitability volatile.
    - A subsidiary's assets might consist of intangible assets, or other assets with highly subjective values.
- The parent company controls the dividend policy of the subsidiary, enabling it to smooth out profit fluctuations with a steady dividend. Consolidation reveals the underlying profits of the group.
- Over time the net assets of the subsidiary should increase, but the cost of the investment will stay fixed and will soon bear no relation to the true value of the subsidiary.

37 Parsley

Text references. Consolidated financial statements are covered in Chapters 13-16.

Top tips. Points to watch in this question are:

(a) Correct consolidation technique – not proportionate consolidation
(b) Elimination of intra-group transactions
(c) Adjustments to inventory, receivables and cash

(a) <u>Goodwill arising on acquisition of Sage</u>

	$'000	$'000
Consideration transferred		30,000
Net assets acquired:		
Share capital	25,000	
Retained earnings	2,000	
		27,000
Goodwill		3,000

(b) (i) PARSLEY
CONSOLIDATED STATEMENT OF COMPREHENSIVE INCOME
FOR THE YEAR ENDED 31 DECEMBER 20X9

	$'000
Revenue (135m + 74m – 12m)	197,000
Cost of sales (W1)	(89,000)
Gross profit	108,000
Distribution costs	(13,700)
Administrative expenses	(26,784)
Impairment of goodwill (3,000 – 2,250)	(750)
Finance charges (W2)	(12)
Profit before taxation	66,754
Taxation	(19,000)
Profit for the year	47,754

(ii) PARSLEY
CONSOLIDATED STATEMENT OF FINANCIAL POSITION AS AT 31 DECEMBER 20X9

	$'000	$'000
Non-current assets		
Intangible: goodwill		2,250
Property, plant and equipment (net book value):		
$(74,000,000 + 39,050,000)		113,050
		115,300
Current assets		
Inventory (10,630,000 + 4,498,000 – 1,000,000 (W1))	14,128	
Receivables (W3)	20,886	
Bank	14,744	
		49,758
		165,058
Equity and liabilities		
Share capital		80,000
Retained earnings (W5)		48,790
		128,790
	$'000	$'000
Current liabilities		
Payables (W4)	6,118	
Taxation	18,000	
Dividends: Parsley	12,000	
		36,118
Non-current liabilities		
8% loan notes		150
		165,058

Workings

1   Cost of sales

		$'000
Parsley		70,000
Sage		30,000
		100,000
Less intra-group		(12,000)
		88,000
Add back unrealised profit in inventory $(12m – 8m) \times 25\%$		1,000
		89,000

2   Finance charges

	$'000
Per question – Sage	16
Less loan interest payable to Parsley: $50,000 \times 8\%$	(4)
	12

3   Receivables

	$'000	$'000
Parsley		18,460
Sage		12,230
Dividends	8,000	
Loan interest	4	
Intra-group	1,800	
		(9,804)
		20,886

4   Payables

	$'000	$'000
Parsley		6,000
Sage		1,922
Loan interest (W2)	4	
Intra-group	1,800	
		(1,804)
		6,118

5   Retained earnings

	Parsley $'000	Sage $'000
Per question	37,540	15,000
Less provision for unrealised profit (W1)	(1,000)	
Pre-acquisition		(2,000)
		13,000
Goodwill impairment (W6)	(750)	
	35,790	
Share of Sage	13,000	
	48,790	

6   Impairment of goodwill

	$'000
Goodwill at acquisition (part (a))	3,000
Goodwill at 31 December 20X9	2,250
Impairment	750

(c) The purpose of consolidated accounts is to present the financial position of connected companies as that of a **single entity, the group**. This means that, **in the consolidated statement of financial position, the only profits recognised should be those earned by the group in providing services to outsiders.** Similarly, **inventory should be valued at the cost to the group.**

When a company sells goods to another company in the same group, it will recognised revenue and profit in its own books. However, **from the point of view of the group, no sale has taken place**, because the goods have not been sold outside the group. The sale must therefore be eliminated from revenue and **the unrealised profit** (that is profit on inventory not sold outside the group) **must be eliminated from inventory.**

38 Molecule

Text references. The consolidated statement of financial position is covered in Chapter 14. Associates are covered in Chapter 16.

Top Tips. Note that you are specifically asked for a working for retained earnings. The adjustments for intra-group trading may be on the face of the consolidated statement of financial position or in a separate working.

(a) Calculation of goodwill on the acquisition of Atom

	$'000	$'000
Consideration transferred		4,545
Share of net assets acquired		
Share capital	4,000	
Retained earnings	60	
		4,060
Goodwill		485

Note. Goodwill is fully written off and will not appear in the statement of financial position. The impairment will be deducted from retained earnings.

(b) MOLECULE GROUP
CONSOLIDATED STATEMENT OF FINANCIAL POSITION
AS AT 31 OCTOBER 20X7

	$'000	$'000
Non-current assets		
Property, plant and equipment (3,000 + 3,300)		6,300
Investment in associate (W4)		790
Current assets		
Inventory (1,500 + 800 – 20 (W3))	2,280	
Receivables (1,800 + 750 – 30 – 450)	2,070	
Bank (600 + 350)	950	
		5,300
		12,390
Equity and liabilities		
Equity		
$1 Ordinary shares		9,000
Retained earnings (W2)		500
		9,500
Current liabilities		
Payables (1,220 + 200 – 30)	1,390	
Tax (700 + 800)	1,500	
		2,890
Total equity and liabilities		12,390

Workings

1   *Group structure*

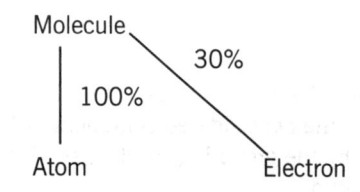

```
        Molecule
       /      \
   100%        30%
     /          \
   Atom       Electron
```

2   *Unrealised profit on intra-group sale*

Profit on intra-group sale is $240,000 \times \dfrac{20}{120} = \$40,000$

∴ Unrealised profit is $40,000 \times 50\% = \$20,000$

Dr retained earnings, Cr group inventory

3   *Investment in associate*

	$'000
Cost of investment	800
Share of post-acquisition retained earnings ((600-300) x 30%)	90
Less impairment	(100)
	790

4   *Retained earnings*

	Molecule $'000	Atom $'000	Electron $'000
Per question	1,325	200	600
Unrealised profit (W3)	(20)		
Less pre-acquisition		(60)	(300)
		140	300
Impairment of goodwill/investment in associate (485+100)	(585)		
Correction of error (write off of receivable from prior year)	(450)		
Atom	140		
Electron (300 x 30%)	90		
	500		

(c) **Significant influence** can usually be determined by the holding of **voting rights** in the entity, generally in the form of shares.

Significant influence may take various forms:

(i)   Participation in the policy making process
(ii) Material transactions between investee and investor
(iii) Board representation
(iv) Provision of technical advice
(v)   An interchange of personnel between the companies

39 Tom, Dick and Harry

Text references. The consolidated statement of financial position is covered in Chapter 14. Associates are covered in Chapter 16.

Top tips. Calculating the goodwill value in part (a) is tricky, however, you should be able to explain the treatment of negative goodwill under IFRS 3 to gain some easy marks. Watch out for the extra depreciation charge created when the fair value exceeds the book value of non-current assets. In this question you have been given the extra depreciation charge, but in your exam you might be asked to calculate it. Remember that to calculate the extra depreciation charge, you need to divide the fair value adjustment by the remaining useful life.

In part (b), don't forget to set out your proforma and insert the easy numbers first.

(a) (i) *Goodwill on acquisition of Dick*

	$
Consideration paid	200,000
Less net assets acquired represented by:	
Share capital	(100,000)
Retained earnings	(90,000)
Plus fair value adjustment	(50,000)
	(240,000)
Goodwill	(40,000)

170 Answers

(ii) *Treatment of negative goodwill under IFRS 3*

The goodwill calculated is negative which means that the aggregate value of the net assets acquired may exceed what the parent company paid for them. Under IFRS 3, this is referred to as a 'bargain purchase'. In this situation, IFRS 3 requires that:

(a) The Tom Group should first re-assess the amounts at which it has measured both the cost of the combination and the acquired net assets. This is to identify any errors in the calculation and to check that a 'bargain purchase' really has occurred.

(b) Any negative goodwill remaining after this exercise should be recognised immediately in profit or loss.

(b) TOM GROUP
CONSOLIDATED STATEMENT OF FINANCIAL POSITION AS AT 31 OCTOBER 20X1

	$'000	$'000
Non-current assets		
Property, plant and equipment (W2)		373
Investment in associate (W5)		117
		490
Current assets		
Inventory (100 + 70 – 2 (W3))	168	
Receivables (170 + 40)	210	
Bank (190 + 30)	220	
		598
		1,088
Equity and liabilities		
Share capital		500
Retained earnings (W6)		448
		948
Current liabilities (110 + 30)		140
		1,088

Workings

1 *Group structure*

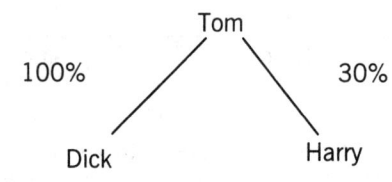

```
            Tom
      100% /   \ 30%
          /     \
        Dick   Harry
```

2 *Property, plant and equipment*

	$
Tom	205,000
Dick	120,000
Fair value adjustment	50,000
Depreciation adjustment	(2,000)
	373,000

3 *Unrealised Profit*

Total profit – 25,000/5 = 5,000

Profit on goods left in stock = 5,000 x 40% = 2,000

DR Retained earnings, CR Group inventory

4   *Investment in associate*

	$'000
Cost of investment	115
Share post-acquisition reserve ((60-50) x 30%)	3
Share of post-acquisition retained earnings ((90-80) x 30%)	3
Impairment	(4)
	117

5   *Retained earnings*

	Tom	Dick	Harry
Per individual statements	370	130	150
Less pre-acquisition		(90)	(130)
		40	20
Unrealised profit (W2)	(2)		
Negative goodwill (part (a))	40		
Depreciation adjustment	(2)		
Impairment of investment in associate	(4)		
Dick 40 x 100%	40		
Harry 20 x 30%	6		
	448		

40 Objective test answers: General principles of taxation

1   (a)   Tax is deducted at source, so non-payment is not an issue
    (b)   The costs of collection are borne by employers
    (c)   The funds are received at the same time each month, which helps financial planning

2   C   The company acts as a tax collector on behalf of the tax authority. Therefore any tax deducted is put in a payable account until the money is actually paid to the tax authority. The balance on the payable account represents the amount collected but not yet paid over.

3   B   The tax authorities do not have the power to detain company officials. Their powers relate to documents and information (eg information held on computer).

4   Direct taxation is charged directly on the **person** or **entity** that is intended to pay the tax.

5   Accounting profit + disallowable expenditure – non-taxable income – tax allowable expenditure = taxable profit

6   C   Equity

7   Tax evasion is manipulation of the tax system by illegal means to avoid paying taxes.

8   • Domestic legislation and legal decisions
        • Tax authority practice
        • International treaties
        • Supranational bodies

9   C   Tax deducted at source before payment of interest or dividends.

10 B   The person or entity that finally bears the cost of the tax.

11   The tax authority within whose area an entity is resident.

12 A   Power of arrest

13 C   Effective incidence

14 A   A progressive tax

15   Any three of the following:

    (1)   To give a date from which penalties and/or interest can accrue
    (2)   To get funds in as quickly as possible for use by central government
    (3)   To reduce backlogs and extra work for the tax department
    (4)   To prevent entities deducting tax at source, eg employers collecting payroll tax, from spending it before it reaches the tax authority

172 Answers

16 A An example of hypothecation is the 'congestion charge' levied on London motorists that can only be spent on London transport.

17 (a) Under group loss relief, it is possible to set the losses of a group member against the profits of another group member. If the profit-making group member pays tax at a higher rate than the one making the loss, the total tax liability of the group for the year can be reduced.

(b) Claiming group loss relief can help improve group cash flows as the loss is relieved more quickly.

18 **Equity**: the tax burden should be fairly distributed

Efficiency: tax should be easy and cheap to collect

Economic effects: the government must consider the effect of taxation policy on various sectors of the economy

19 A

20 A Formal incidence

21 A The classical system

	$'000
Company income tax (400,000 × 25%)	100
Personal income tax (250,000 × 30%)	75
	175

22 C Naturally, tax authorities like to minimise the tax gap.

41 Objective test answers: International tax

1 D The head office is located, and all board meetings take place in, the Cayman Islands. Therefore the place of management is in the Cayman Islands.

2 C International tax treaties (eg double taxation treaties) are a source of tax rules.

The other options are all sources of accounting rules.

3 The EU issues rules on sales taxes, which must be applied by all member states.

4 It is called the schedular system.

5
- Interest payments
- Dividends
- Royalties
- Capital gains accruing to non-residents

6
- Full deduction
- Exemption
- Credit

7 B Double taxable treaties deal with **overseas** income.

8 B A place of management, a workshop, a quarry

9 D The country where most of the entity's products are sold.

10 B

	$
50,000 × 12%	6,000
Less already paid	(5,000)
Balance due:	1,000

11 B Corporate income tax is due on all profits of the branch, not just those remitted.

12 C EA will be deemed resident in Country C, which is its place of management.

13 D A construction project is only a permanent establishment if it lasts more than 12 months.

14 Net assets and consumption

15 C Under the OECD model, an entity is considered to have residence in the country in which it has a permanent establishment, which includes a place of management.

16 $20,000

	$
Net dividend	90,000
Withholding tax	10,000
Gross dividend	100,000

Underlying tax (100,000 × 200,000/1,000,000) $20,000

42 Objective test answers: Indirect taxes

1 A suitable commodity would have the following characteristics:

- A limited number of large producers
- Products that are easily defined
- A commodity produced in large volume

2 C Sales tax is an indirect tax, all the others are direct taxes.

3 B As long as they are registered for sales tax, options A, C and D merely act as tax collectors, it is the end consumer who suffers the tax.

4

			$
DA	Input tax (200 × 15%)		(30)
	Output tax (500 × 15%)		75
	Total due		45
DB	Input tax		(75)
	Output tax (1,000 × 15%)		150
	Total due		75
	Total		120

5

	$
Sale by DA (500 × 7%)	35
Sale by DB (1,000 × 7%)	70
Total paid	105

6 D Sales taxes such as VAT are indirect

7 B $1,450

	$
VAT output tax (200 × 50 × 15%)	1,500
VAT input tax (200 × 35 × 15%)	(1,050)
VAT payable	450
Excise duty payable (200 × 5)	1,000
Total payable	1,450

8 Amount paid = $14,000

	$
Output VAT 120,000 × 20%	24,000
Input VAT 100,000 × 10%	(10,000)
Amount paid	14,000

9

		$			$
CU:	Output tax	37.5	CZ:	Output tax	90.0
	Input tax	(15.0)		Input tax	(37.5)
	Payable	22.5		Payable	52.5

10 VAT paid $15,000

Gross profit $100,000

	$
Output VAT (183,000 × 22/122)	33,000
Input VAT (138,000 × 15/115)	(18,000)
Amount paid	15,000
Revenue (183,000 × 100/122) + 70,000	220,000
Cost of sales (138,000 × 100/115)	(120,000)
Gross profit	100,000

11 C $5,550

Workings	$
Cost	14,000
Excise duty	3,000
	17,000
VAT @ 15%	2,550
	19,550

Taxes paid = $3,000 + $2,500 = $5,550

12

	$'000
Output tax (18,400 × 15/115)	2,400
Input tax (10,000 + 4,000 × 15%)	(2,100)
VAT due from FE	300

Note that VAT is deductible on purchases relating to zero-rated outputs, but not on purchases relating to exempt outputs

43 Objective test answers: Company taxation

1   B

	$	$
Accounting profit		350,000
Add: depreciation	30,000	
disallowed expenses	15,000	
		45,000
		395,000
Less: non-taxable income	25,000	
tax allowable depreciation	32,000	
		(57,000)
Taxable profit		338,000

2   D

	$	$
Taxable profit		350,000
Less: depreciation	30,000	
disallowed expenses	15,000	
		(45,000)
		305,000
Add: non-taxable income	25,000	
tax allowable depreciation	32,000	
		57,000
Accounting profit		362,000

3 A

	$	$
Accounting loss		(350,000)
Add: depreciation	30,000	
disallowed expenses	400,000	
		430,000
		80,000
Less: non-taxable income	25,000	
tax allowable depreciation	32,000	
		(57,000)
Taxable profit		23,000

4 B

	$m	$m
Taxable profit		50
Less: depreciation	15	
disallowed expenses	1	
		(16)
		34
Add: non-taxable income	3	
tax allowable depreciation	4	
		7
Accounting profit		41

5 D

	$	$
Accounting profit		250,000
Add: depreciation	45,000	
disallowed expenses	20,000	
		65,000
		315,000
Less: tax allowable depreciation		(30,000)
Taxable profit		285,000

Tax payable = $285,000 × 30% = $85,500.

6 C

	$	$
Accounting profit		360,000
Add: depreciation	40,000	
disallowed expenses	10,000	
		50,000
		410,000
Less: non-taxable income	35,000	
tax allowable depreciation	30,000	
		(65,000)
Taxable profit		345,000

Tax payable = $345,000 × 20% = $69,000.

7 B

	$	$
Accounting profit		500,000
Add: depreciation	50,000	
disallowed expenses	5,000	
		55,000
		555,000
Less: non-taxable income	25,000	
tax allowable depreciation	60,000	
		(85,000)
Taxable profit		470,000

Tax payable = $470,000 × 25% = $117,500.

Answers

8   **D**

	$	$
Accounting profit		250,000
Add: depreciation	40,000	
disallowed expenses	2,000	
		42,000
		292,000
Less: tax allowable depreciation		(30,000)
Taxable profit		262,000

Tax payable = $262,000 × 30% = $78,600.

9   **D**   Direct tax and earnings tax. (This is the examiner's answer.)

10   Tax due = $22,500

	$
Accounting profit	95,000
Less non-taxable income	(15,000)
Add non–allowable expenditure	10,000
Taxable profit	90,000

Tax = $90,000 × 25%
     = $22,500

11 $4,000

	$'000
Revenue	45
Operating costs	(23)
Finance costs	(4)
Taxable allowance	(2)
Taxable amount	16
Tax @ 25%	4

12

		$
30 September 20X3	Tax on trading profits = 200 × 20% =	40,000
30 September 20X4	Tax on trading profit = (150 – 120) × 20% =	6,000
30 September 20X5	Tax on capital gains = (130 – 100) × 20% =	6,000
		12,000

13   **B**   The company income tax that has already been paid is **imputed** to the shareholder as a tax credit.

14   **A** $320,000 less prior year over-provision ($290,000 – $280,000)

15

	Accounting book value	Tax basis	Difference	Deferred tax balance
	$	$	$	$
Cost 1.4.X4	500,000	500,000		
Depreciation to 31.3.X5	(100,000)			
Capital allowance 50%	-	(250,000)	-	-
	400,000	250,000	150,000	45,000
Depreciation to 31.3.X6	(100,000)			
Capital allowance 20%	-	(50,000)	-	-
	300,000	200,000	100,000	30,000
Revaluation 1.4.X6	120,000			
	420,000			
Depreciation (42,000/3)	(140,000)			
Capital allowance 20%	-	40,000	-	-
	280,000	160,000	120,000	36,000

	$
Deferred tax balance 31.3.X6	30,000
Deferred tax balance 31.3.X7	36,000
Income statement charge X6/X7	6,000

16   $42,900

	$
Purchase cost	630,000
Surveyors and legal fees (3,500 + 6,500)	10,000
Renovation costs	100,000
	740,000
Indexation of purchase cost (630,000 x 50%)	315,000
Indexation of renovation costs (100,000 x 50%)	50,000
Total costs	1,105,000
Sale less disposal costs (1,250,000 – 2,000)	1,248,000
Taxable profit on disposal	143,000
Tax due at 30%	42,900

44 Objective test answers: Deferred tax

1   A

	$
Over provision for prior period	(2,000)
Provision for current period	50,000
Increase in deferred tax charge	5,000
Charge to income statement	53,000

2   C

	$
Under provision for prior period	200
Provision for current period	30,000
Decrease in deferred tax charge	(5,000)
Charge to income statement	25,200

3   A   Item 2 consists of permanent differences, all the rest are temporary differences.
4   D   All four items have a carrying amount equal to their tax base.
5   B   IAS 12 states that deferred tax assets and liabilities should not be discounted.

6   D

	$
Taxable temporary differences b/f	850,000
Depreciation for tax purposes	500,000
Depreciation charged in the financial statements	(450,000)
Revaluation surplus	250,000
Taxable temporary differences c/f	1,150,000
Deferred tax at 30%	345,000

7   D

	$
Over provision for prior period	(27,500)
Provision for current period	30,000
Decrease in deferred tax charge	(10,000)
Credit to income statement	(7,500)

8   It is an imputation system.

9   D

	$
Under provision for prior period	2,800
Provision for current period	28,000
Increase in deferred tax charge	5,000
Charge to income statement	35,800

Answers

10   Deferred tax balance = $66,750

Tax written down value:

	$
1 Oct 20X3 cost	900,000
20X4 tax allowance – 50% × 900,000	(450,000)
30 Sept 20X4 tax written down value	450,000
20X5 tax allowance – 25% × 450,000	(112,500)
30 Sept 20X5 tax written down value	337,500

Accounting carrying value:

	$
Cost	900,000
Depreciation 2 × (900-50)/5	(340,000)
30 Sept 20X5 accounting carrying value	560,000

Temporary difference = $560,000 – 337,500
= $222,500

Deferred tax balance = $222,500 × 30%
= $66,750

11

	$
Taxable profit for the year	946,000
Tax at 22%	208,120
Prior year over-provision	(31,000)
Increase in deferred tax provision	117,000
Charge to income statement	294,120

12   Deferred tax balance at 31 March 20X7 = $34
Deferred tax balance at 31 March 20X8 = ($2)

Tax written down value:

	$ '000
1 Apr 20X5 cost	600
20X6 tax allowance (50% × 600,000)	(300)
31 Mar 20X6 tax written down value	300
20X7 tax allowance (25% × 300,000)	(75)
31 Mar 20X7 tax written down value	225
20X8 tax allowance (25% × 225,000)	(56)
31 Mar 20X8 tax written down value	169

Accounting carrying value:

	$
Cost	600
Depreciation (2 × (600/5))	(240)
31 Mar 20X7 carrying value	360
1 Apr 20X7 impairment review	(120)
1 Apr 20X7 carrying value	240
Depreciation X7/X8 (240/3)	(80)
31 Mar 20X8 carrying value	160

31 March 20X7
Temporary difference = $360 – $225 = $135
Deferred tax balance = $135 × 25% = $34

31 March 20X8
Temporary difference = $160 – $169 = ($9)
Deferred tax balance = ($9) × 25% = ($2)

Note. The question specifies working to the nearest $1,000.

13 $200,250

	$
Accounting profits	822,000
Entertaining expenses	32,000
Political donation	50,000
	904,000
Government grant	(103,000)
Taxable profit	801,000
Tax at 25%	200,250

14 $49,500

	Carrying value $	Tax base $
1 October 20X5	400,000	400,000
Depreciation 25%	(100,000)	–
First year allowance	–	(400,000)
Balance 30 Sept 20X6	300,000	–
Depreciation 25%	(75,000)	–
Balance 30 Sept 20X7	225,000	–

Difference between carrying value and tax base = $225,000

Deferred tax at 22% = $49,500

15

	Carrying value $	Tax base $	Difference $
1 April 20X7	220,000	220,000	
Depreciation (220,000/8)	(27,500)	–	
First year allowance 30%	–	(66,000)	
Balance 30 March 20X8	192,500	154,000	38,500
Revaluation	50,000	–	
	242,500	154,000	
Depreciation (242,500/7)	(34,643)	–	
Writing down allowance 20%	–	(30,800)	
Balance 30 March 20X9	207,857	123,200	84,657

Deferred tax balance at 30 March 20X9 = 84,657 × 25% = $21,164

Deferred tax balance at 30 March 20X8 = 38,500 × 25% = $9,625

Movement on deferred tax balance at 30 March 20X9 = 21,164 - 9,625 = $11,539

16

	Temporary difference	
B/f (12,500 – 5,000)	7,500	
20X3 (2,120 – 1,630)	490	
20X4 (1,860 – 1,590)	270	
20X5 (1,320 – 1,530)	(210)	
Balance at 31 December 20X5	8,050	× 25% = 2,012.50

45 Section B answers: Taxation I

(a)

> **Top tips.** We have given three examples here as this is all that is needed. Other acceptable answers would be a trust fund, a partnership or any other body set up to carry out a trade for profit (eg the bar at a golf club).

The person liable to pay tax is called a **taxable person**.

Examples include the following.

- An individual
- An estate of a deceased person
- A limited company

A taxable person usually pays tax in the country where he or she is resident. The tax authority able to charge tax is called the **competent jurisdiction**.

(b) (i) **Indirect taxation** is charged indirectly on the final consumer of the goods or services. An example is a sales tax (eg VAT in the UK; TVA in France). As value is added, the tax increases cumulatively.

Indirect taxes are not actually paid by the business. Instead, the business acts as a tax collector on behalf of the tax authorities. For example, a business charges sales tax on its sales (output tax) and it pays sales tax on its purchases (input tax). The difference between output tax and input tax is paid over to the tax authorities.

(ii) **Unit taxes** are based on the number or weight of items, eg excise duties on the number of cigarettes or on the weight of tobacco.

Ad valorem taxes are based on the value of the items, eg a sales tax or value added tax.

(c)

	$'000
INCOME STATEMENT (EXTRACT)	
Income tax expense (W1)	1,145
STATEMENT OF FINANCIAL POSITION (EXTRACT)	
Non-current liabilities	
Deferred tax (W2)	1,750
Current liabilities	
Income tax	1,000

Workings

1   Income statement

	$
Income tax for year	1,000,000
Over-provision in previous year	(5,000)
Increase in deferred tax	150,000
Income tax expense	1,145,000

2   Deferred tax

	$
Opening balance	1,600,000
Increase in year	150,000
Closing balance	1,750,000

(d)

> **Examiner's comments.** Most candidates could define withholding tax whilst many candidates found difficulty defining underlying tax. A common error Part (ii) was not grossing up the amount received before calculating withholding tax. As many candidates did not know what underlying tax was they could not calculate it.

(i) **Withholding tax** is deducted at source by the tax authority before a payment is made. This occurs most commonly when dividends are paid to non-residents. The tax authority has no power to tax the non-resident, so it taxes the dividend at source.

Underlying tax is the tax which has already been suffered by the profits from which a dividend is paid. When the recipient pays tax on his dividend income, this means that the dividend has effectively been taxed twice. To mitigate this, some tax authorities operate an imputation system, by which the recipient obtains relief for the underlying tax.

(ii) $45,000 represents 9/10 of the amount prior to withholding tax, so withholding tax is therefore $45,000/9 = $5,000.

(iii) The amount of dividend prior to withholding tax was $50,000. This has already been taxed at 20% (100/500). Therefore $50,000 is 80% and the other 20% is the underlying tax - $12,500.

(e)

> **Examiner's comments**. It was surprising how many candidates could not correctly calculate VAT when the figure inclusive of VAT was given.

(i)

		$
Revenue (40,250 × 100/115)		35,000
Cost of sales:		
Purchases plus excise duty	12,000	
Repackaging (6,900 × 100/115)	6,000	
		(18,000)
Net profit		17,000

(ii)

	$
VAT output tax (35,000 × 15%)	5,250
VAT input tax (18,000 × 15%)	(2,700)
Due to VAT authorities	2,550

46 Section B answers: Taxation II

(a) (i) Governments might apply specific excise duties:

- to discourage people from consuming too much of a substance which is harmful to health – such as alcohol and tobacco

- to raise funds to pay for the consequences of the consumption of these harmful substances – for example, the additional health care required for patients with smoking-related illnesses

- to discourage the excessive use of products which damage the environment, such as the use of petrol or diesel in vehicles and aircraft

- to raise maximum revenue by targeting goods which are widely used and relatively expensive.

(ii) A single stage sales tax is chargeable at a single point in the supply chain, usually at the point of sale to the final customer. An example of a single stage sales tax is the retail sales tax applied in the USA.

A multi stage sales tax is chargeable and deductible at different points in the supply chain, such as VAT in the UK. As value is added the tax increases cumulatively. However with VAT, the business deducts the VAT it pays and pays over the balance to the government. The incidence of the tax is therefore on the final consumer of the goods or services.

(b) <u>Power to review and query filed returns</u>

The tax authorities usually have the power to ask for further information if they are not satisfied with a filed return. These queries must be answered or there may be legal penalties.

Power to request special reports or returns

The special report may take the form of asking for details of pay and tax deducted from an individual employee, where there are indications that the tax rules have been broken. There have been instances of casual employees having a number of jobs but using a number of false names, so that the tax authority has been defrauded.

Power to examine records

Most tax authorities have the power to inspect business records to ensure compliance. If mistakes in returns have been made, the tax authority may be able to re-open earlier years and collect back taxes owed.

Powers of entry and search

Where the tax authority believes fraud has occurred, it can obtain warrants to enter a business's premises and seize the records.

Exchange of information with tax authorities in other jurisdictions

This has become very important as a counter-terrorism measure in recent years. One tax authority may become aware of funds being moved to another country in suspicious circumstances. It will then warn the tax authority in that other jurisdiction. Exchange of information is also useful in dealing with drug smuggling and money laundering.

(c) If a company makes payments to an individual or another company resident in a different tax jurisdiction, it may have to pay **withholding tax** to the tax authority of its own jurisdiction.

The reason for this is to stop companies paying all their earnings abroad and then stopping trading without paying any tax to the tax authorities of the country where they are resident. Therefore the local tax authority will take a payment on account of the final tax liability by deducting at source a withholding tax from all payments sent abroad. The withholding tax can be as low as 5% or as high as 40%.

Payments affected are usually interest payments or dividends.

> **Alternative answers.** You would also have scored marks for stating royalties or capital gains accruing to non-residents.

(d) Double taxation treaties

In order to establish more clearly which tax authority has jurisdiction, countries enter into **double taxation treaties**. These treaties seek to avoid a business having to pay tax twice on its income simply because it deals with two tax authorities.

A double taxation treaty (eg that between the UK and the USA) sets out which tax authority has jurisdiction. So a company incorporated in the UK that trades with the USA will be taxed primarily in the UK. The treaty defines a **permanent establishment** and directs that the business will be taxed in the country where it has its permanent establishment.

Where a double taxation treaty exists, provisions are usually made to reduce withholding taxes, or even to avoid paying withholding tax at all.

Another feature of a double taxation treaty is that where a company pays tax in Country A, but is resident in Country B, the tax authorities of Country B will give relief for the tax paid in Country A.

Methods of giving relief

One way is to give full **deduction** for foreign taxes paid. However this is not always appropriate, particularly if the country where the tax is paid has a high tax rate and the other has a low rate.

Relief may be given by **exemption**. In this case, if income is taxed in Country A, then it will not be taxed in Country B.

Another way of giving relief is by **credit**. This usually occurs where the tax rate in Country A is higher than that in Country B. Instead of deducting the full amount of tax paid in Country A, Country B credits the amount it would have paid in Country B. For example, the income is $10,000 and the tax rate in Country A is 30%, while that in Country B is 20%. The tax paid in Country A will be $3,000 but the double tax relief allowed in Country B will be $2,000 (20% × $10,000).

(e)

> **Examiner's comments.** Most candidates were able to explain the meaning of avoidance and evasion, with fewer highlighting the difference between them. Some candidates gave odd examples of tax avoidance, such as 'claiming capital allowances' or 'claiming loss relief'. These are not examples of tax avoidance, they are proper application of the tax legislation and are not 'loopholes'.
>
> Several candidates stated that giving double taxation relief on overseas profits was a means of preventing tax avoidance, which is incorrect.
>
> Many candidates did not give enough examples or sufficient detail within the examples to earn full marks.

(i) **Tax avoidance** is successful tax planning. It is arranging the financial affairs of an individual or an entity in such a manner as to minimise tax liability. It is perfectly legal.

Tax evasion is the use of illegal means to avoid paying tax, such as not declaring income, claiming deduction for non-deductible expense, or contravening tax legislation.

(ii) Although only evasion is illegal, avoidance is just as much of a problem for government. Methods that governments can use to reduce avoidance and evasion are:

- Anti-avoidance legislation. This outlaws specific avoidance schemes.
- Deducting tax at source such as the PAYE system in the UK.
- Keeping the tax system as simple as possible to minimise the number of factors that can be manipulated.
- Making sure that penalties for evasion are high enough to act as a deterrent.
- Increasing the efficiency of the tax collection and investigation machinery.
- Having a tax system which is not generally perceived as unfair. An unfair system makes people feel justified in avoiding tax.

47 Section B answers: Taxation III

(a) **Deferred tax – disclosure and note**

	$m
Temporary differences on non-current assets	0.56
Provision at 30 April 20X3	0.69
Deferred tax credit in income statement	(0.13)
Provision at 30 April 20X4	0.56

Working

Deferred tax

	$m
Temporary difference at 30 April 20X3	2.30
Temporary difference at 30 April 20X4	2.00
Deferred tax at 30 April 20X3 (2.30 × 30%)	0.69
Deferred tax at 30 April 20X4 (2.00 × 28%)	0.56
Reduction in deferred tax provision	0.13

> **Alternative approach**
>
> The reduction in provision is made up of two elements.
>
> | | $m |
> |---|---|
> | Reversal of temporary differences ((2.30 – 2.00) × 30%) | 0.09 |
> | Change in tax rate (2.00 × (30% – 28%)) | 0.04 |
> | | 0.13 |

(b) **Tax on profit on ordinary activities – note to income statement**

	$m
Current tax	
Tax on profit for the period	1.40
Overprovision for previous period ($750,000 – $720,000)	(0.03)
Deferred tax	
Increase in provision ($300,000 – $250,000)	0.05
Total tax charge	1.42

Statement of financial position

	$m
Payables	
Current tax	1.40
Deferred tax	0.30

(c)

> **Examiner's comments.** Part (i) was fairly well done; most candidates seem to be getting the idea of temporary differences and deferred tax balances. However, some had trouble with the dates. The asset had been owned for three years but many candidates calculated four or even five years before working out the temporary difference.

	Accounting value $	Tax value $
Cost	200,000	200,000
Depreciation 20X3 – 20X5	(120,000)	(131,400)*
Balance 30 September 20X5	80,000	68,600
Disposal proceeds	(60,000)	(60,000)
Loss	20,000	8,600

(i) Timing difference at 30 September 20X5 (80,000 – 68,600) = 11,400

Tax at 20% = 2,280

(ii) The carrying value of the asset at 30 September 20X6 is $80,000. Disposal at $60,000 will give rise to an accounting loss of $20,000.

(iii) At the date of disposal the tax WDV of the asset is $68,600. Disposal at $60,000 gives rise to a balancing allowance of $8,600.

* (60,000 + 42,000 + 29,400)

(d)

> **Examiner's comments.** Very few candidates provided a fully correct answer to this question, and some demonstrated very little knowledge of deferred tax.
>
> Some candidates used the wrong periods, some failed to apply the tax rate to the year end balances and some described the credit to the income statement as a charge.

Year ended	Cost	Depreciation	Tax allowance
31.3.X4	250,000	50,000	125,000
31.3.X5	250,000	50,000	31,250
		100,000	156,250

(i) Deferred tax balance: 31.3.X4: (125,000 – 50,000) × 30% = $22,500
(ii) Deferred tax balance: 31.3.X5: (156,250 – 100,000) × 30% = $16,875
(iii) Income statement credit: year ended 31.3.X5 = (22,500 – 16,875) = $5,625

(e)

> **Examiner's comments.** Some candidates filled a page or more with calculations but did not show how the results would be used. You must answer the question asked, in this case the question asked for tax payable so the answer must state the taxable profits and tax payable otherwise the question has not been answered.

		$
Profit before tax		29,800
Gain on disposal		(4,000)
Depreciation		14,200
		40,000
Capital allowances:		
Buildings (80,000 × 5%)		(4,000)
Plant and equipment	– first year (30,000 × 50%)	(15,000)
	– disposal balancing allowance (11,812 – 5,000)	(6,812)
Taxable profit		14,188
Tax due for year ended 30 April 20X8 at 20%		2,838

(f)

> **Examiner's comments.** Most candidates gained reasonable marks for this question. The majority of candidates were able to calculate the adjusted profit before tax relief for non-current assets although the tax depreciation was often calculated incorrectly.

		$
Profit before tax		33,950
Local government tax		950
Entertaining		600
Depreciation		21,600
		57,100
Capital allowances:		
Buildings (70,000 × 4%)		(2,800)
Plant and equipment	- existing (80,000 × 73% × 27%)	(15,768)
	- addition (20,000 × 50%)	(10,000)
Taxable profit		28,532

Tax due:	$
$10,001 - $25,000 @ 15%	2,250
$25,001 - $28,532 @ 25%	883
Total due for 20X6	3,133

MOCK EXAMS

CIMA
Paper F1 (Operational)
Financial Operations

Mock Exam 1

Question Paper		
Time allowed:	Reading time	20 mins
	Answering question paper	3 hours
This paper is divided into three sections		
Section A	Answer ALL sub-questions in this section	
Section B	Answer ALL of the six short answer questions	
Section C	Answer BOTH of these questions	

DO NOT OPEN THIS PAPER UNTIL YOU ARE READY TO START UNDER EXAMINATION CONDITIONS

SECTION A – 20 marks

Answer ALL sub-questions in this section

Question 1

1.1 A has a taxable profit of $100,000. The book depreciation was $10,000 and the tax allowable depreciation was $25,000. What was the accounting profit? **(2 marks)**

1.2 Company W makes an accounting profit of $300,000 during the year. This includes non-taxable income of $10,000 and depreciation of $35,000. In addition, $5,000 of the expenses are disallowable for tax purposes. If the tax allowable depreciation totals $30,000, what is the taxable profit?

    A $290,000
    B $295,000
    C $300,000
    D $310,000 **(2 marks)**

1.3 Which of the following is a source of tax rules?

    A   International accounting standards
    B   Supranational tax agreements
    C   Local company legislation
    D   Domestic accounting practice **(2 marks)**

1.4 Company E has sales of $230,000, excluding sales tax, in a period. Its purchases total $151,000, including sales tax. Purchases of $10,000 are zero rated. Sales tax is 17.5%. What is the sales tax payable for the period?

    A $7,830
    B $9,580
    C $13,825
    D $19,250 **(2 marks)**

1.5 A company is resident in Country A. It has a branch in Country B. The branch has taxable profits of $100,000, on which tax of $15,000 is paid. The tax rate in Country A is 20% and there is a double taxation treaty between Countries A and B that allows tax relief on the credit basis. If the company has total taxable profits, including those of the branch of $150,000, how much tax will it pay in Country A?

    A $10,000
    B $15,000
    C $20,000
    D $30,000 **(2 marks)**

1.6 IAS 10 *Events after the reporting period* distinguishes between adjusting and non-adjusting events.

Which of the following is an adjusting event?

    A   One month after the year end, a customer lodged a claim for $1,000,000 compensation. The customer claimed to have suffered permanent mental damage as a result of the fright she had when one of the entity's products malfunctioned and exploded. The outcome of the court case cannot be predicted at this stage.

    B   There was a dispute with the workers and all production ceased one week after the year end.

    C   A fire destroyed all of the entity's inventory in its furnished goods warehouse two weeks after the year end.

    D   Inventory valued at the year end at $20,000 was sold one month later for $15,000. **(2 marks)**

1.7 X signed a finance lease agreement on 1 October 20X2. The lease provided for five annual payments, in arrears, of $20,000. The fair value of the asset was agreed at $80,000.

Using the sum of digits method, how much should be charged to the statement of comprehensive income for the finance cost in the year to 30 September 20X3?

A $4,000
B $6,667
C $8,000
D $20,000

(2 marks)

1.8 D purchased a non-current asset on 1 April 20X0 for $200,000. The asset attracted writing down tax allowances at 25% on the reducing balance. Depreciation was 10% on the straight-line basis. Assume income tax is at 30%.

The deferred tax balance for this asset at 31 March 20X3 is:

A $9,000
B $16,688
C $27,000
D $55,625

(2 marks)

1.9 C started work on a contract to build a dam for a hydro-electric scheme. The work commenced on 24 October 20X1 and is scheduled to take four years to complete. C recognises profit on the basis of the certified percentage of work completed. The contract price is $10 million.

An analysis of C's records provided the following information:

Year to 30 September	20X2	20X3
Percentage of work completed and certified in year	30%	25%
	$'000	$'000
Total cost incurred during the year	2,900	1,700
Estimated cost of remaining work to complete contract	6,000	3,900
Total payments made for the cost incurred during the year	2,500	2,000

How much profit should C recognise in its statement of comprehensive income for the years ended:

	30 September 20X2	30 September 20X3
	$'000	$'000
A	100	375
B	330	375
C	330	495
D	500	825

(2 marks)

1.10 S announced a rights issue of 1 for every 5 shares currently held, at a price of $2 each. S currently has 2,000,000 $1 ordinary shares with a quoted market price of $2.50 each. Directly attributable issue costs amounted to $25,000.

Assuming all rights are taken up and all money paid in full, how much will be credited to the share premium account for the rights issue?

A $200,000
B $308,333
C $375,000
D $400,000

(2 marks)

(Total for Section A = 20 marks)

SECTION B – 30 marks

Answer ALL six sub-questions

Question 2

(a) At the beginning of the accounting period, D had a credit balance of $40,000 on its current tax account, which was paid during the period. The opening balance on the deferred tax account was $250,000 credit.

The provision for tax for the current period is $50,000 and the balance on the deferred tax account is to be reduced to $225,000.

Required

Prepare extracts from the statement of comprehensive income, statement of financial position and notes to the accounts showing these tax related items

(Total for sub-question (a) = 5 marks)

(b) IAS 12 *Income taxes* requires entities to publish an explanation of the relationship between taxable income and accounting profit. This can take the form of a numerical reconciliation between the tax expense and the product of the accounting profit and the applicable tax rate. Explain why this explanation is helpful to the readers of financial statements.

(Total for sub-question (b) = 5 marks)

(c) Discuss the usefulness of the audit report to a potential investor.

(Total for sub-question (c) = 5 marks)

The following data are to be used to answer questions (d) and (e)

The financial statements of GK for the year to 31 October 20X8 were as follows:

STATEMENT OF FINANCIAL POSITION AT	31 October 20X8		31 October 20X7	
	$'000	$'000	$'000	$'000
Assets				
Non-current tangible assets	10,000		10,500	
Property	5,000	15,000	4,550	15,050
Plant and equipment				
Current assets				
Inventory	1,750		1,500	
Trade receivables	1,050		900	
Cash and cash equivalents	310		150	
		3,110		2,550
Total assets		18,110		17,600
Equity and liabilities				
Ordinary shares @ $.050 each	6,000		3,000	
Share premium	2,500		1,000	
Revaluation reserve	3,000		3,000	
Retained earnings	1,701		1,000	
		13,201		8,000
Non-current liabilities				
Interest-bearing borrowings	2,400		7,000	
Deferred tax	540	2,940	450	7,450

Current liabilities
Trade and other payables 1,060 1,400
Tax payable 909 750
1,969 2,150
18,110 17,600

STATEMENT OF COMPREHENSIVE INCOME FOR THE YEAR 31 OCTOBER 20X8

	$'000	$'000
Revenue		16,000
Cost of sales		10,000
Gross profit		6,000
Administrative expenses	(2,000)	
Distribution costs	(1,200)	(3,200)
		2,800
Finance cost		(600)
Profit		2,200
Income tax expense		(999)
Profit for the year		(1,201)

Additional information:

1. Trade and other payables comprise:

	31 October 20X8	31 October 20X7
	$'000	$'000
Trade payables	730	800
Interest payable	330	600
	1,060	1,400

2. Plant disposed of in the year had a net book value of $35,000; cash received on disposal was $60,000.

3. GK's statement of comprehensive income includes depreciation for the year of $1,110,000 for properties and $882,000 for plant and equipment.

4. Dividends paid during the year were $500,000.

(d) Using the data relating to GK above, calculate the cash generated from operations that would appear in GK's statement of cash flows, using the indirect method, for the year ended 31 October 20X8, in accordance with IAS 7 *Statement of cash flows*

(Total for sub-question (d) = 5 marks)

(e) Using the data relating to GK above, calculate the cash flow from investing activities and cash flows from financing activities sections of GK's statement of cash flows for the year ended 31 October 20X8, in accordance with IAS 7 *Statement of cash flows*.

(Total for sub-question (e) = 5 marks)

(f) IAS 8 *Accounting policies, changes in accounting estimates and errors* distinguishes between accounting policies and accounting estimates. Explain the distinction between accounting policies and accounting estimates, give an example of each and explain their treatment under IAS 8.

(Total for sub-question (f) = 5 marks)

(Total for Section B = 30 marks)

SECTION C – 50 marks

Answer BOTH of these questions

Question 3

HI, listed on its local stock exchange, is a retail organisation operating several retail outlets. A reorganisation of the entity was started in 20X2 because of a significant reduction in profits. This reorganisation was completed during the current financial year.

The trial balance for HI at 30 September 20X3 was as follows:

	$'000	$'000
Retained earnings at 30 September 20X2		1,890
Administrative expenses	715	
Bank and cash	1,409	
Buildings	11,200	
Cash received on disposal of equipment		11
Cost of goods sold	3,591	
Distribution costs	314	
Equipment and fixtures	2,625	
Interim ordinary dividend paid	800	
Inventory at 30 September 20X3	822	
Investment income received		37
Available-for-sale investments at market value 30 September 20X2	492	
Ordinary shares of $1 each, fully paid		5,000
Provision for deferred tax		256
Provision for reorganisation expenses at 30 September 20X2		1,010
Allowances for depreciation at 30 September 20X2		
Buildings		1,404
Equipment and fixtures		1,741
Reorganisation expenses	900	
Revaluation surplus		172
Sales revenue		9,415
Share premium		2,388
Trade payables		396
Trade receivables	852	
	23,720	23,720

Additional information provided

(a) The reorganisation expenses relate to a comprehensive restructuring and reorganisation of the entity that began in 20X2. HI's financial statements for 20X2 included a provision for reorganisation expenses of $1,010,000. All costs had been incurred by the year end, but an invoice for $65,000, received on 2 October 20X3, remained unpaid and is not included in the trial balance figures. No further restructuring and reorganisation costs are expected to occur and the provision is no longer required.

(b) Available-for-sale investments are carried in the financial statements at market value. The market value of the available-for-sale investments at 30 September 20X3 was $522,000. There were no movements in the investments held during the year.

(c) On 1 November 20X3, HI was informed that one of its customers, X, had ceased trading. The liquidators advised HI that it was very unlikely to receive payment of any of the $45,000 due from X at 30 September 20X3.

(d) Another customer is suing for damages as a consequence of a faulty product. Legal advisers are currently advising that the probability of HI being found liable is 75%. The amount payable is estimated to be the full amount claimed of $100,000.

(e) The income tax due for the year ended 30 September 20X3 is estimated at $1,180,000 and the deferred tax provision needs to be increased to $281,000.

(f) During the year, HI disposed of old equipment for $11,000. The original cost of this equipment was $210,000 and accumulated depreciation at 30 September 20X2 was $205,000. HI's accounting policy is to charge no depreciation in the year of the disposal.

(g) Depreciation is charged using the straight-line basis on non-current assets as follows.

Buildings	3%
Equipment and fixtures	20%

Depreciation is regarded as a cost of sales.

Required

Prepare the statement of comprehensive income for HI for the year to 30 September 20X3 and a statement of financial position at that date, in a form suitable for presentation to the shareholders, in accordance with the requirements of IFRS.

Notes to the financial statements are **not** required.

(25 marks)

Question 4

The draft statements of financial position of Hornet, its subsidiary company Wasp and its associate Ant at 31 October 20X5 are as follows.

	Hornet $'000	Wasp $'000	Ant $'000
Assets			
Non-current assets			
Land and buildings	315,000	278,000	145,000
Plant	145,000	220,000	55,000
	460,000	498,000	200,000
Investment			
Shares in Ant at cost	100,000		
Current assets			
Inventory	357,000	252,000	52,000
Receivables	375,000	126,000	78,000
Bank	208,000	30,000	10,000
	940,000	408,000	140,000
	1,500,000	906,000	340,000
Equity and liabilities			
Equity			
$1 ordinary shares	700,000	600,000	200,000
Retained earnings	580,000	212,000	80,000
	1,280,000	82,000	280,000
Current liabilities			
Payables	220,000	94,000	60,000
Total equity and liabilities	1,500,000	906,000	340,000

The following information is also available.

(a) Hornet purchased all 600 million shares in Wasp on 1 November 20X4 for a consideration of $0.25 per share plus 1 new $1 share issued in Hornet for every 2 shares in Wasp. At the date of acquisition, Wasp had a credit balance of $150 million in retained earnings. The acquisition has not been reflected in the books of Hornet as at 31 October 20X5.

(b) Each $1 share in Hornet had a fair value of $2.5 on 1 November 20X4.

(c) Hornet purchased 30% of the shares in Ant some time ago for $100 million. The retained earnings of Ant at that date were $60 million. Hornet's investment in Ant is deemed to be impaired by $10 million at 31 October 20X5.

(d) At the date of acquisition, the property, plant and equipment of Wasp was valued at $70 million in excess of its carrying value. The valuation was attributable to:

- freehold land, valued at $40 million in excess of carrying value.

- freehold properties, valued at $30 million in excess of carrying value. The properties had a useful life of 20 years from the date of acquisition of Wasp and are measured at depreciated cost in Wasp's own financial statements at 31 October 20X5.

The revaluations were not recorded in the accounts of Wasp.

(e) Wasp's inventory includes goods purchased from Hornet at a price that includes a profit to Hornet of $12 million.

(f) At 31 October 20X5 Wasp owes Hornet $25 million for goods purchased during the year.

Required

(a) Calculate the goodwill on acquisition of Wasp. **(5 marks)**

(b) Prepare the consolidated statement of financial position for Hornet as at 31 October 20X5. **(20 marks)** (Show clearly any workings.)

(Total = 25 marks)

(Total for Section C = 50 marks)

Answers

**DO NOT TURN THIS PAGE UNTIL YOU HAVE
COMPLETED MOCK EXAM 1**

A plan of attack

As you turned the page to start this exam any one of a number of things could have been going through your mind. Some of them may have been quite sensible, some of them may not.

The main thing to do is take a deep breath and do not panic. It's best to sort out a plan of attack before the actual exam so that when the invigilator tells you that you can begin and the adrenaline kicks in you are using every minute of the three hours wisely.

Your approach

This paper has three sections. The first section contains 10 multiple choice questions which are compulsory. The second has six short compulsory questions. The third has two compulsory questions totalling 50 marks.

OTs first again

However you find the paper, chances are you should **start with the objective test questions**. You should be able to do at least a few and answering them will give you a boost. **Don't even look at the other questions before doing Section A**. Remember how long to allocate to the OTs? That's right, 36 minutes.

You then have a **choice**.

- Read through and answer Section B before moving on to Section C
- Read the questions in Section C, answer them and then go back to Section B

Time spent at the start of each Section B and the Section C questions confirming the requirements and producing a plan for the answers is time well spent.

Doing the exam

Actually doing the exam is a personal experience. There is not a single *right way*. As long as you submit complete answers to the MCQs in Section A, the six Section B questions and the questions in Section C, your approach obviously works.

One approach

Having done or guessed at the MCQs, I would work straight through Section B. The possible pitfall would be getting sucked too deeply into Section B and leaving insufficient time for Section C.

So lets look at the Section B questions in the paper:

- Question (a) is a straightforward calculation of income tax liability. It would be a good idea to begin by putting the information into T accounts. Then the information just needs to be correctly presented. This can easily be done in 9 minutes.

- Question (b) is a discussion question on the relationship of accounting profit to taxable profit. Make a few notes before you start.

- Question (c) is a trap. You can probably think of lots of things to say about this and the worst thing you can do is to start writing them all down. You have 9 minutes for this, no more. Your plan (and you must have one) should be something like: 1. Ways in which it is useful 2. Limitations on its usefulness 3. Ways in which its usefulness is overestimated. Then think of the valid points you want to make in these three areas and make them briefly. Our answer does not use bullet points, but that would have been an equally valid approach.

- Questions (d) and (e) are on statements of cash flows. Don't waste time digesting the whole of the financial statements. Look at the question to see what information you need to extract and get on with it. A methodical approach is really needed here.

- Question (f) is difficult and requires a good knowledge of IAS 8. If you had trouble with it, do revise this, as it could well come up.

Having hacked your way through Section B, taking no more than 9 minutes per question, you should now be left with 90 minutes to do your Section C questions. These are worth 50 marks and you must aim to secure as many of them as possible. Read the questions **twice** if you need to.

For the Section C Questions you must proceed in a methodical way. Set out your formats and then work through the question requirements, doing neat, readable calculations and fill out the figures. Even if you do not finish, you will get marks for what you have done, so do the easy bits first.

Time allocation

Be disciplined. Allocate your time according to the marks available but never go over the time allocation. The last few marks in a question are the hardest to earn.

Be sure to follow the requirements. If four advantages are required, give four. No extra credit will be given for five. Two advantages will only get you half marks.

Answer all of the question. Having a go at every part of all the Section B questions you are required to do will put you in a better position to pass than, say, only doing five questions. However difficult that sixth question seems at first, there are marks to be earned.

If you have time left at the end of the exam ensure that you have attempted every part of every question. If you have, then scan through and ensure you complete any part of an answer you left earlier. Use the full three hours working towards a pass.

Marking the exam

When you mark your exam, be honest. Don't be too harsh though. Give yourself credit for the things you did well, but don't kid yourself with 'I would have done that in the real exam'. It may be worth your while making two lists; strengths and weaknesses.

Strengths will be areas of the syllabus you are confident with and also good exam technique. (Maybe you produced correct financial statement formats.)

Weaknesses will be holes in your knowledge and poor exam technique (maybe you ran out of time and couldn't answer all the requirements of the last question).

Making this list will help you focus your last days of revision on the areas which require attention whilst reminding you of the areas you excel in.

SECTION A

Question 1

1.1
	$
Taxable profit	100,000
Less: depreciation	10,000
	90,000
Add: tax allowable depreciation	25,000
Accounting profit	115,000

1.2 The correct answer is C.

	$	$
Accounting profit		300,000
Add: depreciation	35,000	
disallowed expenses	5,000	
		40,000
		340,000
Less: non-taxable income	10,000	
tax allowable depreciation	30,000	40,000
Taxable profit		300,000

1.3 The correct answer is B. Supranational tax agreements (eg the EU rules on sales tax) are a source of tax rules. The other options are all sources of accounting rules.

1.4 The correct answer is D.

	$
Output tax (230,000 x 17.5%)	40,250
Input tax ((151,000 – 10,000)/117.5 × 17.5)	21,000
Payable	19,250

1.5 The correct answer is B.

Total tax due is $30,000 ($150,000 x 20%) less double taxation relief of $15,000 (less than $100,000 x 20%), leaves $15,000 to pay.

1.6 D The subsequent sale provides evidence of the net realisable value of the inventory as at the year end.

1.7 B $$\$(100,000 - 80,000) \times \frac{5}{5+4+3+2+1} = \$20,000 \times \frac{5}{15}$$

$$= \$6,667$$

1.8 B WDA

	$	Capital allowance $
Cost 1.4 X0	200,000	
WDA 25%	50,000	50,000
WDV 31.3 X1	150,000	
WDA 25%	(37,500)	37,500
WDV 31.3 X2	112,500	
WDA 25%	(28,125)	28,125
WDV 31.3 X3	84,375	
Capital allowances claimed		115,625
Depreciation w/off		
3 yrs @ 10% straight line		60,000
Accelerated allowances		55,625
Tax rate		× 30%
		16,688

1.9 C

	20X2 $'000	20X3 $'000
Costs to date	2,900	4,600
Costs to complete	6,000	3,900
Estimated total cost	8,900	8,500
Projected profit	1,100	1,500
Contract price	10,000	10,000
Completed	30%	55%
Cumulative profit	330	825
Profit recognised	330	495

1.10 C Number of shares issued:

$$\frac{2,000,000}{5} = 400,000 \text{ shares}$$

	$
Issue price	2
Nominal value	1
Premium	1

	$
∴ Total premium	400,000
Less issue costs	25,000
Net to share premium	375,000

SECTION B

Question 2

Marking scheme

	Marks
(a) Tax expense	1
Tax payable	1
Deferred tax balance	1
Notes	1
Presentation	1
	5

	$
Statement of comprehensive income (extract)	
Tax expense (Note 1)	25,000
Statement of financial position (extract)	
Current liabilities	
Tax payable	50,000
Non-current liabilities	
Deferred tax (Note 2)	225,000

Notes to the financial statements

1	Tax expense	$
	Provision for the current period	50,000
	Decrease in deferred tax provision	(25,000)
		25,000

2	Deferred tax	$
	Balance brought forward	250,000
	Decrease in provision	(25,000)
	Balance carried forward	225,000

Marking scheme

	Marks
(b) 1 mark per well-presented point	5

In many sets of financial statements, there **may appear to be little relationship** between the figure reported as the profit before tax and the actual tax charge that appears in the statement of comprehensive income. In a simple tax system, the tax charge would be the reported profit multiplied by the tax rate. However this will not normally be the case in real life, due to the complexities of the tax system and the estimates and subjective decisions that the directors must make in estimating the tax charge for the year.

The purpose of the reconciliation between the actual tax charge and the reported profit multiplied by the standard rate of tax is to highlight to the users of the financial statements these estimates and judgements. This reconciliation should **clarify the effect of adjustments** such as changes in tax rates, estimated tax charges differing from final agreed tax liabilities and other factors that have affected the amount that appears as the tax charge in the statement of comprehensive income. Another factor which may affect the tax charge is deferred tax. The reconciliation will therefore draw attention to factors which may lead to an increased tax charge in the future.

Marking scheme

		Marks
(c)	Types of report	1
	Expression of opinion	1
	Compliance with legislation and standards	1
	Cannot be expected to detect fraud	1
	May not uncover going concern issues	1
		5

Types of report

Any potential investor will of course examine a company's latest set of audited accounts and will expect to see an unqualified audit report. If the report is **qualified** she/he will ask further questions. If it is a disclaimer or an adverse report, he will probably decide to invest elsewhere.

Unqualified reports

So, assuming that the report is unqualified, how useful will it be to him? The audit report is the expression of the auditor's **opinion**. The auditor has given his opinion that the accounts present fairly the financial position of the company and comply with the relevant legislation and accounting standards. The report will state that he has sought to obtain 'reasonable assurance' that the accounts are free from 'material misstatement'.

The reason he auditor feels able to give nothing more than 'reasonable assurance' is that he did not prepare the accounts and he will not have had time to examine all of the transactions. The auditor will begin by testing the internal control system. If the internal controls appear to be effective, he will reduce the time spent on substantive testing. If fraud or errors are well-hidden, and the auditor's suspicions have not been aroused, the chances of him stumbling across the discrepancy are not that high.

Other matters

While the auditor will certainly give attention to any going concern issues, the audit report cannot be taken as any guarantee of the future viability of the entity. Nor does it assure the effectiveness or efficiency of management. These are probably the two factors which most interest an investor. The audit report is a **useful addition** to whatever other information the investor is able to obtain, but the above points mean that it cannot be used to frame an investment decision.

Marking scheme

		Marks
(d)	Net profit before taxation	½
	Depreciation	1
	Profit on disposal	1
	Finance cost	½
	Working capital adjustments	1½
	Cash generated from operations	½
		5

	$'000
Net profit before taxation	2,200
Depreciation (1,110 + 882)	1,992
Profit on disposal of plant (60 – 35)	(25)
Finance cost	600
Increase in trade receivables (1,050 – 900)	(150)
Increase in inventories (1,750 – 1,500)	(250)
Decrease in trade payables (730 – 800)	(70)
Cash generated from operations	4,297

Marking scheme

		Marks	
(e)	Cash flows from investing activities		
	Purchase of property, plant and equipment	1	
	Proceeds from sale of plant	1	
			2
	Cash flows from financing activities		
	Proceeds from share issues	1½	
	Dividends paid	½	
	Borrowings repaid	1	
			3
			5

Cash flows from investing activities

	$'000
Purchase of property, plant and equipment (W)	(1,977)
Proceeds from sale of plant	60
Net cash used in investing activities	(1,917)

Cash flows from financing activities

	$'000
Proceeds from issue of share capital (6,000 – 3,000 + 2,500 – 1,000)	4,500
Dividends paid	(500)
Borrowings repaid (7,000 – 2,400)	(4,600)
Net cash used in financing activities	(600)

Workings

PROPERTY, PLANT AND EQUIPMENT

	$'000		$'000
Balance b/f	15,050	Depreciation (1,110 + 882)	1,992
Additions (bal fig)	1,977	Disposal	35
		Balance c/f	15,000
	17,027		17,027

Marking scheme

		Marks	
(f)	Accounting policies / accounting estimates distinction	1	
	Example of each	2	
	Treatment of each	2	
			5

Accounting policies

Accounting policies are defined in IAS 8 as the 'specific principles, bases, conventions, rules and practices adopted by an entity in preparing and presenting financial statements'. In practice, accounting policies are formulated by reference to the appropriate IAS or IFRS. They should be applied consistently from one period to the next and for all similar transactions within a period.

An example of an accounting policy would be that non-current assets are held at historical cost and depreciated over their useful lives.

Accounting estimates

In applying an accounting policy, it is often necessary to make estimates. When a non-current asset is purchased, its expected life can only be estimated. An entity may have to estimate the expected level of bad debts, the possibility of some of its inventory becoming obsolescent, the fair value of assets and liabilities.

An example of an accounting estimate would be the method by which an asset was depreciated – this is the means by which the accounting policy of depreciation is applied. So a change from straight-line to reducing balance depreciation would be accounted for as a change of accounting estimate.

Changes

Changes of accounting policy are relatively rare and should be accounted for using **retrospective restatement**. The corresponding figures for previous periods are restated, so that the new policy is applied to transactions and events as if it had always been in use. Changes of accounting estimate are accounted for using **prospective restatement** – the change of estimate is applied to the current period and to future periods if they are affected.

SECTION C

Question 3

Text references. Provisions are dealt with in Chapter 9: *Miscellaneous standards*.

Top tips. As with all Section C questions, read the requirements carefully. Notes to the accounts are not required, so you should not have wasted time preparing them. However workings need to be clear and almost a substitute for notes, for example non-current assets.

Easy marks. Property, plant and equipment workings are important as they affect both the statement of comprehensive income and statement of financial position, so do these carefully. You may have had trouble with the reorganisation costs and the tax but, once you had handled property, plant and equipment, the rest of the statement of comprehensive income and statement of financial position would give you plenty of easy marks.

Marking scheme

	Marks	
Statement of comprehensive income		
Revenue	½	
Cost of sales	1	
Distribution costs	½	
Administrative expenses	2	
Overprovision	2	
Profit on disposal	1	
Investment income	½	
Income tax expense	2	
Other comprehensive income	2	
		11½
Statement of financial position		
Property, plant and equipment	3	
Available for sales investments	1½	
Receivables	1	
Revaluation surplus	1½	
Retained earnings	1½	
Deferred tax	1	
Other provisions	1	
Taxation	1	
Restructuring accrual	1½	
		13
Presentation		½
		25

HI
STATEMENT OF COMPREHENSIVE INCOME FOR THE YEAR ENDED 30 SEPTEMBER 20X3

	$'000
Revenue	9,415
Cost of sales (W2)	(4,410)
Gross profit	5,005
Distribution costs	(314)
Administrative expenses (W3)	(860)
Reorganisation costs overprovision (W4)	45
Profit on disposal of asset (W1)	6
Investment income	37
Profit before tax	3,919
Income tax expense (W5)	(1,205)
Profit for the year	2,714
Other comprehensive income:	
Gain on available-for-sale investments	30
Total comprehensive income for the year	2,744

HI
STATEMENT OF FINANCIAL POSITION AS AT 30 SEPTEMBER 20X3

	$'000	$'000
Assets		
Non current assets		
Property, plant and equipment (W1)		9,856
Available-for-sale investments (W6)		522
		10,378
Current assets		
Inventory	822	
Receivables (852 – 45)	807	
Cash at bank and in hand	1,409	
		3,038
		13,416
Equity and liabilities		
Equity		
Ordinary shares of $1 each	5,000	
Share premium	2,388	
Revaluation surplus (W6)	202	
Retained earnings (1,890 + 2,714 – 800)	3,804	
		11,394
Non current liabilities		
Deferred tax	281	
Other provisions (W3)	100	
		381
Current liabilities		
Trade payables	396	
Taxation	1,180	
Accruals: restructuring (W4)	65	
		1,641
		13,416

Workings

1   Property, plant and equipment

	Buildings $'000	Equipment and fixtures $'000	Total $'000
Cost			
Opening balance	11,200	2,625	13,825
Additions	–	–	–
Disposals	–	(210)	(210)
	11,200	2,415	13,615
Accumulated depreciation			
Opening balance	1,404	1,741	3,145
On disposals	–	(205)	(205)
Charge for year			
• $11,200 × 3%	336	–	–
• $2,415 × 20%	–	483	819
Closing balance	1,740	2,019	3,759
Carrying value	9,460	396	9,856

Profit on disposal:

	$'000	$'000
Sale proceeds		11
Carrying value		
Cost	210	
Accumulated depreciation	(205)	
		5
Profit		6

2   Cost of sales

	$'000
Per trial balance	3,591
Depreciation (W1)	819
	4,410

3   Administrative expenses

	$'000
Per trial balance	715
Bad debt written off (Note 1)	45
Provision for legal claim re faulty product (Note 2)	100
	860

Notes

1   Although the customer went into liquidation after the year end, this provides additional evidence of conditions existing at the year end. It is thus an adjusting event under IAS 10.

2   The obligation is probable, therefore a provision must be made.

4   Reorganisation costs

	$'000	$'000
Provision in 20X2 accounts		1,010
Reorganisation expenses	900	
Invoice received after y/e	65	
		965
Provision surplus		45

5   Taxation

	$'000	$'000
Income tax payable		1,180
Deferred tax		
Provision b/fwd	256	
Provision required	281	
∴ Increase required		25
Charge to statement of comprehensive income		1,205

6   *Investments and revaluation surplus*

	Investments $'000	Revaluation surplus $'000
Per trial balance	492	172
Revaluation of investments to market value	30	30
	522	202

Question 4

Text references: The consolidated statement of financial position is covered in Chapter 14.

Top tips: There are some tricky parts to this question, including the share for share exchange and the excess depreciation you had to calculate on the fair value adjustments to buildings, however there were easy marks available in other areas. Remember to work methodically through the question and tackle the bits you are confident with first.

Easy marks: There were some easy marks here once you had the formats down correctly. Once you had calculated the unrealised profit, marks were available on receivables, payables and inventory.

Marking scheme

			Marks
(a)	Goodwill on acquisition		5
(b)	*Consolidated statement of financial position*		
	Goodwill	1	
	Land and building	3	
	Plant	½	
	Investment in associate	3	
	Inventory	1½	
	Receivables	1½	
	Bank	2	
	Share capital	2	
	Retained earnings	3½	
	Payables	1½	
	Presentation	½	
			20
			25

(a) *Calculation of goodwill*

		$'000
Consideration transferred		
Cash (600,000 x $0.25)		150,000
Share exchange (600,000 x ½ x $2.5)		750,000
		900,000
Net assets acquired		
Share capital	600,000	
Retained earnings	150,000	
Fair value adjustment – land	40,000	
Fair value adjustment – buildings	30,000	
		820,000
Goodwill		80,000

(b) HORNET GROUP
CONSOLIDATED STATEMENT OF FINANCIAL POSITION AS AT 31 OCTOBER 20X5

	$'000	$'000
Assets		
Non-current assets		
Goodwill (a)		80,000
Land and buildings (W3)		661,500
Plant		365,000
Investment in associate (W4)		96,000
		1,202,500
Current assets		
Inventory (W2)	597,000	
Receivables (375 + 126 – 25)	476,000	
Bank (208 + 30 – 150 (a))	88,000	
		1,161,000
		2,363,500
Equity and liabilities		
$1 ordinary shares (700 + 300 (a))		1,000,000
Share premium		450,000
Retained earnings (W5)		624,500
		2,074,500
Current liabilities		
Payables (220 + 94 – 25)		289,000
Total equity and liabilities		2,363,500

Workings

1   Group structure

```
           Hornet
      100%  /    \  30%
          Wasp    Ant
```

2   Inventory

	$m	$m
Hornet		357
Wasp	252	
Less unrealised profit	(12)	
		240
		597

3   Land and Buildings

	$m	$m
Hornet		315.0
Wasp	278.0	
Land revaluation	40.0	
Buildings revaluation	30.0	
Less excess depreciation (30/20)	(1.5)	
		346.5
Total land and buildings		661.5

4   Investment in associate

	$m
Cost of investment	100
Impairment of associate	(10)
Share of post acquisition retained earnings (20 x 30%)	6
	96

5   Retained earnings

	Hornet $m	Wasp $m	Ant $m
Per question	580.0	212	80
Less impairment of associate	(10.0)		
Less unrealised profit	(12.0)		
Less excess depreciation	(1.5)		
Pre-acquisition		(150)	(60)
		62	20
Wasp	62.0		
Ant (20 × 30%)	6.0		
	624.5		

CIMA
Paper F1 (Operational)
Financial Operations

Mock Exam 2

Question Paper		
Time allowed:	Reading time	20 mins
	Answering question paper	3 hours
This paper is divided into three sections		
Section A	Answer ALL sub-questions in this section	
Section B	Answer ALL of the six short answer questions	
Section C	Answer BOTH of these questions	

DO NOT OPEN THIS PAPER UNTIL YOU ARE READY TO START UNDER EXAMINATION CONDITIONS

SECTION A – 20 marks

Answer ALL sub-questions in this section

Question 1

1.1 Which of the following statements most closely defines double taxation relief?

   A   The group is treated as one entity for tax purposes
   B   Losses of one group member can be offset against the profits of another.
   C   Capital gains tax is deferred until an asset is sold outside the group.
   D   Tax paid by a company in one country is offset against the tax due in another country.   **(2 marks)**

1.2 Company T has sales of $230,000, including sales tax, in a period. Its purchases, excluding sales tax, total $180,000, of which $20,000 are zero-rated. Sales tax is 15%. What is the sales tax payable for the period?

   A $6,000
   B $6,522
   C $10,500
   D $11,022   **(2 marks)**

1.3 Company P makes an accounting loss of $320,000 during the year. This includes non-taxable income of $20,000 and depreciation of $33,000. In addition, $40,000 of the expenses are disallowable for tax purposes. If the tax allowable depreciation totals $45,000, what is the taxable amount?

   A $182,000 loss
   B $300,000 loss
   C $312,000 loss
   D $328,000 loss   **(2 marks)**

1.4 An asset has to meet two recognition criteria before being recognised in financial statements. One of these is the probability that future economic benefits will flow to the entity. The other criterion is:

   A   The asset has a cost or value that can be measured reliably
   B   The future economic benefits will be received within the current accounting period
   C   The future economic benefits can be reliably measured
   D   The asset has an open market value   **(2 marks)**

1.5 Which of the following are covered by the auditors' report?

   1   Statement of cash flows
   2   Statement of changes in equity
   3   Statement of financial position

   A   All three are covered.
   B   1 and 2 only
   C   2 and 3 only
   D   1 and 3 only   **(2 marks)**

1.6 IAS 1 *Presentation of financial statements* defines the classification of liabilities as current or non-current.

Which of the following liabilities should be included within current liabilities?

1 Loan notes issued five years ago, due for repayment within one year, which have been agreed to be refinanced on a long-term basis before the financial statements are approved

2 Trade payables due for settlement more than twelve months after the year end, within the normal course of the operating cycle

3 Trade payables due for settlement within twelve months after the year end, within the normal course of the operating cycle

4 Bank overdrafts

A All four items
B 1, 3 and 4 only
C 1 and 2 only
D 2, 3 and 4 only **(2 marks)**

1.7 The following figures apply to a construction contract at the end of the first year:

	$'000
Total contract price	36,000
Costs to date	10,000
Expected costs to completion	20,000
Cash received from customer	24,000

What amounts will be included as attributable profit in the statement of comprehensive income and shown under *amounts due to customers* in the statement of financial position?

	Profit $'000	Amounts due to customers $'000
A	16,000	14,000
B	6,000	14,000
C	2,000	12,000
D	6,000	12,000

(2 marks)

1.8 Which of the following statements about IAS 17 *Leases* are correct?

1 A finance lease is one which transfers substantially all the risks and rewards of the ownership of an asset to a lessee.

2 A leased asset should be depreciated over the shorter of the lease term and the useful life of the asset.

3 All obligations under finance leases will appear in the statement of financial position under the heading of 'Current liabilities'.

4 An asset held on an operating lease should appear in the lessee's statement of financial position as a non-current asset and be depreciated over the term of the lease.

A 1 and 3 only
B 1 and 2 only
C 2 and 4 only
D All four statements are correct **(2 marks)**

1.9 An asset with a fair value of $15,400 is acquired under a finance lease on 1 January 20X1 with a deposit on that date of $4,000 and four further annual payments in arrears of $4,000 each. The interest rate implicit in the lease is 15%.

What figure would appear in the statement of financial position at 31 December 20X1 under the heading of current liabilities?

    A $2,634
    B $4,000
    C $6,476
    D $9,110

(2 marks)

1.10 Which of the following is a non-adjusting event after the reporting period in accordance with IAS 10 for financial statements prepared to 30 June 20X6 and approved on 3 October 20X6?

    A   Final agreement of the price for the sale of a building which had been under contract since 28 June 20X6

    B   Receipt of the financial statements for the year ended 31 May 20X6 of an unlisted company in which the business owns 10% of the share capital showing that it is going into liquidation

    C   A decision made on 1 July 20X6 to close a division of the business which made significant losses in the year ending 30 June 20X6

    D   Information showing that a long-term contract on which profit had been taken in the year ending 30 June 20X6 will in fact not be profitable due a defect in materials used in January 20X6

(2 marks)

(Total for Section A = 20 marks)

SECTION B – 30 marks

Answer ALL six sub-questions

Question 2

(a) Tax rules arise from four main sources. List the sources and describe two of these in detail.

(Total for sub-question (a) = 5 marks)

(b) Discuss briefly the problems encountered in attempting to regulate financial reporting in the absence of a conceptual framework.

(Total for sub-question (b) = 5 marks)

(c) Jedders Co has three long leasehold properties in different parts of the region each of which had an original life of 50 years. As at 1 January 20X0, their original cost, accumulated depreciation to date and carrying (book) values were as follows.

	Cost $'000	Depreciation $'000	Carrying value 1.1.20X0 $'000
Property in North	3,000	1,800	1,200
Property in Central	6,000	1,200	4,800
Property in South	3,750	1,500	2,250

On 1 January an independent surveyor provided valuation information to suggest that the value of the South property was the same as book value, the North property had fallen against carrying value by 20% and the Central property had risen by 40% in value against the carrying value.

The directors wish to show all their properties at a revalued amount in the accounts as at 31 December 20X0.

Required

Calculate the charges to the statement of comprehensive income and the non-current asset extracts in the statement of financial position for all the properties for the year ended 31 December 20X0. You should follow the requirements of IAS 16 *Property, plant and equipment*.

(Total for sub-question (c) = 5 marks)

(d) IAS 10 distinguishes between 'adjusting' and 'non-adjusting' events.

Required

Explain what is meant by 'adjusting events' and 'non-adjusting events' and give three examples of each.

(Total for sub-question (d) = 5 marks)

(e) The International Accounting Standards Committee Foundation (IASCF) oversees a number of other International committees, two of which are the Standards Advisory Council (SAC) and the International Financial Reporting Interpretations Committee (IFRIC).

Required

Explain the role of the SAC and the IFRIC in assisting with developing and implementing International Financial Reporting Standards.

(Total for sub-question (e) = 5 marks)

(f) GJ commenced business on 1 October 2005 and, on that date, it acquired property, plant and equipment for $220,000. GJ uses the straight line method of depreciation. The estimated useful life of the assets was five years and the residual value was estimated at $10,000. GJ's accounting year end is 30 September.

All the assets acquired qualified for a first year tax allowance of 50% and then an annual tax allowance of 25% of the reducing balance.

On 1 October 2007, GJ revalued all of its assets; this led to an increase in asset values of $53,000.

GJ's applicable tax rate for the year is 25%.

Required

Calculate the amount of the deferred tax provision that GJ should include in its statement of financial position at 30 September 2008, in accordance with IAS 12 Income Taxes.

(Total for sub-question (f) = 5 marks)

(Total for Section B = 30 marks)

SECTION C – 50 marks

Answer BOTH of these questions

Question 3

The statements of financial position of YZ are given below:

STATEMENT OF FINANCIAL POSITION AT

	30 September 20X3		30 September 20X2	
	$'000	$'000	$'000	$'000
Assets				
Property, plant and equipment		634		510
Current assets				
Inventory	420		460	
Trade receivables	390		320	
Interest receivable	4		9	
Short term Investments	50		0	
Cash in bank	75		0	
Cash in hand	7		5	
		946		794
Total assets		1,580		1,304
Equity and liabilities				
Equity				
Ordinary shares $0.50 each	363		300	
Share premium account	89		92	
Revaluation surplus	50		0	
Retained earnings(loss)	93		(70)	
		595		322
Non-current liabilities				
10% loan notes	0		40	
5% loan notes	329		349	
		329		389
Current liabilities				
Bank overdraft	0		70	
Trade payables	550		400	
Income tax	100		90	
Accruals	6		33	
		656		593
Total equity and liabilities		1,580		1,304

Additional information

(a) On 1 October 20X2, YZ issued 60,000 $0.50 ordinary shares at a premium of 100%. The proceeds were used to finance the purchase and cancellation of all its 10% loan notes and some of its 5% loan notes, both at par. A bonus issue of one for ten shares held was made on 1 November 20X2; all shares in issue qualified for the bonus.

(b) The current asset investment was a 30 day government bond.

(c) Property, plant and equipment include certain properties which were revalued in the year.

(d) Property, plant and equipment disposed of in the year had a net book value of $75,000; cash received on disposal was $98,000. The balance on the disposal account has been added to sales revenue.

(e) Depreciation charged for the year was $87,000.

(f) The accruals balance is interest payable of $33,000 at 30 September 20X2 and $6,000 at 30 September 20X3.

(g) Interim dividends paid during the year were $23,000.

(h) Sales revenue for the year was reported as $2,900,000 and purchases were $1,694,000. Other expenses (not including depreciation) were $775,000. YZ earned investment income of $5,000 and finance costs for the year were $19,000. The tax charge is estimated at $104,000.

Required

Prepare the following for YZ for the year ended 30 September 20X3:

(a) A statement of comprehensive income **(10 marks)**
(b) A statement of cash flows, using the indirect method **(15 marks)**

(Total 25 marks)

Question 4

The following are the financial statements relating to Straw, a limited liability company, and its subsidiary company Berry.

STATEMENT OF COMPREHENSIVE INCOME
FOR THE YEAR ENDED 31 DECEMBER 20X5

	Straw $'000	Berry $'000
Sales revenue	235,000	85,000
Cost of sales	(140,000)	(52,000)
Gross profit	95,000	33,000
Distribution costs	(12,000)	(5,000)
Administrative expenses	(45,000)	(8,000)
Dividend income from Berry	5,000	–
Profit before tax	43,000	20,000
Tax	(13,250)	(5,000)
Profit for the year	29,750	15,000

STATEMENTS OF FINANCIAL POSITION
AS AT 31 DECEMBER 20X5

	Straw $'000	Straw $'000	Berry $'000	Berry $'000
Assets				
Non-current assets				
Property, plant and equipment		100,000		40,000
Investments				
30,000,000 $1 ordinary shares in Berry at cost		34,000		–
		134,000		40,000
Current assets				
Inventory, at cost	13,360		3,890	
Trade receivables and dividend receivable	14,640		6,280	
Bank	3,500		2,570	
Total assets		31,500		12,740
		165,500		52,740
Equity and liabilities				
Equity				
$1 Ordinary shares		100,000		30,000
General reserve		9,200		1,000
Retained earnings		27,300		9,280
		136,500		40,280
Current liabilities				
Trade payables	9,000		2,460	
Dividend payable	20,000		10,000	
Total equity and liabilities		29,000		12,460
		165,500		52,740

Additional information

(a) Straw purchased its $1 ordinary shares in Berry on 1 January 20X1. At that date the balance on Berry's general reserve was $0.5 million and the balance of retained earnings was $1.5 million.

(b) At 1 January 20X5 the total goodwill arising from the acquisition of Berry was valued at $960,000. Straw's impairment review of this goodwill at 31 December 20X5 valued it at $800,000.

(c) During the year ended 31 December 20X5 Straw sold goods which originally cost $12 million to Berry. Straw invoiced Berry at cost plus 40%. Berry still has 30% of these goods in inventory at 31 December 20X5.

(d) Berry owed Straw $1.5 million at 31 December 20X5 for some of the goods Straw supplied during the year.

Required

(a) Calculate the goodwill arising on the acquisition of Berry. **(2 marks)**

(b) Prepare the following financial statements for Straw.

    (i) The consolidated statement of comprehensive income for the year ended 31 December 20X5.

(8 marks)

    (ii) The consolidated statement of financial position as at 31 December 20X5. **(15 marks)**

Disclosure notes are not required. **(Total = 25 marks)**

(Total for Section C = 50 marks)

Answers

**DO NOT TURN THIS PAGE UNTIL YOU HAVE
COMPLETED MOCK EXAM 2**

A plan of attack

This is the second mock exam, so you will now have some feel of what you have to get done in the exam.

Your approach

This paper has three sections. All sections, and all questions, are compulsory. The first section contains 20 multiple choice questions. The second has six short questions. The third has one accounts preparation question which carries 30 marks.

OTs first again

However you find the paper, chances are you should **start with the objective test questions**. You should be able to do a good number of them and answering them will give you a boost. Remember how long to allocate to the OTs? That's right, 36 minutes.

You then have a **choice**.

- Read through and answer Section B before moving on to Section C
- Answer the questions in Section C, and then go back to Section B

Time spent at the start of each Section B and C question confirming the requirements and producing a plan for the answers is time well spent.

Doing the exam

Actually doing the exam is a personal experience. There is not a single *right way*. As long as you submit complete answers to the MCQs in Section A, the six Section B questions and the two questions from Section C, your approach obviously works.

One approach

Having done or guessed at the MCQs, I would work straight through Section B. The possible pitfall would be getting sucked too deeply into Section B and leaving insufficient time for Section C.

So lets look at the Section B questions in the paper:

- Question (a) is fairly easy but to score marks you must do exactly as specified in the question – list **four** and describe **two** (not one or three).
- Question (b) looks easy but is not. It is very easy to write off the point in a question like this. So before you start, list out the problems, and then briefly discuss each one.
- Question (c) is more straightforward than it looks, but you must read it carefully so that you know exactly what to do. Then write your answer out methodically.
- Question (d) should have given you no trouble as long as you were clear about what constitutes an 'adjusting event'. You are asked for three examples of each – six altogether – so do exactly that.
- Question (e) is on SAC and IFRIC. You should know enough about these to answer the questions. Don't spend too long on it.
- Question (f) needs to be written out carefully so that you don't miss any steps.

Having worked your way through Section B, taking no more than 9 minutes per question, you should now be left with 90 minutes to do your Section C questions.

For the Section C Questions you must proceed in a methodical way. Set out your format and then work through the question requirements, doing neat, readable calculations and fill out the figures. Even if you do not finish, you will get marks for what you have done, so do the easy bits first.

Time allocation

Be disciplined. Allocate your time according to the marks available but never go over the time allocation. The last few marks in a question are the hardest to earn.

Be sure to follow the requirements. If four advantages are required, give four. No extra credit will be given for five. Two advantages will only get you half marks.

Answer all of the question. Having a go at every part of all the Section B questions you are required to do will put you in a better position to pass than, say, only doing five questions. However difficult that sixth question seems at first there are marks to be earned.

If you have time left at the end of the exam ensure that you have attempted every part of every question. If you have, then scan through and ensure you complete any part of an answer you left earlier. Use the full three hours working towards a pass.

Marking the exam

Marking the MCQs is not too difficult. You only have 2-4 marks to award. In the longer questions, give yourself credit where you used the correct method, even if your answer was wrong.

Most important, list out all the items you did not know or got wrong, and make sure you revise them.

SECTION A

Question 1

1.1   D   Option A is the definition of group relief and options B and C show aspects of group relief.

1.2   A

		$
Output tax $\frac{230,000}{115} \times 15$		30,000
Input tax $((180,000 - 20,000) \times 15\%)$		24,000
Payable		6,000

1.3   C

	$	$
Accounting loss		(320,000)
Add: depreciation	33,000	
disallowed expenses	40,000	
		73,000
		(247,000)
Less: non-taxable income	20,000	
tax allowable depreciation	45,000	
		(65,000)
Taxable loss		(312,000)

1.4   A   The cost or value can be measured reliably.

1.5   A   An audit report covers all three.

1.6   A   Item (1) is now included as a current liability after the revision of IAS 1.

1.7   C

	$'000
Total contract price	36,000
Total expected costs (10,000 + 20,000)	30,000
Total expected profit	6,000
Profit to date = 6,000,000 × 10/30	2,000
Due to customer:	
Progress billings	24,000
Costs to date	(10,000)
Profit to date	(2,000)
Balance due to customer	12,000

1.8   B   3   Obligations under finance leases due after twelve months will be shown under *non-current* liabilities.

            4   An asset held under an operating lease is *not* capitalised by the lessee.

1.9   A

FINANCE LEASE ACCOUNT

	$m		$m
20X1 1 Jan deposit	4,000	Non-current assets	15,400
31 Dec – instalment	4,000	Interest 15% × $11,400	1,710
Balance c/d	9,110		
	17,110		17,110
		Balance b/d	9,110
20X2 31 Dec – instalment	4,000	Interest 15% × 9,110	1,366

31 December 20X1

Current liabilities = 4,000 – 1,366
                  = $2,634

1.10 C

> Theory underlying answer
>
> The decision to close the division was taken after the year end and therefore does not affect the accounts for the year to 30 June 20X6 even though the division was loss-making. Option A confirms the final price of a transaction entered into before the year end and is therefore an adjusting event. Option B provides evidence of a diminution in value of an investment held at the year end and is therefore an adjusting event. Option D provides evidence that the previous estimate of accrued profit was inaccurate and therefore an adjustment should be made.

SECTION B

Question 2

Marking scheme

		Marks
(a)	4 main sources - ½ mark each	2
	Describe 2 in detail - 1½ marks each	3
		5

The four main sources are as follows.

- Domestic tax legislation and court rulings
- Domestic tax authority practice
- Supranational bodies
- International tax treaties

Domestic tax legislation and court rulings

The main source of tax rules arises from the domestic tax legislation of the country, eg in the UK, the annual Finance Act. Although the legislators try to think of all possible situations, business is always changing and so the law may have to be interpreted by the courts. This gives rise to court rulings that have the force of law.

Domestic tax authority practice

Every tax authority develops its own practice on how the law is applied. For example, UK tax law states that employees should be taxed on all 'benefits' supplied by the employer. However, in practice, certain benefits are exempted from the rules because it would be too time consuming and yield little in the way of tax.

Alternative answers. You could have chosen to explain any of the four main sources and so would have gained credit for the following.

Supranational bodies

Supranational bodies, such as the European Union (EU), can affect tax rules. The EU has a number of rules on value added or sales tax, which have to be applied by all members of the EU.

International tax treaties

Some businesses trade in many different countries of the world, so called 'multi-national' companies. This means that their profits will be subject to tax in the local countries they trade in, as well as the country where the company has its headquarters. This could mean that the company pays tax on certain profits twice. In order to avoid this 'double tax', countries enter into tax treaties which set out which country taxes the profits. These treaties also allow relief for local taxes paid, for example withholding taxes.

Marking scheme

		Marks
(b)	Define conceptual framework	1
	Problems – 1 mark for each well-explained point – max 4	4
		5

A conceptual framework provides the theoretical basis upon which financial reporting can be regulated. It establishes generally agreed-upon principles and accounting standards can be developed in accordance with this. Lack of a conceptual framework can lead to the following problems:

(i) Standards being developed in a **firefighting fashion**, in response to problems or abuses as they arise. Standards developed in this way are unlikely to be well thought-out and may need further revision as more problems are identified.

(ii) Because standards are not being developed as part of a consistent whole, there may be **conflicts** and **inconsistencies** between different standards. Also issues may be addressed in more than one standard, leading to duplication of effort and confusion.

(iii) If there is no overall framework to which reference can be made, standard setters will feel the need to cover every eventuality. This can lead to standards becoming very detailed and **prescriptive**. This has already been observed in the USA with the FASB standards.

(iv) A conceptual framework provides some sort of **protection from political pressure** from vested interests. A new standard developed as part of a conceptual framework cannot be amended in a way which will bring it into conflict with the conceptual framework.

Marking scheme

	Marks
(c) Depreciation charges	2
Revaluation loss	1
Property, plant and equipment	2
	5

STATEMENT OF COMPREHENSIVE INCOME (EXTRACTS)

	$'000
Depreciation charge	
North (($1.2m × 80%)/20 years)	48
Central (($4.8m × 140%)/40 years)	168
South ($2.25m/30 years)	75
	291
Loss on revaluation (20% × $1.2m)	240

STATEMENT OF FINANCIAL POSITION (EXTRACTS)

	Cost/revaluation $'000	Depreciation $'000	Carrying value $'000
North	960	48	912
Central	6,720	168	6,552
South	2,250	75	2,175
	9,930	291	9,639

At 1 January 20X0 the accumulated depreciation of the Central property is $1.2m, which represents 10 years' worth of depreciation, leaving 40 years remaining life. For the South and North properties, the respective lives in these calculations are 30 and 20 years. If there is no previous revaluation surplus on the North property, then the loss in the current year is classed as an impairment, and must be taken to profit or loss.

Marking scheme

	Marks
(d) Definition adjusting / non adjusting event	2
Examples adjusting event – ½ mark each	1½
Examples non-adjusting event – ½ mark each	1½
	5

Adjusting events are events that provide further evidence of conditions that existed at the reporting date.

Examples of adjusting events include:

(i) The subsequent determination of the purchase price or of the proceeds of sale of non-current assets purchased or sold before the year-end

(ii) The renegotiation of amounts owing by customers or the insolvency of a customer

(iii) Amounts received or receivable in respect of insurance claims which were in the course of negotiation at the year end

Non-adjusting events are indicative of conditions that arose subsequent to the end of the reporting period.

Examples of non-adjusting events might be:

(i) Losses of non-current assets or inventories as a result of a catastrophe such as fire or flood
(ii) Closing a significant part of the trading activities if this was not begun before the year-end
(iii) The value of an investment falls between the year end and the date the accounts are authorised

Marking scheme

		Marks
(e)	1 mark per well-presented point	5

Standards Advisory Council (SAC)

The SAC provides a forum for groups and individuals to give advice to the International Accounting Standards Board (IASB), the board responsible for setting IFRS. The committee members are from diverse geographical and functional backgrounds to allow them to gather opinions from a wide range of representatives.

The committee meets three times a year and advises the IASB on its agenda and priorities for setting new IFRS. Consultation with the SAC continues throughout the development of an IFRS. In particular, the SAC advises the IASB on issues related to the practical application and implementation of new IFRS. It also advises on the advantages and disadvantages of different proposals.

International Financial Reporting Interpretations Committee (IFRIC)

The IFRIC provides timely guidance on the application and interpretation of IFRS. It normally deals with complex accounting issues that could give rise to a diversity of accounting treatments. In this way it assists the IASB in setting and improving IFRS.

IFRIC produces interpretations which, once finalised, are ratified and issued by the IASB. The IASB may choose to add an item to its own agenda if an interpretation is not ratified.

Marking scheme

		Marks
(f)	Tax WDV	1½
	Accounting carrying value	1½
	Deferred tax provision	2
		5

Deferred tax provision = $16,865

Tax written down value:

	$
1 Oct 2005 cost	220,000
2006 tax allowance 50% × 220,000	(110,000)
30 Sept 2006 tax written down value	110,000
2007 tax allowance 25% × 110,000	(27,500)
30 Sept 2007 tax written down value	82,500
2008 tax allowance 25% × 82,500	(20,625)
30 Sept 2008 tax written down value	61,875

Accounting carrying value:

	$
Cost	220,000
Depreciation 2 × (220,000-10,000)/5	(84,000)
30 Sept 2007 accounting carrying value	136,000
	53,000
Revaluation	189,000
Depreciation $(189 – 10)/3	(59,667)
30 September 2008 carrying value	129,333

	$
Accounting net book value	129,333
Tax written down value	(61,875)
Temporary difference	67,458
Deferred tax @ 25%	16,856

SECTION C

Question 3

> **Text references.** Statements of cash flows are covered in Chapter 8: *IAS 7 Statement of cash flows*.
>
> **Top tips.** This is fairly straightforward, especially the statement of comprehensive income, although the bonus issue may have confused you. If so, leave the more difficult calculation to the end and concentrate on those areas you can do confidently. Be methodical and don't get bogged down in one part of the question. Write out for yourself a reconciliation of the movement on share capital and share premium and you will see that the only cash flow is $60,000 from the share issue.
>
> **Easy marks** Start with the statement of comprehensive income and then the cash flow proforma and get cash flows from operating activities done. You can get easy marks on all of this. You will need to do a working for property, plant and equipment, but you have done a statement of comprehensive income, so the rest of the statement of cash flows is relatively easy. If you have worked out property, plant and equipment, you will also get the marks on investing activities.

Marking scheme

	Marks	
Statement of comprehensive income		
Sales revenue	1	
Cost of sales	1	
Other income	1	
Other expenses	1	
Investment income	1	
Finance cost	1	
Income tax expense	1	
Other comprehensive income	2	
Presentation	1	
		10
Statement of cash flows		
Cash flows from operating activities		
Profit before tax	1	
Finance cost	1	
Depreciation	1	
Profit on disposal	1	
Working capital adjustments - ½ each	1½	
Interest paid	1	
Income taxes paid	1	
		7½
Cash flows from investing activities		
Purchase of PPE	1½	
Proceeds of sale of PPE	1	
Interest received	1	
		3½
Cash flows from financing activities		
Proceeds from issue of share capital	1½	
Purchase of loan notes	1	
Dividends paid	1	3½
Cash and cash equivalents		½
Total		15
		25

(a) YZ
STATEMENT OF COMPREHENSIVE INCOME FOR THE YEAR TO 30 SEPTEMBER 20X3

	$'000	$'000
Sales revenue (2,900 – 23)		2,877
Cost of sales (460 + 1,694 – 420)		(1,734)
Gross profit		1,143
Other income – profit on disposal (W1)		23
Other expenses (775 + 87 (W1))		(862)
		304
Investment income (W4)	5	
Finance cost (W2)	(19)	(14)
Profit before tax		290
Income tax expense (W3)		(104)
Profit for the year		186
Other comprehensive income:		
Gain on revaluation of properties		50
Total comprehensive income for the year		236

(b) YZ
STATEMENT OF CASH FLOWS
FOR THE YEAR ENDED 30 SEPTEMBER 20X3

	$'000	$'000
Cash flows from operating activities		
Profit before tax	290	
Adjustments for		
Finance cost	14	
Depreciation	87	
Profit on disposal (W1)	(23)	
Operating profit before working capital changes	368	
Decrease in inventory	40	
Increase in receivables	(70)	
Increase in payables	150	
Cash generated from operations	488	
Interest paid (W2)	(46)	
Income taxes paid (W3)	(94)	
Net cash from operating activities		348
Cash flows from investing activities		
Purchase of property, plant and equipment (W1)	(236)	
Proceeds from sale of property, plant and equipment	98	
Interest received (W4)	10	
Net cash used in investing activities		(128)
Cash flows from financing activities		
Proceeds from issuance of share capital (W5)	60	
Repurchase of loan notes	(60)	
Dividends paid	(23)	
Net cash used in financing activities		(23)
Net increase in cash and cash equivalents		197
Cash and cash equivalents at beginning of period		(65)
Cash and cash equivalents at end of period		132

Workings

1 Property, plant and equipment

PROPERTY, PLANT AND EQUIPMENT

	$'000		$'000
Bal b/fwd (carrying value)	510	Disposals	75
Revaluation	50	Depreciation	87
Additions (bal fig)	236	Balance c/fwd (carrying value)	634
	796		796

DISPOSALS

	$'000		$'000
Property, plant and equipment	75	Bank proceeds	98
Profit on sale	23		
	98		98

2 *Interest paid*

INTEREST PAYABLE

	$'000		$'000
Paid (bal. fig)	46	Balance b/fwd	33
Balance c/fwd	6	Statement of comprehensive income	19
	52		52

3 *Income taxes paid*

TAXATION

	$'000		$'000
∴ Paid (bal.fig)	94	Balance b/fwd	90
Balance c/fwd	100	Statement of comprehensive income	104
	194		194

4 *Interest received*

INTEREST RECEIVABLE

	$'000		$'000
Balance b/fwd	9	Cash received	10
Statement of comprehensive income	5	Balance c/fwd	4
	14		14

5 *Share capital issue*

	Share capital $'000	Share premium $'000
Bal b/f	300	92
Share issue for cash	30	30
Bonus issue ($1/10 \times 330$)	33	(33)
	363	89

Question 4

Marking scheme

		Marks
(a)	Goodwill calculation	2
(b)	**Consolidated statement of comprehensive income**	
	Revenue	1½
	Cost of sales	2
	Distribution costs	1
	Administrative expenses	1½
	Tax	1
	Profit for the year	1
		8

(c) **Consolidated statement of financial position** Marks

Goodwill	1
Property, plant and equipment	1
Inventory	1½
Trade receivables	1½
Bank	1
Share capital	1
Retained earnings	2½
General revenue	1½
Trade payables	1½
Dividend payable	1½
Presentation	1
	15
Total	25

(a) **Calculation of goodwill**

	$	$
Consideration transferred		34,000
Net assets acquired		
Share capital	30,000	
Share premium	500	
Retained earnings	1,500	
		32,000
Goodwill		2,000

(b) (i) STRAW GROUP
CONSOLIDATED STATEMENT OF COMPREHENSIVE INCOME
FOR THE YEAR ENDED 31 OCTOBER 20X5

	$'000
Revenue (235 + 85 – 16.8 (W1))	303,200
Cost of sales (140 + 52 – 16.8 + 1.44 (W1))	(176,640)
Gross profit	126,560
Distribution costs (12 + 5)	(17,000)
Administrative expenses (W2)	(53,160)
Profit before tax	56,400
Tax (13,250 + 5,000)	(18,250)
Profit for the year	38,150

(ii) STRAW GROUP
CONSOLIDATED STATEMENT OF FINANCIAL POSITION AS AT 31 OCTOBER 20X5

	$'000	$'000
Assets		
Goodwill	800	
Property, plant and equipment (100 + 40)	140,000	
		140,800
Current assets		
Inventory (W4)	15,810	
Trade receivables (W5)	9,420	
Bank (3,500 + 2,570)	6,070	
		31,300
Total assets		172,100

Equity and liabilities		
Share capital	100,000	
Retained earnings (W8)	32,440	
General reserve (W7)	9,700	
		142,140
Current liabilities		
Trade payables (W6)	9,960	
Dividends	20,000	
		29,960
Total equity and liabilities		172,100

Workings

1 *Intragroup sale*

Sale price to be eliminated from consolidated revenue:

	$'000
Cost to Straw	12,000
40% mark up	4,800
Cost to Berry	16,800

Unrealised profit in inventory: $4,800,000 × 30% = $1,440,000

Gross profit = $95,000,000 + $33,000,000 − $1,440,000
= $126,560,000

2 *Administrative expenses*

	$'000
Straw	45,000
Berry	8,000
Impairment of goodwill (W3)	160
	53,160

3 *Impairment of goodwill*

	$'000
Impairment at 1.11.20X4 (2,000 − 960)	1,040
Impairment during year (bal. fig.)	160
Impairment at 31.12.X5 (2,000 − 800)	1,200

4 *Inventory*

	$'000
Straw	13,360
Berry	3,890
Less unrealised profit (W1)	(1,440)
	15,810

5 *Trade receivables*

	$'000	$'000
Straw	14,640	
Less dividend receivable	(10,000)	
		4,640
Berry		6,280
Less intragroup		(1,500)
		9,420

6 *Trade payables*

	$'000
Straw	9,000
Berry	2,460
Less intragroup	(1,500)
	9,960

7   *General reserve*

	Straw $'000	Berry $'000
Per question	9,200	1,000
Less pre-acquisition		(500)
		500
Share of Berry 500 × 100%	500	
	9,700	

8   *Retained earnings*

	Straw $'000	Berry $'000
Per question	27,300	9,280
Less PUP	(1,440)	
	25,860	
Less pre-acqn.		(1,500)
		7,780
Share of Berry: 100%	7,780	
Impairment of goodwill (2,000 – 800)	(1,200)	
	32,440	

MATHEMATICAL TABLES

PRESENT VALUE TABLE

Present value of £1 ie $(1+r)^{-n}$ where r = interest rate, n = number of periods until payment or receipt.

Periods (n)	1%	2%	3%	4%	5%	6%	7%	8%	9%	10%
1	0.990	0.980	0.971	0.962	0.952	0.943	0.935	0.926	0.917	0.909
2	0.980	0.961	0.943	0.925	0.907	0.890	0.873	0.857	0.842	0.826
3	0.971	0.942	0.915	0.889	0.864	0.840	0.816	0.794	0.772	0.751
4	0.961	0.924	0.888	0.855	0.823	0.792	0.763	0.735	0.708	0.683
5	0.951	0.906	0.863	0.822	0.784	0.747	0.713	0.681	0.650	0.621
6	0.942	0.888	0.837	0.790	0.746	0.705	0.666	0.630	0.596	0.564
7	0.933	0.871	0.813	0.760	0.711	0.665	0.623	0.583	0.547	0.513
8	0.923	0.853	0.789	0.731	0.677	0.627	0.582	0.540	0.502	0.467
9	0.914	0.837	0.766	0.703	0.645	0.592	0.544	0.500	0.460	0.424
10	0.905	0.820	0.744	0.676	0.614	0.558	0.508	0.463	0.422	0.386
11	0.896	0.804	0.722	0.650	0.585	0.527	0.475	0.429	0.388	0.350
12	0.887	0.788	0.701	0.625	0.557	0.497	0.444	0.397	0.356	0.319
13	0.879	0.773	0.681	0.601	0.530	0.469	0.415	0.368	0.326	0.290
14	0.870	0.758	0.661	0.577	0.505	0.442	0.388	0.340	0.299	0.263
15	0.861	0.743	0.642	0.555	0.481	0.417	0.362	0.315	0.275	0.239
16	0.853	0.728	0.623	0.534	0.458	0.394	0.339	0.292	0.252	0.218
17	0.844	0.714	0.605	0.513	0.436	0.371	0.317	0.270	0.231	0.198
18	0.836	0.700	0.587	0.494	0.416	0.350	0.296	0.250	0.212	0.180
19	0.828	0.686	0.570	0.475	0.396	0.331	0.277	0.232	0.194	0.164
20	0.820	0.673	0.554	0.456	0.377	0.312	0.258	0.215	0.178	0.149

Periods (n)	11%	12%	13%	14%	15%	16%	17%	18%	19%	20%
1	0.901	0.893	0.885	0.877	0.870	0.862	0.855	0.847	0.840	0.833
2	0.812	0.797	0.783	0.769	0.756	0.743	0.731	0.718	0.706	0.694
3	0.731	0.712	0.693	0.675	0.658	0.641	0.624	0.609	0.593	0.579
4	0.659	0.636	0.613	0.592	0.572	0.552	0.534	0.516	0.499	0.482
5	0.593	0.567	0.543	0.519	0.497	0.476	0.456	0.437	0.419	0.402
6	0.535	0.507	0.480	0.456	0.432	0.410	0.390	0.370	0.352	0.335
7	0.482	0.452	0.425	0.400	0.376	0.354	0.333	0.314	0.296	0.279
8	0.434	0.404	0.376	0.351	0.327	0.305	0.285	0.266	0.249	0.233
9	0.391	0.361	0.333	0.308	0.284	0.263	0.243	0.225	0.209	0.194
10	0.352	0.322	0.295	0.270	0.247	0.227	0.208	0.191	0.176	0.162
11	0.317	0.287	0.261	0.237	0.215	0.195	0.178	0.162	0.148	0.135
12	0.286	0.257	0.231	0.208	0.187	0.168	0.152	0.137	0.124	0.112
13	0.258	0.229	0.204	0.182	0.163	0.145	0.130	0.116	0.104	0.093
14	0.232	0.205	0.181	0.160	0.141	0.125	0.111	0.099	0.088	0.078
15	0.209	0.183	0.160	0.140	0.123	0.108	0.095	0.084	0.074	0.065
16	0.188	0.163	0.141	0.123	0.107	0.093	0.081	0.071	0.062	0.054
17	0.170	0.146	0.125	0.108	0.093	0.080	0.069	0.060	0.052	0.045
18	0.153	0.130	0.111	0.095	0.081	0.069	0.059	0.051	0.044	0.038
19	0.138	0.116	0.098	0.083	0.070	0.060	0.051	0.043	0.037	0.031
20	0.124	0.104	0.087	0.073	0.061	0.051	0.043	0.037	0.031	0.026

CUMULATIVE PRESENT VALUE TABLE

This table shows the present value of £1 per annum, receivable or payable at the end of each year for n years $\dfrac{1-(1+r)^{-n}}{r}$.

Periods (n)	1%	2%	3%	4%	5%	6%	7%	8%	9%	10%
1	0.990	0.980	0.971	0.962	0.952	0.943	0.935	0.926	0.917	0.909
2	1.970	1.942	1.913	1.886	1.859	1.833	1.808	1.783	1.759	1.736
3	2.941	2.884	2.829	2.775	2.723	2.673	2.624	2.577	2.531	2.487
4	3.902	3.808	3.717	3.630	3.546	3.465	3.387	3.312	3.240	3.170
5	4.853	4.713	4.580	4.452	4.329	4.212	4.100	3.993	3.890	3.791
6	5.795	5.601	5.417	5.242	5.076	4.917	4.767	4.623	4.486	4.355
7	6.728	6.472	6.230	6.002	5.786	5.582	5.389	5.206	5.033	4.868
8	7.652	7.325	7.020	6.733	6.463	6.210	5.971	5.747	5.535	5.335
9	8.566	8.162	7.786	7.435	7.108	6.802	6.515	6.247	5.995	5.759
10	9.471	8.983	8.530	8.111	7.722	7.360	7.024	6.710	6.418	6.145
11	10.368	9.787	9.253	8.760	8.306	7.887	7.499	7.139	6.805	6.495
12	11.255	10.575	9.954	9.385	8.863	8.384	7.943	7.536	7.161	6.814
13	12.134	11.348	10.635	9.986	9.394	8.853	8.358	7.904	7.487	7.103
14	13.004	12.106	11.296	10.563	9.899	9.295	8.745	8.244	7.786	7.367
15	13.865	12.849	11.938	11.118	10.380	9.712	9.108	8.559	8.061	7.606
16	14.718	13.578	12.561	11.652	10.838	10.106	9.447	8.851	8.313	7.824
17	15.562	14.292	13.166	12.166	11.274	10.477	9.763	9.122	8.544	8.022
18	16.398	14.992	13.754	12.659	11.690	10.828	10.059	9.372	8.756	8.201
19	17.226	15.679	14.324	13.134	12.085	11.158	10.336	9.604	8.950	8.365
20	18.046	16.351	14.878	13.590	12.462	11.470	10.594	9.818	9.129	8.514

Periods (n)	11%	12%	13%	14%	15%	16%	17%	18%	19%	20%
1	0.901	0.893	0.885	0.877	0.870	0.862	0.855	0.847	0.840	0.833
2	1.713	1.690	1.668	1.647	1.626	1.605	1.585	1.566	1.547	1.528
3	2.444	2.402	2.361	2.322	2.283	2.246	2.210	2.174	2.140	2.106
4	3.102	3.037	2.974	2.914	2.855	2.798	2.743	2.690	2.639	2.589
5	3.696	3.605	3.517	3.433	3.352	3.274	3.199	3.127	3.058	2.991
6	4.231	4.111	3.998	3.889	3.784	3.685	3.589	3.498	3.410	3.326
7	4.712	4.564	4.423	4.288	4.160	4.039	3.922	3.812	3.706	3.605
8	5.146	4.968	4.799	4.639	4.487	4.344	4.207	4.078	3.954	3.837
9	5.537	5.328	5.132	4.946	4.772	4.607	4.451	4.303	4.163	4.031
10	5.889	5.650	5.426	5.216	5.019	4.833	4.659	4.494	4.339	4.192
11	6.207	5.938	5.687	5.453	5.234	5.029	4.836	4.656	4.486	4.327
12	6.492	6.194	5.918	5.660	5.421	5.197	4.988	4.793	4.611	4.439
13	6.750	6.424	6.122	5.842	5.583	5.342	5.118	4.910	4.715	4.533
14	6.982	6.628	6.302	6.002	5.724	5.468	5.229	5.008	4.802	4.611
15	7.191	6.811	6.462	6.142	5.847	5.575	5.324	5.092	4.876	4.675
16	7.379	6.974	6.604	6.265	5.954	5.668	5.405	5.162	4.938	4.730
17	7.549	7.120	6.729	6.373	6.047	5.749	5.475	5.222	4.990	4.775
18	7.702	7.250	6.840	6.467	6.128	5.818	5.534	5.273	5.033	4.812
19	7.839	7.366	6.938	6.550	6.198	5.877	5.584	5.316	5.070	4.843
20	7.963	7.469	7.025	6.623	6.259	5.929	5.628	5.353	5.101	4.870

Notes

Notes

Review Form & Free Prize Draw - Paper F1 Financial Operations (1/10)

All original review forms from the entire BPP range, completed with genuine comments, will be entered into one of two draws on 31 July 2010 and 31 January 2011. The names on the first four forms picked out on each occasion will be sent a cheque for £50.

Name: _____ Address: _____

How have you used this Kit?
(Tick one box only)
- [ ] Home study (book only)
- [ ] On a course: college _____
- [ ] With 'correspondence' package
- [ ] Other _____

Why did you decide to purchase this Kit?
(Tick one box only)
- [ ] Have used the complementary Study text
- [ ] Have used other BPP products in the past
- [ ] Recommendation by friend/colleague
- [ ] Recommendation by a lecturer at college
- [ ] Saw advertising
- [ ] Other _____

During the past six months do you recall seeing/receiving any of the following?
(Tick as many boxes as are relevant)
- [ ] Our advertisement in *Financial Management*
- [ ] Our advertisement in *Pass*
- [ ] Our advertisement in *PQ*
- [ ] Our brochure with a letter through the post
- [ ] Our website www.bpp.com

Which (if any) aspects of our advertising do you find useful?
(Tick as many boxes as are relevant)
- [ ] Prices and publication dates of new editions
- [ ] Information on product content
- [ ] Facility to order books off-the-page
- [ ] None of the above

Which BPP products have you used?

Text	[ ]	Success CD	[ ]
Kit	[✓]	Interactive Passcards	[ ]
Passcard	[ ]	i-Pass	[ ]

Your ratings, comments and suggestions would be appreciated on the following areas.

	Very useful	Useful	Not useful
Passing F3	[ ]	[ ]	[ ]
Planning your question practice	[ ]	[ ]	[ ]
Questions	[ ]	[ ]	[ ]
Top Tips etc in answers	[ ]	[ ]	[ ]
Content and structure of answers	[ ]	[ ]	[ ]
'Plan of attack' in mock exams	[ ]	[ ]	[ ]
Mock exam answers	[ ]	[ ]	[ ]

Overall opinion of this Kit   Excellent [ ]   Good [ ]   Adequate [ ]   Poor [ ]

Do you intend to continue using BPP products?   Yes [ ]   No [ ]

The BPP author of this edition can be e-mailed at: rebeccahill@bpp.com

Please return this form to: Nick Weller, CIMA Publishing Manager, BPP Learning Media Ltd, FREEPOST, London, W12 8BR

Review Form & Free Prize Draw (continued)

TELL US WHAT YOU THINK

Please note any further comments and suggestions/errors below.

Free Prize Draw Rules

1. Closing date for 31 July 2010 draw is 30 June 2010. Closing date for 31 January 2011 draw is 31 December 2010.
2. Restricted to entries with UK and Eire addresses only. BPP employees, their families and business associates are excluded.
3. No purchase necessary. Entry forms are available upon request from BPP Learning Media Ltd. No more than one entry per title, per person. Draw restricted to persons aged 16 and over.
4. Winners will be notified by post and receive their cheques not later than 6 weeks after the relevant draw date.
5. The decision of the promoter in all matters is final and binding. No correspondence will be entered into.

	Dr	Cr
Sales →	12k	→ 12k
COS		→ 1
INV	→ 1	
COS		

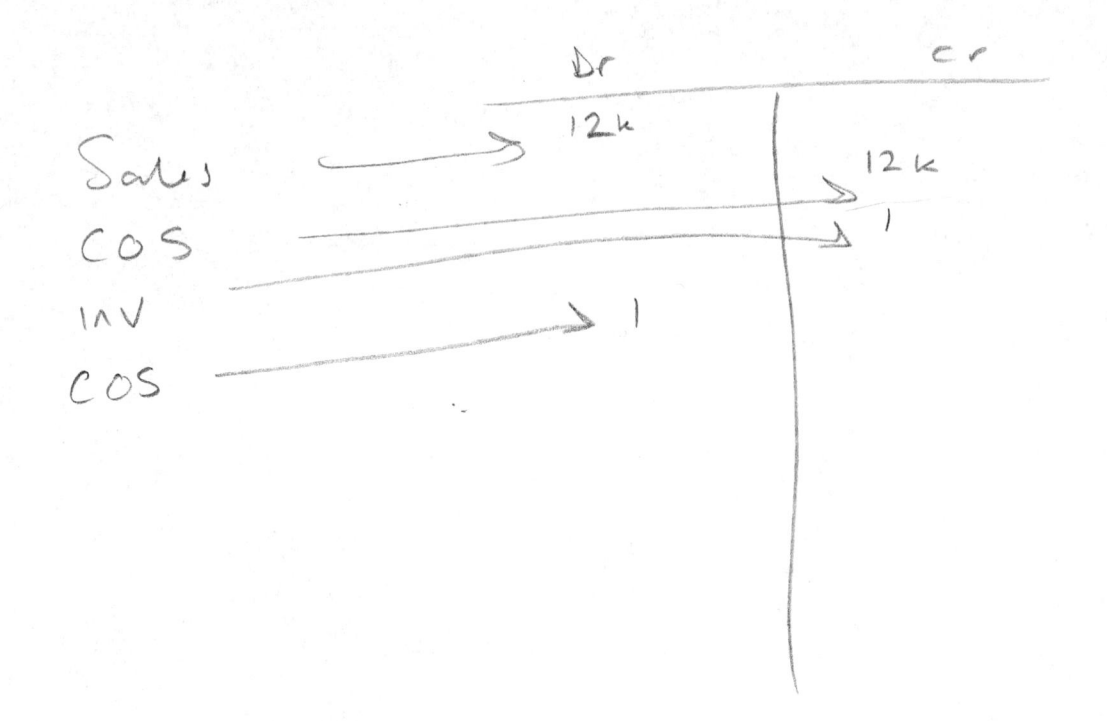